ALL ABOUT
ESCROW

**OR HOW TO BUY THE BROOKLYN
BRIDGE AND HAVE THE LAST LAUGH!**

DEDICATION

This book is dedicated to my Grandfather Church, the first banker in my life.

ALL ABOUT
ESCROW

OR HOW TO BUY THE BROOKLYN BRIDGE AND HAVE THE LAST LAUGH!

FOURTH EDITION

WRITTEN BY
Sandy Gadow

ILLUSTRATED BY
Dave Patton

EDITED BY
Leigh Robinson

PUBLISHED BY

P.O. Box 1639, El Cerrito, CA 94530-4639

First Edition	April, 1981
Revised	April, 1982
Second Edition	August, 1984
Third Edition	May, 1987
Reprinted	May, 1988
Fourth Edition	February, 1989
Reprinted	August, 1989
Revised	March, 1990

Library of Congress Catalog Card Number: 81-65603

International Standard Book Number: 0-932956-14-9

Printed in the United States of America

PREFACE

After years of working as an escrow officer, guiding confused buyers and anxious sellers through their various escrow documents, I began to realize that there wasn't a single book available which could answer their many questions about escrow, one which explained the subject all by itself. Usually it is buried in a few pages of a real estate book or a how-to-make-a-million guide. You'd have to spend hours, and you'd have to buy numerous separate books, just to be sure you had the most basic escrow information.

I have always been amazed, too, at how readily most buyers and sellers sign their names to the various legal documents involved in a real estate transaction although they have but a faint understanding of what those mysterious documents are.

Besides the lack of available information, there are three basic reasons why the subject is such a mystery to most people:

- The primary one is emotional involvement. Most people simply want to get escrow over with as quickly as possible to achieve their primary objective, the acquisition or disposition of property. The buyer says, "I want that house, that piece of property. Let's get it into escrow right away. I'll sign, I'll sign. Just let me have it." And the seller says, "Where's my money?"

- Then there are the lengthy contract forms and the "fine print" which are so forbidding that few people are inclined to read them at all.

- Lastly, there's the jargon: "due-on-sale clauses, grantors, impounds, prorations, quitclaim deeds, reconveyances, subject to's, wraparounds," and so on (yes, they're all in the glossary).

Your real estate agent, your banker, your attorney, and even your friends can all give you some information about escrow, but you really ought to have this information all gathered together in one book, a guidebook to help you through the final stages of your real estate transaction. You need an unbiased, clearly stated explanation of what escrow does and how escrow works.

After all, it is your money and your property that must go through escrow, and no matter what it is you are buying, a house as shelter for yourself or an income property as a nestegg for your retirement, that property is an important investment. Just as you wouldn't really want to trust someone else to take your money and buy you a car or some jewelry or undergarments, neither should you leave your real estate affairs wholly in the hands of someone else. Your real estate investment is bound to be the largest financial commitment you will make during your entire lifetime. It's very important to you, and you should be satisfied that it's handled correctly. Because no one else has your best interests in mind more than you do, you should know something about escrow yourself.

ACKNOWLEDGEMENTS

I wish to acknowledge my husband, Bob, for his long-term, whole-hearted support; my Aunt Evy, from whose advice grew my "real estate mentality"; Kay Goff, for his advice and criticisms; Bob Johnson, who supplied the necessary mechanical and technical tools to write this book; Jackie and Junior, who started me in the escrow business many years ago; Adele, for her help and understanding; Clyde Royston, for sharing his invaluable knowledge; my family and friends, who waited patiently and always gave me encouragement; Jeffrey Cunningham, for sharing his considerable expertise on reconveyance; and Leigh Robinson, who put everything together.

TABLE OF CONTENTS

INTRODUCTION

Let's suppose that you've taken a lot of time and gone to a lot of trouble to find exactly the property you want to buy, a property which suits your various and complex needs. You've spent many hours talking price and terms with the seller; you've finally agreed upon a purchase price; and you've even agreed to put up a deposit to confirm the contract.

What happens next? How does this property, this real estate, actually change hands? And what do you need to do now to insure that the transaction will occur precisely according to the terms you have negotiated?

Well, the very next thing you need to do is "open escrow," a procedure known variously in some parts of the country as "title closing" or "settlement." To do that, you simply give your entire deposit and all your instructions regarding the transaction to an impartial third party, most likely an escrow company, but it may be a title company, an abstract company, an abstract attorney, or a real estate attorney. This third party then has the responsibility of handling all the details necessary for the property to change hands. You are relieved of the details from then on.

When you do go ahead and open escrow, you are most likely told that everything is in good hands and will be taken care of for you. Don't worry, people say. Everything will be okay. But wait a minute! Don't you have any questions about this mysterious escrow procedure? After all, you are entrusting some very important papers and some very large sums of money to perfect strangers, not to mention the responsibility you're giving them. Are you doing it all blindly? Wouldn't you feel better if you knew what in the world was about to happen in escrow? Sure you would. Most anybody would.

All right, then, let's proceed to determine how much you already know about escrow. Let's figure out your escrow I.Q. Do your best to answer these representative questions:

- What information is needed to open escrow?

- Why is it important that your deposit check be held in escrow rather than given directly to the seller?

- What does the escrow agent do with the deposits?

- What papers will you be asked to sign, and how will these papers be prepared?

- How will your loan be processed?

- What is title insurance, and why do you need it?

- What problems might arise in escrow to prevent your purchase from coming to a close?

- How can you be certain that the papers you sign are correct?

- Who decides when escrow will close?

- Can you change the way you hold title after escrow closes?

Okay, how did you do? If you were able to answer all of these questions to your own satisfaction, your escrow I.Q. is probably high enough for you to figure you're a know-it-all about escrow, and you're excused from reading this book. Ah, but if you were unsure about some of your answers, your escrow I.Q., whatever it is, could most certainly be raised by reading this book.

To learn the answers to these questions and others about escrow, we'll go step-by-step, clearly and simply, through ordinary escrow instructions and common loan documents; we'll check for completeness and accuracy; we'll find out what problems to watch out for; and you'll learn how to feel confident that your own escrow will close promptly. By the time you have finished reading this book, you should have the escrow I.Q. of a genius, and, what's more, you'll even be able to communicate knowledgeably with your escrow officer. You'll be speaking her language, "escrowese." It's easy. Really it is!

This book is designed to give you a good understanding of what your escrow officer should be doing for you. It provides you with all the information you need to ask her about your transaction. Perhaps after reading it, you'll even be able to inform her of some things she didn't know about before or had forgotten. Escrow officers are not infallible, you know.

Most important of all, with what you learn from reading this book, you should feel confident enough to follow your purchase or sale all the way through escrow and know what's happening at each step.

Following your escrow is easier than you may think, and it is well worth the small investment of your time.

By the way, I will refer throughout this book to escrow officers as women because they generally are. Your own escrow officer, however, may very well be a man. My referring to them repeatedly as women is not meant in any way to imply that one gender is more qualified than the other but just that you are more likely to encounter an escrow officer who is female than one who is male.

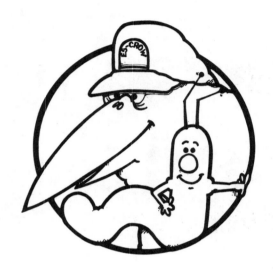

1
ESCROW OVERVIEW

WHAT IS ESCROW?

Basically, escrow is a means for enabling ownership transfers to occur fairly and squarely. Escrow involves an impartial third party brought into a transaction to see that the primary parties, the buyer and seller, perform as they have agreed they would. Escrow enables a buyer and seller to do business with minimum risk because the responsibility for handling the funds and documents is placed in the hands of someone who is not the least bit affected by the outcome. The escrow holder is a disinterested go-between for the parties involved in the transaction, one whose legal obligation is to safeguard the interests of everyone who is affected by the outcome.

Although there may be an escrow involved in many different kinds of transactions, such as refinancing, sales of notes, sales of businesses, sales of business assets, transfers of liquor licenses, and even the release of the American hostages from Iran back in 1981 (remember that the Bank of England was chosen to be the escrow holder), escrow is used most extensively in the sale of real estate. In this context, which is the one this book is all about, escrow may assist in the transfer of real estate, in the transfer of personal property included with real property, or in the processing of a loan. In short, an escrow is useful whenever a third party is needed to assure impartiality, to keep or hold any funds or documents safely until all the details have been settled. This third party handles all of the details necessary to complete the transaction and then, after the details have all been taken care of, disburses the documents and monies to the proper parties at the proper time.

You may have wished at times that there were some kind of escrow arrangement available when you sent off your cash, check, or money order for some mail-order merchandise because you never know whether you'll receive your order or not and you never know whether you'll be satisfied once you do receive it. Unfortunately, there is no such arrangement available. You just have to hope that the mail-order company is honest enough to send you the merchandise after it receives your money and that it will handle promptly any complaint you might have.

The amount of money involved in any single mail order transaction is generally insignificant, however, when compared to the amounts of money involved in real estate transactions. That's why escrow is so important to your real estate purchase, sale, or trade. It enables the transfer to take place with the fewest problems possible and ensures full satisfaction of the contract.

WHAT ARE THE REQUIREMENTS FOR ESCROW?

Escrow is said to exist when a buyer of real property agrees by a valid written contract to relinquish all control over his purchase money in exchange for the seller's grant deed. A contract sufficient to involve an escrow must comply with the four basic requirements for any valid contract, namely, that there must be competent parties, a valid consideration, a property as subject matter, and mutual agreement as to the terms and conditions. The buyer and seller then become the primary parties or "principals" in the escrow, and when there is a lender involved, the lender becomes a primary party in need of escrow protection, too.

The written contract used to initiate most real estate escrows is called a real estate purchase agreement and receipt for deposit. Later, this contract is accompanied by written escrow instructions. When properly written and signed by the principal parties, these instruments become binding contracts fully enforceable in a court of law. Just as the principals have to comply with the terms of the contracts they have signed, so, too, must the escrow agent comply with the terms of the escrow instructions.

WHY SHOULD I OPEN ESCROW?

You should open escrow in order to assure yourself of concurrent performance. "Concurrent performance" means that the grant deed is recorded at the same time or on the same day that your money is released from escrow, that is, after all obligations, such as loans, inspection fees, monies for termite clearance, title fees, and the like, have been paid. Escrow guarantees that your money is taken care of properly and legally and that your real estate transaction will occur with concurrent performance.

Escrow also assures you that your money and important papers are safely in the hands of a disinterested third party who has the legal responsibility to protect them. In essence, escrow provides a clearing house for funds and documents and a means for seeing that all the conditions of your real estate transaction are met before the property changes hands. All parties to the escrow have legal protection during the period of escrow, and everything is managed by the disinterested escrow holder, thereby minimizing the possibility of fraud or violation of any terms of the agreement.

WHAT DOES THE ESCROW OFFICER DO?

The officer assigned to your escrow acts as your personal secretary, no matter whether you are the buyer or the seller. By law she must comply with the terms and conditions of your instructions, and she must keep your funds safely deposited in a separate escrow account. She will also strive to be as confidential as possible.

The escrow officer acts as the impartial party in the transaction and performs all the necessary clerical duties involved in order to close your escrow. Among these duties are the following:

- Ordering the preliminary title report;

- Securing payoff demands and/or beneficiary statements from existing lenders and requesting full reconveyances of any deeds of trust to be paid off in escrow;

- Obtaining instructions and loan documents from the new lender (buyer's lender);

- Obtaining documents to clear any outstanding liens against the property;

- Issuing receipts for deposits of documents and funds and holding funds in a separate account (if a deposit of, say $1,000 or more, is to be held in escrow for more than a few days, you should request that it be deposited into a high-yielding in-

BUYER

ESCROW HOLDER
CARRIES OUT ESCROW INSTRUCTIONS
CLEARS TITLE
CALCULATES PRORATIONS
DRAWS UP DEED
RECORDS DEED
DISTRIBUTES DOCUMENTS & MONEY

SELLER

PURCHASE MONEY AND ESCROW FEES

ESCROW FEES AND DEED

DEED

PURCHASE MONEY

terest-bearing savings account; any interest accumulated is then credited to you at the close of escrow);

• Prorating taxes, interest, rents, etc.;

• Preparing buyer's and seller's escrow instructions and seeing that all documents are properly executed; determining when everything's going to be completed so the transaction can close;

• Obtaining title insurance for the buyer and/or the lender;

• Arranging timely transfer of the fire insurance policy or seeing that the buyer secures a new policy;

• Recording the necessary documents, such as grant deeds, deeds of trust, powers of attorney, substitutions of liability, and reconveyances, when all the conditions of the transaction have been met; and

• Disbursing all funds to the proper parties, delivering documents, and preparing the final closing statements.

HERE'S A TIP ABOUT ESCROW OFFICERS: Remember that one of the many extra services which escrow companies offer is information. Your escrow officer will be happy to answer your questions about escrow in general and your own escrow in particular, so long as your questions are not, strictly speaking, the kind of legal questions you ought to be asking an attorney. You will find that your escrow officer frequently

knows the answers to escrow questions, or she knows where the answers can be found. Indeed, she should be the first person you call whenever a question arises. She knows the status of your escrow at any given moment and will be happy to discuss it with you. Be frank and open with her because only if she has all of the pertinent facts available can she make sure that your title and escrow questions are answered and that your escrow will close on time. She really is a personal secretary for you. Don't be afraid to ask her your questions, and don't let yourself be rushed into signing anything you don't understand. Ask her your questions first. Sign your papers second.

> *PLEASE NOTE WELL*
> Escrow officers have quite a responsibility. They are supposed to be as impartial as a bench-sitting judge and as secretive as a mother confessor. They are supposed to know whose eyes should see which documents and to keep one party's prying eyes from seeing the other party's private papers. Above all, they are supposed to preserve the confidentiality of every escrow they handle. Theirs is not an easy job.

HOW DOES THE ESCROW HOLDER GET PAID?

A single escrow fee, determined by the amount of money involved in the transaction, covers all of the usual escrow services except for the title insurance fees.

Customs unique to a particular geographical area generally dictate who will pay

the fees (see Appendix). In some areas, the buyer customarily pays the title and the escrow fees, whereas in other areas, the seller customarily pays half of the fees and the buyer half. In still other areas, for some unknown reason, the seller pays all of the escrow fees. But just as real estate sales commissions are negotiable, so, too, is the responsibility for paying these fees. At some time before signing the purchase agreement, though, the buyer and seller ought to determine who will pay the fees so there won't be any argument later about who is supposed to be paying them.

IS THERE SUCH A THING AS A TIMETABLE FOR THE TYPICAL ESCROW?

Yes and no. Just as there is no typical American or typical child, there is no typical escrow, not in real life anyway. They're all different. Still, there are many similarities among escrows, enough so that it is possible to create a timetable for a so-called "typical" escrow. Take a look at the table below. It shows how long you might expect the various escrow activities to take.

TIMETABLE–TYPICAL ESCROW	
WEEK	**ACTIVITY**
1	Open escrow
2-4	Order the preliminary title report Shop for a loan
5-6	Complete the loan application Check the preliminary title report for liens, judgments, problems, etc. Review the termite report
6-8	Prepare escrow instructions Sign the loan documents. Buyer: Deposit balance of money due Seller: Sign the deed and escrow instructions
8-10	Close escrow Record the documents Release the seller's money Pay off the old loans and miscellaneous charges Deliver the grant deed to the buyer Prepare the closing statements

2
OPENING ESCROW

WHAT'S INVOLVED IN OPENING ESCROW?

Opening escrow involves simply visiting the office of any firm which handles escrows, then handing over the deposit monies and giving instructions for the transaction. Both the buyer and the seller submit escrow instructions, and so does the lender if there is one.

That's all there is to opening escrow. It's something that anyone who's involved in the transaction may do—the buyer, the seller, the lender, or the real estate agent. It doesn't matter who opens the escrow just so long as those involved in the transaction have designated someone to do it when they sign the final purchase agreement. Generally, the real estate agent, being the one most familiar with escrow procedures, takes the initiative and opens the escrow, but the agent doesn't have to be the one to do it. Anyone may.

A COMMON MISUNDERSTANDING: Mike and Liz like a certain house that's for sale, but because it's for sale by its owner, they decide to pass it up. After all, without a real estate agent involved, who would protect their deposit money and who would take care of all the escrow details?

THE WAY THINGS REALLY ARE: Mike and Liz could make an offer on this house with complete confidence that their interests would be protected. All they need to do is select a reputable escrow company and a knowledgeable escrow officer.

In for-sale-by-owner transactions, which involve no agent at all, either the buyer or the seller or both together may open escrow.

HOW SHOULD I SELECT MY ESCROW AGENT?

In selecting an escrow agent to handle your transaction, consider the following criteria:

- *Reputation of the Company in the Community*—Because you want to protect yourself and your property with a dependable escrow agent, you would be wise to ask your friends and acquaintances who have had experience with real estate transactions to recommend a company they have been pleased with, one which met their expectations.

- *Managerial Experience*—The escrow agent you select should be professional and reliable and should employ skilled escrow officers. Your escrow officer should be knowledgeable, efficient, friendly, and confidential. After reading this book, you'll be prepared to ask questions of escrow officers to determine which one you want to handle your transaction.

- *Office Location*—Since you will have to visit the escrow agent's office in person at least once and perhaps several times to prove your identity and sign numerous papers, try to select an agent with an office conveniently located near your home or work so you can reach it during normal business hours in just a few minutes. The escrow office itself should be neat and orderly, and it should provide you and your escrow officer with quiet, dignified surroundings.

• *Fees*—The fees charged by escrow agents do vary. Whenever possible, try to se-

lect the most reputable and professional one you can find, one which also charges reasonable fees.

In certain circumstances, you may have no choice when the time comes to select an escrow agent, for some institutional lenders have their own escrow departments and prefer to use them exclusively for their own loans. You can find out by asking lenders when you apply for a loan whether they handle their own escrows.

You will always have a choice of title insurance companies, however, and you may want to shop around for one, for they vary in both rates and coverage.

The most commonly used escrow agents are title insurance companies, trust companies, banks, savings and loan associations, real estate companies, and independent escrow companies, all of which are strictly regulated by the government. Lawyers, too, sometimes serve as escrow agents. No matter who acts as the escrow agent, though, the function of the agent is basically the same. Only the specific procedures which they follow will vary somewhat.

Be aware that the entire practice of handling escrow does vary from place to place just as the party responsible for paying the fees varies. Even from county to county within states it varies. In Northern California, for instance, title insurance companies usually process the escrow and the issuance of a title insurance policy together, whereas in Southern California, independent escrow agents handle most of the escrows, and title companies issue the title insurance separately.

In some parts of the country, particularly in the East, the buyer and seller hire different lawyers, who, in turn, see that their clients fulfill every obligation necessary to complete the transaction. There is some consultation between the lawyers, and then, at closing, there is an exchange, an examination, and a signing of the documents. This is a more casual escrow procedure, but it still involves a third party (or parties) entrusted to carry out the desires of buyer and seller.

WHAT INFORMATION WILL I NEED TO OPEN ESCROW?

To open escrow you will need to provide the escrow company the following information regarding your transaction:

- Purchase price, address, and description of property;

- Seller's name and address;

- Buyer's name and address;

- Real estate agent, if any, his address, and the commission agreed upon;

- Parties to whom preliminary title reports are to be sent (generally they are the buyer, seller, lender, and real estate agent);

WORKSHEET FOR OPENING ESCROW

DATE July 2, 1990

PERSON OPENING ESCROW Donald Duncan, Agent

ADDRESS 312 3rd St., Boonville, CA 11002

TELEPHONE (123) 987-4567

PROPERTY ADDRESS 12 Allendale Ct., Boonville, CA

OWNER Samuel P. Seller, A married Man

ADDRESS 12 Allendale Ct., Boonville, CA 11002

TELEPHONE (123) 456-7890

BUYER Bruce B. Buyer + Barbara A. Buyer, His Wife

ADDRESS 525 Mesa Dr., Targaret City, CA 11004

TELEPHONE (123) 109-8765

SALES PRICE $100,000   DEPOSIT $1,000

TOTAL DOWN PAYMENT (INCLUDING DEPOSIT) $10,000

COMMISSION

6 % PAID TO Valley Real Estate

% PAID TO

1ST DEED OF TRUST — LENDER First Federal Trust

AMOUNT $80,000   TERMS Best Available Interest Rate — 30 years

2ND DEED OF TRUST — LENDER Samuel P. Seller

AMOUNT $10,000   TERMS 10%, $212.48 monthly pmts — Due in 5 years

TERMITE REPORT COMPANY Gettem Termite Control Co.

TERMITE REPORT COPIES SENT TO Buyer, Seller, Agent

BILL OF SALE (PERSONAL PROPERTY INCLUDED) Washer/Dryer, Stove, Refrigerator, some window coverings, Chandelier in Dining Room

CLOSING DATE August 10, 1990

CLOSING COSTS

TITLE INSURANCE PAID BY Buyer

ESCROW FEES PAID BY Buyer

TRANSFER TAXES PAID BY Seller

TITLE

PURCHASER TO TAKE TITLE AS Joint Tenants

MISCELLANEOUS Seller to pay up to $250 for termite work

- Termite report information;

- Amount of deposit to be held in escrow (if your deposit is $1,000 or more, stipulate that it be put into a high-yielding interest-bearing account);

- Buyer's fire insurance agent;

- Financing information;

- Personal property involved in the sale, if any (this would include such things as washer, dryer, refrigerator, stove, window coverings, chandeliers, etc.);

- Rents, if any, including due dates and refundable deposits;

- Miscellaneous information peculiar to your purchase;

- Closing date; and

- Current tax bills and most recent title policy (helpful but not absolutely necessary).

Whether you select an escrow officer yourself or have one assigned to you by the escrow company, she must have all of this information available to her in order to prepare your escrow instructions properly. The better informed she is, the faster she can process your escrow. On the previous page you'll find a worksheet which is designed to help you organize all of this information for your escrow officer. There's a blank copy in the back of this book for you to use.

WHAT SHOULD A PURCHASE AGREEMENT INCLUDE?

Often buyers and sellers have questions about making up a written purchase agreement of their own, especially when they come to terms without the aid of a real estate agent. Their agreement may take any number of forms, but it should spell out the basic plan for their real estate transaction, and it must be dated and signed by both the buyer and the seller. The agreement must state clearly the terms of the sale and what must occur before the property can change hands.

Although either the buyers or the sellers may draw up an agreement of their own using a model which includes the standard safeguards, they would be wise to buy a standard purchase agreement form at a stationery store or from a publisher which sells these agreements to real estate agents. One such firm is Professional Publishing Company, 122 Paul Drive, San Rafael, CA 94903, which sells a "Purchase Agreement and Deposit Receipt" basic form for relatively simple transactions. Having a lawyer draw up the agreement is another alternative, of course, one which may be necessary for more complicated transactions. Typically, on the West Coast, lawyers do not become involved in drafting purchase, sale, or exchange agreements unless circumstances, such as a pending probate, a lawsuit, or divorce proceedings, complicate the matter. The real estate agent, buyer, or seller normally draws up the agreement. On the East Coast, however, lawyers do play a large part in real estate transactions, in some areas drawing up the purchase agreement, examining the title, and preparing the necessary legal documents, such as the deed, deeds of trust, promissory notes, and so

NCR (No Carbon Required)

RESIDENTIAL PURCHASE AGREEMENT AND DEPOSIT RECEIPT

RECEIVED FROM __BRUCE A. BUYER and BARBARA A. BUYER, HIS WIFE__

hereinafter designated as PURCHASER, the sum of $ __1,000.00 (One Thousand and no/100ths----------------__)(DOLLARS)

evidenced by ☐ Cash, ☒ Personal Check, ☐ Cashier's Check, ☐ Other _____ to be deposited upon

acceptance with: __SECURE TITLE COMPANY__

on account of the PURCHASE PRICE of $ __100,000.00   One hundred thousand and no/100ths------------__ DOLLARS)

for the real property situated in the City of __Boonville__, County of __Barrett__, State of __California__

described as: __12 Allendale Ct., A.P. #184-162-21__ upon the following TERMS and CONDITIONS:

1. **DEPOSIT INCREASE.** The deposit shall be increased to $ __N/A__ within _____ days from acceptance, evidenced by Cash.

2. **PRORATIONS.** Rents, taxes, interest and other expenses of the property to be prorated as of the date of recordation of the deed. Security deposits, advance rentals, or considerations involving future lease credits shall be credited to Purchaser.

3. **CLOSING.** On or before __8/10/90__ or within __30__ days from acceptance, whichever is later, both parties shall deposit with an authorized escrow holder all funds and instruments necessary to complete the sale in accordance with the terms hereof. Thereafter any party, including Agent, may disclose the terms of sale. The representations and warranties herein shall not be terminated by conveyance of the property. Escrow fee to be paid by ___

4. **PHYSICAL POSSESSION.** Physical possession, with all keys and garage door openers, shall be delivered to Purchaser (check either item [1] or [2]):
   ☒ 1. *Upon recordation of the deed.*
   ☐ 2. *After recordation*, but not later than midnight of _____. Unless Seller has vacated the premises prior to recordation, Seller shall pay Purchaser _____ per day from recordation to date of possession and leave in escrow a sum equal to the above per diem amount multiplied by the number of days from date of closing to date allowed for delivery of possession. Said sum to be disbursed to the persons entitled thereto on the date possession is delivered.

5. **EVIDENCE OF TITLE** in the form of ☒ a policy of title insurance, ☐ other: _____ to be paid for by __Buyer__

6. **EXAMINATION OF TITLE.** Fifteen (15) days from date of acceptance hereof are allowed the Purchaser to examine the title to the property and to report in writing any valid objections thereto. Any exceptions to the title which would be disclosed by examination of the records shall be deemed to have been accepted unless reported in writing within said fifteen (15) days. If Purchaser objects to any exceptions to the title, Seller shall use due diligence to remove such exceptions at his own expense before close of escrow. But if such exceptions cannot be removed before close of escrow, all rights and obligations hereunder may, at the election of the Purchaser, terminate and end, and the deposit shall be returned to Purchaser, unless he elects to purchase the property subject to such exceptions.

7. **ENCUMBRANCES.** In addition to any encumbrances referred to herein, Purchaser shall take title to the property subject to: (1) Real Estate Taxes not yet due and (2) Covenants, conditions, restrictions, rights-of-way and easements of record, if any, which do not materially affect the value or intended use of the property. The amount of any bond or assessment which is a lien shall be ☒ paid, ☐ assumed, by __Seller__

8. **FIXTURES.** All items permanently attached to the property including attached floor coverings, draperies with hardware, shades, blinds, window and door screens, storm sash, combination doors, awnings, light fixtures, TV antennas, electric garage door openers, outdoor plants, and trees, are included free of liens.

9. **PERSONAL PROPERTY.** The following personal property, on the premises when inspected by Purchaser, is included in the purchase price and shall be transferred to Purchaser by a Warranty Bill of Sale at close of escrow. No warranty is implied as to the condition of said property: __Washer/dryer, refrigerator, stove, window coverings, chandelier in living room.__

10. **MAINTENANCE.** Seller covenants that the heating, air-conditioning (if any), electrical, sewer, drainage, sprinkler (if any) and plumbing systems including the water heater, as well as built-in appliances and other mechanical apparatus shall be in normal working order on the date physical possession is delivered. Seller shall replace any cracked or broken glass including windows, mirrors, shower and tub enclosures. Until physical possession is delivered, Seller shall maintain existing landscaping, grounds and pool (if any). The following items are specifically excluded from the above: __None__

11. **NOTICES.** By acceptance hereof, Seller warrants that he has no notice of violations relating to the property, from City, County, or State agencies.

12. **PROVISIONS ON THE REVERSE SIDE.** The provisions checked below are included in this agreement on the reverse side.
   ☒ A. Pest Control Inspection, paid by ☒ Purchaser, ☐ Seller
   ☐ B. Existing Pest Control Report dated _____ By _____
   ☐ C. "As is," but Subject to Purchaser's Approval
   ☐ D. Waiver of Pest Control Inspection
   ☒ E. Roof Inspection within __5__ days of acceptance
   ☐ F. City and County Inspections
   ☐ G. Condominium Disclosure
   ☐ H. Home Protection Contract for $ _____ paid by _____
   ☐ I. Maintenance Reserve of $ _____
   ☐ J. Inspection of Property Condition, Pool, Septic Tank, and Energy Efficiency
   ☐ K. VA Appraisal Clause
   ☐ L. FHA Appraisal Clause
   ☒ M. Smoke Detectors Provided by Seller
   ☐ N. Flood Hazard Zone
   ☐ O. Contingent upon the sale of _____

13. **ACCESS TO PROPERTY.** Seller agrees to provide reasonable access to the property to Purchaser, inspectors and appraisers representing Purchaser.

14. **LIQUIDATED DAMAGES.** By initialing this provision Purchaser: [BAB BAB] and Seller: [SPS] agree that in the event Purchaser defaults in the performance of this agreement, Seller shall retain the amount of the deposit, or three percent of the purchase price, whichever is lesser, as liquidated damages for such default. The remainder of the deposit, if any, shall be refunded to Purchaser. The parties agree to confirm this provision upon making the additional deposit with the escrow holder.

15. **DEFAULT.** In the event that Purchaser shall default in the performance of this agreement, unless the parties have agreed to a provision for liquidated damages, Seller may, subject to any rights of the agent herein, retain Purchaser's deposit on account of damages sustained and may take such action as he deems appropriate to collect such additional damages as may have been actually sustained, and Purchaser shall have the right to take such action as he deems appropriate to recover such portion of the deposit as may be allowed by law. In the event that Purchaser shall so default, unless Purchaser and Seller have agreed to liquidated damages, Purchaser agrees to pay to the brokers entitled thereto such commissions as would be payable in the absence of such default. Purchaser's obligation to said brokers shall be in addition to any rights which said brokers may have against Seller in the event of default. In the event legal action is instituted by the broker or any party to this agreement to enforce the terms of this agreement, or arising out of the execution of this agreement or the sale, or to collect commissions, the prevailing party shall be entitled to receive from the other party a reasonable attorney fee to be determined by the court in which such action is brought.

16. **EXPIRATION.** This offer shall expire unless a copy hereof with Seller's written acceptance is delivered to Purchaser or his Agent within __5__ days.

17. **TIME.** Time is of the essence of this agreement.

18. **ADDITIONAL TERMS AND CONDITIONS:** __Subject to buyer obtaining a loan in the amount of 80% of the purchase price at current interest rate for 30 years. All loan fees to be paid by buyer. Seller to take back a 2nd Note & Deed of Trust in the amount of $10,000.00, at 10% interest, payable in monthly installments of $212.48 and due in 5 (five) years. Seller to pay up to $250.00 for termite repair work.__

The undersigned Purchaser has read both sides of this agreement and acknowledges receipt of a copy hereof. Purchaser acknowledges further that he has not received or relied upon any statements or representations by the undersigned Agent which are not herein expressed.

__Valley Real Estate__ Real Estate Company   DATED: __July 1, 1990__ TIME: __11:30 A.M.__

By __Donald Duncan__ Agent   __Bruce A. Buyer__ Purchaser

Broker's Initials: __DD__ Dated: __July 1, 1990__   __Barbara A. Buyer__ Purchaser

ACCEPTANCE

Seller accepts the foregoing offer and agrees to sell the herein described property for the price and on the terms and conditions herein specified.

COMMISSION. Seller hereby agrees to pay to __Valley Real Estate Company__

the Broker in this transaction, in Cash from proceeds at close of escrow, for services rendered: __in the sale of 12 Allendale Ct., Boonville, California__

In the event that Purchaser defaults and fails to complete the sale, the Broker shall be entitled to receive one-half of Purchaser's deposit, but not more than the commission earned, without prejudice to Broker's rights to recover the balance of the commission from Purchaser. The mutual rescission of this agreement by Purchaser and Seller shall not relieve said parties of their obligations to Broker hereunder. This agreement shall not limit the rights of Broker provided for in any listing or other agreement which may be in effect between Seller and Broker, except that the amount of the commission shall be as specified herein.

The undersigned Seller hereby acknowledges receipt of a copy hereof.   DATED: __July 1, 1990__ TIME: __5:00 P.M.__

__Valley Real Estate__ Real Estate Company   __Samuel P. Seller__ Seller

By __Donald Duncan__   _____ Seller

FORM 101 CAL (1-86) COPYRIGHT © 1986, BY PROFESSIONAL PUBLISHING CORP. 122 PAUL DR., SAN RAFAEL, CA 94903

PROFESSIONAL PUBLISHING

forth (see Appendix).

Whether you use a pre-printed form such as the one shown on the previous page or a tailor-made agreement, your agreement should provide the following as safeguards:

- The deposit received from the buyer and what will happen to it if the agreement is canceled;

- Personal property to be included in the sale, spelled out very specifically (take the time to list all the movable items which are to be included with the real property transfer and avoid numerous problems later. Are the curtains considered "window coverings"? Will a naked light bulb be substituted for the hanging Tiffany lamp? Are the towel bars considered attached and hence real property, or are they personal property?);

- Date for the close of escrow and what will happen if the close is delayed;

- Prorations and the date to be used for computing them;

- Default provisions or what will happen if one party doesn't live up to the agreement;

- Termite inspection, including who pays for the inspection and who pays for remedying any deficiencies disclosed in the inspection, as well as who pays for the recommended preventive measures listed in the report;

- Other property inspections (might include a roofing inspection or a general building inspection);

- Financing arrangements;

- Occupancy date when the buyer may move in (will the seller remain in residence after the close of escrow, and if so, what will his rent be?); and

- Stipulation for payment of real estate commissions, if applicable (commissions are paid only upon close of escrow, and the agreement should provide for payment).

Be sure that your purchase agreement provides ample protections for both buyer and seller.

PLEASE NOTE WELL

If there is anything in the agreement which does not make sense to you, ask your escrow officer or consult an attorney. Do not sign until you thoroughly understand, and feel that you can accept, all the conditions stipulated in the agreement. You don't want to be stuck with something you didn't bargain for, and you surely don't want to take a chance on losing either the property or your deposit money.

WHAT IS A REAL ESTATE TRANSFER DISCLOSURE STATEMENT?

A transfer disclosure statement is a document which reveals a property's known defects. As of January 1, 1987, sellers of California residential property consisting of one to four units (houses through fourplexes) must furnish their buyers with a completed "Real Estate Disclosure Statement" for every such property sold.

These are typical of the questions which sellers must answer in writing for their buyers:

- Is the house built on filled or unstable ground?

- Do you know of any flooding problems on your property or on any adjacent property?

- Do you know of any structural additions or alterations, or the installation, alteration, repair, or replacement of significant components of the structure upon the property, completed during the term of your ownership or that of a prior owner, completed with or without an appropriate permit?

- Do you know of any inspection reports, surveys, studies, or notices concerning the property?

- Do you know of any violations of government regulations, ordinances, or zoning laws regarding this property?

- Has the roof ever leaked while you have owned the property?

- Are the water supply pipes copper, galvanized, or plastic?

- Are you aware of any excessive rust stains in the tubs, lavatories, or sinks?

- Are there any extension cords stapled to baseboards or underneath carpets or rugs?

- Is the furnace room or furnace closet adequately vented?

- Are you aware of any built-in appliances which are in need of repair or replacement?

- Are you aware of any other conditions that could affect the value or desirability of the property?

The buyer must receive a copy of the disclosure statement at some time before the title is transferred. If possible, it should be in his hands *before* he signs the purchase agreement. Should he receive it *after* signing the purchase agreement, he will have between three and five days during which to cancel the sale.

Real estate agents provide the necessary forms for handling this disclosure requirement as a matter of course. Whenever there's no agent involved, the seller has to do it. Forms for this purpose are available through Professional Publishing, as well as through your local Board of Realtors' office.

PLEASE NOTE WELL

If you suspect that the sellers have remodeled or altered their house recently, check with the local building department to make sure that they secured a building permit for the work. If they didn't get a permit and you buy the house, you may get stuck with the consequences. You may have to get a permit yourself and then see that the work passes inspection. If you don't take care of the matter once you own the house, you will have to disclose the matter when you eventually sell the property.

Does all this sound as if Ralph Nader has discovered that real estate buyers need more protection than what they've had in the past? You're right. *Caveat emptor* no longer applies to smaller real estate transactions. Sellers are the ones who now must beware, not buyers. Under the new California law, they're liable for any damages the buyer incurs because of their negligence or failure to comply with the disclosure statement regulations.

A COMMON MISUNDERSTANDING: The real estate agent told Tom and Priscilla that since the house they were buying was a probate sale, they wouldn't be getting a disclosure statement. After all, the previous owners were dead.

THE WAY THINGS REALLY ARE: Probate sales don't merit an exemption from the disclosure requirements. Whoever is selling the property has to make a disclosure. If they can't do it, then they'd better have the property inspected by a professional and make the findings available to the buyers.

WHAT SHOULD I LOOK FOR WHEN I'M MAKING MY OWN INSPECTION OF THE PROPERTY?

Because the seller might neglect to disclose some of the property's defects (the seller might honestly be ignorant about them), you ought to make a critical inspection yourself. Look all around for clues that there might be potential problems which will have to be corrected sooner or later.

On the outside of the structure, look for the following:

• Drainage problems;

• Soil instability and erosion;

• Failing retaining walls;

• Hazardous or overgrown vegetation (you might want to check with your local agricultural extension office for information about the large vegetation on the property; identify it, and then ask whether it has any special requirements, whether it is resistant to insects, whether it is drought-resistant, and how frequently it requires trimming);

• Hazardous railings or stairs;

- Hazardous sidewalks, walkways, or steps;

- Cracks in the sidewalks, driveways, or patio;

- Cracks in the foundation (you might want to determine whether the structure is bolted to its foundation; mudsills which merely rest in a bed of concrete provide little stress resistance);

- Distortions in the overall structure or in any part of it;

- Damage to the crawlspace ventilation screens;

- Cracks in the brickwork, especially the chimney;

- Cracks in the stucco;

- Drain gutter or roof deterioration;

- Missing or damaged window screens;

- Swimming pool cracks;

- Old or malfunctioning swimming pool equipment;

- Hazardous playhouse.

On the inside, look for any of the following:

- Cracks in the basement walls;

- Water stains or white powder on the basement walls;

- Sump pump below ground level (as evidence that there's a ground-water or drainage problem);

- Cracks in the tile or concrete floors;

- Sloping floors;

- Hazardous steps or stairs;

- Cracks in the fireplace;

- Sticking doors or windows (open and close every one of them);

- Uneven spaces between doors and frames (check them when the doors are closed);

- Water stains on the ceilings or around the windows;

- Wall or ceiling cracks;

- Camouflaged wall cracks ("Powder and paint cover what ain't." New paint may be covering old wall cracking; look closely; if present, cracking is likely to be more of a problem in plaster walls than in sheetrock walls.);

- Sagging beams;

- Burned or damaged electrical outlets (look for smudges and broken plastic);

- Extension cords under the carpets or stapled to the walls (don't be concerned about speaker wire; it may look like electrical cord, but it's generally thinner, and it's certainly of no danger unless it's in the way);

- Exposed wiring;

- Accessibility, adequacy, and type of the electrical panel (circuit breakers are preferable over fuses);

- Accessibility of the gas and water shut-off valves (check to see that the shut-off valves work; some rust in an open position and won't budge when you try to turn them off; in that case, they're useless);

- Hazardous water heater (Does it have a temperature-pressure relief valve which drains to the outside? Is it located where leakage won't damage the floors?);

- Evidence of illegal additions.

Also look for the following items designed for household safety:

- Grounded outlets (outlets should accommodate a three-prong plug);

- Polarized outlets (hardware stores sell an inexpensive testing device);

- Ground-fault interrupters (GFI) on electrical circuits in the kitchen, bath, garage, and outdoor areas (both GFI outlets and GFI circuit breakers will provide ground-fault protection for an entire circuit; a GFI outlet will be visible on the wall; it takes the place of an ordinary outlet; a GFI circuit breaker will be located in the electrical panel);

- Fire extinguishers;

- Operable smoke detectors (check type, too; ionization types are good; photocell types are better; combination types are best);

- Safety-glass markings on glass doors and on windows in doors;

- Safety wire on the garage door springs.

As a buyer, you need to know as much as possible about what you're buying *before* you buy it. If the property has certain deficiencies, you'll want the seller to correct them, so you won't be the one paying for them after you become the owner. If the seller won't correct the deficiencies, then the cost for the corrections should be reflected in the price you pay for the property.

ARE THERE ANY OTHER DISCLOSURES WHICH HAVE TO BE MADE?

Sometimes real estate agents act as the seller's agent; sometimes they act as the buyer's agent; and sometimes they do a kind of balancing act, acting on behalf of both seller and buyer. The nature of their relationship can influence a transaction significantly in one way or another, so the principals ought to know who's working for whom.

California law now requires real estate agents to disclose their relationship and their duties to buyers and sellers whenever a transaction involves a single-family residence or a small income property (one to four units).

The agent must first explain whether he's working for the seller, the buyer, or for both the seller and the buyer, and then all parties must sign a disclosure statement to this effect.

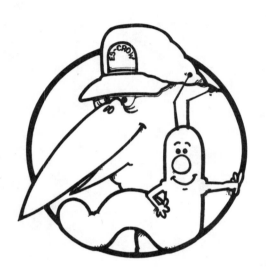

3
THE TITLE SEARCH

WHAT HAPPENS RIGHT AFTER ESCROW OPENS?

Right after escrow is opened, the escrow officer orders that a title search be conducted to trace the chain of title back through every available record. This title search will determine whether the person representing himself as the current owner actually has legal ownership and hence the right to sell the property at all. The search will also reveal what, if any, defects exist on the title. Just as a life insurance company will not insure a person without a thorough physical examination, a title insurance company won't issue a policy of title insurance without doing a thorough title search.

The results of this search are compiled into what is called in most Western states a preliminary title report or "prelim." In some states, it's called a commitment of title; in others, it's called an encumbrance report. No matter what it's called, it reflects the conditions under which a title company is willing to issue a policy of title insurance. Still other states handle their title search results somewhat differently. Their title search firms issue an abstract of title, "abstract" for short, which reflects the various documents in the chain of title without giving any determination as to the title's condition.

HOW IS A TITLE SEARCH PERFORMED?

In order to trace a property's chain of title, a title company examiner searches the records of the county recorder, county assessor, and other government taxing agencies to locate any and all documents which might affect the title to a given property. Most title companies have their own "plant" department where they keep duplicates of recorded documents, along with copies of certain recorded documents from offices and courts at the federal, state, county and municipal levels, any of which may affect titles. Thus, the examiner generally doesn't even have to leave his building to search through these documents.

In his search, the title examiner has four primary determinations to make:

• The exact description of the property;

• The estate or interest in the property;

• The vesting of the estate or interest; and

• The exceptions (liens, encumbrances, and defects) affecting the particular vested interest.

The first step the examiner takes is to locate the property. He does this either by the county assessor's parcel number or by his company's own indexing system. I should note that each title company may have a slightly different system for indexing its documents. Some use a tract- or lot-book system, which is a hand-posted system of recording and indexing documents according to the property description and assessor's parcel number. Some use an outside service which supplies the information to them on microfiche or computer printouts that have specific codes designed for efficiency and ease in tracing the complete history of a particular property.

The county recorder's office itself indexes by name only, using something called a grantor-grantee index. This system is not efficient enough for a title company's search, however, because it lists documents alphabetically by name only, without cross-referencing them to property description. Using this index alone, the examiner could easily confuse one piece of property a person owns with other parcels he may own in the same county.

After locating the property and the assessor's parcel number, then, the examiner notes the current property taxes and looks for any delinquent taxes, assessment bonds, or tax liens.

A COMMON MISUNDERSTANDING: Sears and Macy's filed several judgments against Howard some time ago, but they were in another county. Surely they won't show up during escrow.

THE WAY THINGS REALLY ARE: Howard's escrow company will do a "GI" name run on him and will find all the outstanding judgments against him. They'll have to be paid in escrow.

Next he searches the chain of title, often back through the 1800's, to determine whether there has been a "break" in the chain. Every buyer's and seller's name and every document recorded against that particular piece of property must be checked and verified for authenticity and correctness. The examiner actually pulls out and carefully examines each and every copy of the pertinent documents which have been recorded. He looks up the names of all the grantors and grantees in the general index, an index which lists all the things which apply to a person by name, such as liens,

judgments, assignments, and powers of attorney, whether related to a piece of property or not. The examiner must check the name of every owner thoroughly to be sure it is okay. Often a middle initial is used on some documents and omitted on others. He must ascertain if the different names all refer to the same person. Are Shelley B. Smith, Shelley Bradford Smith, and Shelley Smith all the same person, or are they three different people? In a situation where title is in the name of Shelley B. Smith and she conveys title as Shelley A. Smith, the error would definitely be considered as critical, and it would not be passed by a title company.

He next examines the parcel maps and surveys to report every open easement and right-of-way. He reads every pertinent document to be sure the property description is exactly the same as the parcel in question. He looks at adjoining properties to see if there is an easement or right-of-way which might have been recorded at some later date in the chain. He then reports on every existing deed of trust, judgment, lien, or other encumbrance on the property.

This checking of the title by owners' names, property address, and property description is an efficient and thorough method for locating and verifying information.

Your escrow officer can explain in detail how the search was conducted and how documents were located for your property, and if you are interested in seeing for yourself just how a search is made, your escrow officer can even arrange a tour of the title plant she uses to show you how the documents are indexed and a title is searched. As someone involved in a property transaction, you should feel free to call

"WILL THE REAL SHELLEY B. SMITH PLEASE STAND UP!"

the title plant for further information or to request copies of recorded documents.

HOW LONG DOES A TITLE SEARCH TAKE?

Depending upon the number of documents the examiner must review, a title search will take anywhere from one hour to two weeks to complete.

WHAT KINDS OF THINGS DOES THE SEARCH REVEAL?

The report compiled from the title examiner's findings, the first of many escrow documents you will receive, provides the following information to show the condition of title as of a specific date:

- The vested owner's name as disclosed in public records;

- The current real estate property taxes, including whether they are paid or unpaid, and the date of the last property assessment;

- The outstanding liens, restrictions, easements, or other types of encumbrances;

- The property's legal description of record;

- The conditions under which the title company will issue title insurance; and

- A "plat map" (picture or drawing) showing the location and dimensions of the property as found in recorded documents.

For the escrow officer, the preliminary title report is the key which unlocks the door to completing escrow. This information shows her what items, if any, must be cleared up in order for the title to be conveyed from the seller to you as the new buyer under whatever conditions you have agreed to take title. The report makes no guarantees about insuring the title to the property you are buying. It merely informs you of the contents of documents found in the public records exactly as they appear there and guarantees you only that the search made by the title company is complete. You are not protected against title defects which fail to show up in the records, nor are you protected against documents which are part of the records but have been improperly executed. Only a title insurance policy written for the new owner will insure the title which is being sold and will protect the buyer if there are any defects which do not show up in the records.

Copies of the report go to the buyer, seller, lender, and real estate agent for their evaluation. Only after the buyer and lender accept those items which have been reported against the property can title insurance be issued and escrow closed. Any defects which make the title "unmarketable," that is, any defects which deny the seller the legal right to sell the property, must be removed before someone buys it.

Many times the report will reveal that the seller actually owns the property with someone else. If, for instance, title shows up as Samuel P. Seller as to an undivided 1/2 interest and Skip Smith as to an undivided 1/2 interest, both Samuel and Skip would have to sign the deed. If Skip is out of town or unavailable when he's needed, his absence could complicate matters and delay the closing.

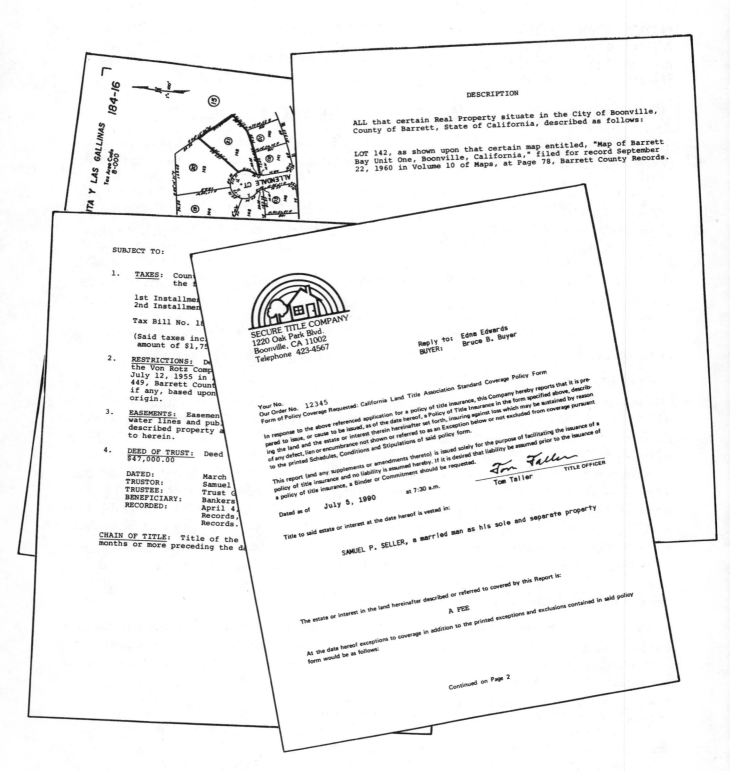

184-16

TA Y LAS GALLINAS

Tax Area Code 8-000

ALLENDALE CT.

DESCRIPTION

ALL that certain Real Property situate in the City of Boonville, County of Barrett, State of California, described as follows:

LOT 142, as shown upon that certain map entitled, "Map of Barrett Bay Unit One, Boonville, California," filed for record September 22, 1960 in Volume 10 of Maps, at Page 78, Barrett County Records.

SUBJECT TO:

1. **TAXES:** Coun
   the f

   1st Installmer
   2nd Installmer

   Tax Bill No. 18

   (Said taxes incl
   amount of $1,75

2. **RESTRICTIONS:** De
   the Von Rotz Comp
   July 12, 1955 in
   449, Barrett Count
   if any, based upon
   origin.

3. **EASEMENTS:** Easement
   water lines and pub
   described property a
   to herein.

4. **DEED OF TRUST:** Deed
   $47,000.00

   DATED: March
   TRUSTOR: Samuel
   TRUSTEE: Trust
   BENEFICIARY: Bankers
   RECORDED: April 4
                     Records,
                     Records.

CHAIN OF TITLE: Title of the
months or more preceding the da

SECURE TITLE COMPANY
1220 Oak Park Blvd.
Boonville, CA 11002
Telephone 423-4567

Reply to: Edna Edwards
BUYER: Bruce B. Buyer

Your No.
Our Order No.   12345
Form of Policy Coverage Requested: California Land Title Association Standard Coverage Policy Form

In response to the above referenced application for a policy of title insurance, this Company hereby reports that it is prepared to issue, or cause to be issued, as of the date hereof, a Policy of Title Insurance in the form specified above, describing the land and the estate or interest therein hereinafter set forth, insuring against loss which may be sustained by reason of any defect, lien or encumbrance not shown or referred to as an Exception below or not excluded from coverage pursuant to the printed Schedules, Conditions and Stipulations of said policy form.

This report (and any supplements or amendments thereto) is issued solely for the purpose of facilitating the issuance of a policy of title insurance and no liability is assumed hereby. If it is desired that liability be assumed prior to the issuance of a policy of title insurance, a Binder or Commitment should be requested.

Tom Taller   TITLE OFFICER
Tom Taller

Dated as of   **July 5, 1990**   at 7:30 a.m.

Title to said estate or interest at the date hereof is vested in:

SAMUEL P. SELLER, a married man as his sole and separate property

The estate or interest in the land hereinafter described or referred to covered by this Report is:

A FEE

At the date hereof exceptions to coverage in addition to the printed exceptions and exclusions contained in said policy form would be as follows:

Continued on Page 2

A COMMON MISUNDERSTANDING: Margaret and her Aunt Sally own forty-one acres of land on the outskirts of Fresno, and a developer has offered Margaret a price which she considers quite attractive. The problem is that Aunt Sally lives on a commune in Readfield, Maine, and is pretty hard to get hold of. Margaret feels pretty sure that her aunt would approve of the transaction, but getting her approval could take a lot longer than the developer is willing to wait. Margaret decides to sign all the papers herself and to send her aunt half of the proceeds.

THE WAY THINGS REALLY ARE: Margaret cannot sell the entire parcel without Aunt Sally's written approval. Aunt Sally's name will appear on the preliminary title report as an owner, and her signature will be required on the grant deed.

Sometimes title shows up as being held by a trust, or it might be in probate pending final disposition of an estate. Either situation would delay the close. When children inherit property from their parents, they frequently assume that they can go ahead and sell the property right away. They don't realize all the time-consuming legal procedures they must follow before they can legally transfer title. For example, there must be a confirmation of the parents' deaths, as well as a confirmation of the validity of whatever trusts are involved. Even when a surviving joint tenant wants to dispose of property which had been held in joint tenancy with someone now deceased, there must be evidence both of the other joint tenant's death and of payment of inheritance taxes. Getting all those papers together takes time.

If a defect, such as a lien or encumbrance, appears on the report and you have not agreed to take title subject to the defect, notify the seller or your escrow officer of your disapproval. For example, if back taxes are due on the property and you don't want to be held liable for them, get them paid in escrow; if a lien exists against the seller and you don't care to assume it, get it paid off in escrow as well; if there's a judgment recorded against the property, get it cleared and obtain the releases showing clearance. If the seller has not removed these defects by the closing date, you can usually stop the purchase and take steps to have what money you have paid returned to you. Ask to look at all the documents listed as encumbrances on the title so you can examine them before the close of escrow. These would include copies of the covenants, conditions, and restrictions, any easement rights, etc.

WHO PAYS FOR THE TITLE SEARCH?

Most often the cost of the title search and the resulting report is included in the title insurance policy premium, which may be paid by either the buyer or the seller or split between both of them, depending upon local customs or the terms which they have negotiated.

WHAT SHOULD I DO WITH THE TITLE REPORT?

Look your title report over very carefully, and do the following:

• Verify that the stated escrow number is correct;

- Note the date on the report because it indicates that the title is as indicated only up to that date, not after;

- Note how title is given and find out whether the vested owner can legally convey title, that he's not a minor, for example;

- Look over the listed exceptions, the things which the title insurance company will not cover, and ask yourself whether you should take any steps to eliminate them;

- Secure a copy of any CC & R's (covenants, conditions, and restrictions) mentioned in the report and determine whether you would be able to abide by them; and

- Obtain copies of any easements; ask the title insurance company to draw them on the plat map for you; and figure out whether they will interfere with any future proposed uses you have for the property.

A COMMON MISUNDERSTANDING: Easements and rights-of-way are so common that Greg figures there's no need to locate them exactly on his plat map. They couldn't possibly interfere with his plans to put a pool in his backyard.

THE WAY THINGS REALLY ARE: An easement or right-of-way could easily be located right where Greg plans to put his pool. He should check his plat map carefully and identify any easements before calling in the pool company.

If you find anything objectionable or unclear about the title report, ask questions about it now. Clear up the matter while you can still do something about it, and if it cannot be settled or answered to your satisfaction, stop the purchase until the matter is resolved. Your escrow officer should be able to explain any item listed in the preliminary report and should be able to answer any questions you may have. Ask, by all means.

PLEASE NOTE WELL

Be sure you check with the local zoning department about zoning restrictions and future planned use of your property. Title companies cannot and do not insure against zoning changes.

MIGHT SOMEONE ORDER A TITLE REPORT ON A PROPERTY EVEN IF IT'S NOT IN ESCROW?

Yes, anyone may order a title search and report alone for a fee of $150-200 in situations involving neither an escrow nor title insurance.

SHOULD I INSPECT THE PROPERTY AGAIN AFTER RECEIVING THE REPORT?

Yes, do take the time to inspect the property personally with report in hand, and ask questions about it when you do. Compare the apparent boundary lines with those shown on the plat map. Don't assume that a fence, a row of trees, or a hedge marks the actual boundaries. That fence may very well be five feet inside the neighbor's yard, and you wouldn't want to move into a new home only to start arguing with your neighbors right away about moving their dilapidated fence.

There are other things you might check that affect title to real property, things which normally do not appear in the public records. They include zoning restrictions, renters' unrecorded leases or month-to-month rights, water rights, persons with a right to title by adverse possession, and work being done on the property that could possibly lead to the filing of a mechanic's lien *after* you buy the property.

A COMMON MISUNDERSTANDING: Rudy decides to buy a charming Victorian house in Petaluma because it's zoned commercial and would make an ideal professional office. He starts running the ads as soon as he gains possession.

THE WAY THINGS REALLY ARE: Although it is zoned commercial, for the past 50 years this Victorian has been used as a personal residence. To change the use from residential to commercial, regardless of the zoning, Rudy will have to conform with all the applicable commercial codes, both city and county. Conformance may involve adding firewalls, additional bathrooms, wheelchair ramps, and fire escapes. It may even require removing the cooking facilities. Before acquiring it, Rudy should find out what the building requires for change of use.

WHAT ARE CC & R'S?

Covenants, conditions, and restrictions, or CC & R's for short, are limitations placed upon the use of land by its owner. They are usually included in the deed and specify what uses will be permitted or prohibited on the land. They are created in appropriate deed clauses, in special agreements, or in a general plan affecting an entire subdivision.

Covenants are promises to do or not to do certain things. A promise not to raise chickens in your backyard or not to put up a clothesline are examples of covenants.

A COMMON MISUNDERSTANDING: Bill and Jeannine don't feel they need to bother reading the CC and R's for their planned unit development. Aren't all CC and R's standard anyway? The other homeowners will surely love the opportunity to buy fresh eggs from local chickens. Bill's pet rabbit, Charlie, is so cute that everyone will adore him.

THE WAY THINGS ARE: Bill and Jeannine should take the time to read their CC and R's. Expressly forbidden in them could be the raising of chickens and rabbits, and then Bill and Jeannine would be faced with the difficult choice of moving out or getting rid of their menagerie.

Conditions are stipulations or qualifications in a deed which, if not complied with,

may give the grantor or his heirs the right to demand the property back. This is otherwise known as a reversionary right. For example, a seller could specify that he will convey his property to a buyer on the condition that the buyer not sell intoxicating liquors on the property. If this condition is not complied with, the property may revert back to the seller, his heirs, or his successors.

Restrictions encompass a general classification for various types of limitations on the use of real property, and they fall into two categories: *private restrictions* and *public restrictions*.

Private restrictions are those imposed on a property by its owner to assure a degree of uniformity in the development of a neighborhood, such as limiting the use of land to residential purposes only. Such restrictions may not, of course, be unlawful or contrary to public policy, nor may they be unreasonable.

Public restrictions are best exemplified by zoning ordinances, which are said to be designed to "promote public health, safety, comfort, convenience, and general welfare." These ordinances place limitations on the use of land within certain areas in accordance with a general policy that has been adopted. Many communities have developed master plans for zoning that covers the future pattern for freeways, recreational, airport, or shoreline development. You should be aware that zoning ordinances are a separate obligation from CC & R's and that zoning ordinances may not necessarily conform with CC & R's. As an example, say that a buyer gets a zoning variance to put a duplex on his property but that he fails to comply with the CC & R's which call for "a single family dwelling only." Despite the zoning change, the owner may not violate the CC & R's in actual use.

WHAT IS AN EASEMENT?

An easement is a right granted by a property owner to another person allowing some land to be set aside for certain purposes, or it may be a property right reserved by a former owner. Easements are commonly granted for pipelines, telephone cables, access roads, power lines, and the like. Thus, if access to your property is possible only by crossing your neighbor's land, you may try to get an easement from him for the right to use that portion of his property.

Basically, there are two types of easements: *appurtenant easements* and *easements in gross*. An appurtenant easement is an interest in property set aside for things such as roads. Once created, it will normally stay with a property from owner to owner, being transferred with the title whether it is named in the deed or not. Problems could occur if an access across your property is being used by your neighbors so you should try to determine whether your property is subject to this type of easement by making a personal inspection. Obviously, if a road runs through your property and continues onto your neighbor's land, and you can see that someone is using it, you should suspect that an appurtenant easement exists even if it is not mentioned in the title report.

An easement in gross, normally obtained, say, to bring in a telephone line, must be described in the deed in order to pass with the title. As a buyer, one of your main concerns would be to note whether there is an easement in gross located right where you may have plans to build or expand in the future. You surely don't want to add a room to your house only to find out later that it is directly over a utility easement and the utility company has to dig up a broken pipe underneath your living room.

As a buyer, your main concerns about easements are whether they are recorded or not, whether their location and use will disturb your own use of the property, and whether their present uses can be expanded by their terms. How would you be affected if that access road across your land, which now serves a nearby farm, later must carry scores of cars when the farm is sold and the property is developed into a factory? What would you do if the friendly neighbors who now own the common driveway which both of you share should sell to someone who won't help with the pavement patching and the chuckhole filling? Recognize that if there is an easement involved in a property transaction, it may cause you headaches later on.

Here's a sample of one recorded easement which was obviously designed to reduce headaches for those people who live around a golf course: "An easement and specific right of way for ingress and egress and seizure and the immediate search, recapture, retrieving, and recovery of errant golf balls for a period of 5 minutes immediately following the departure of any golf ball from the confines of the club golf links, as reserved in the declaration by Virginia Country Club of Long Beach, a corporation, recorded in book 16402, page 291, Official Records."

And here's an instance where *not* having an easement presented a real problem. Several of my clients were trying to buy 650 acres on the top of a mountain overlooking the Pacific Ocean. Not only was the view magnificent, but the prospects for the property were outstanding because it could be subdivided easily. It was priced reasonably and seemed like a very good deal for the buyers until the title report came out. What a shock that report was! It showed that there was no legal access to the property whatsoever. The snag was that the paved roads surrounding the 650 acres were all privately owned by individuals, not by the county, and these individuals were not willing to give access over their roads. There was no other way to get in except maybe by helicopter. Eventually, after months of negotiations, legal pleadings, and entanglements, the individual owners were persuaded, for a price, of course, to give access rights over their privately owned roads, and escrow finally did close.

The lesson to be learned from this last example is that reading the title report carefully is very important to assure that you can use a property as you intend to use it. Never assume just because your property is surrounded by paved roads that you automatically have the use of them. You don't.

WHAT ARE LIENS AND ENCUMBRANCES?

Liens and encumbrances are the two most common defects on a property's title. By themselves, they do not make a title unmarketable because the seller does have the legal right to sell his property subject to the existing liens and encumbrances, but any buyer should understand them, be aware of them, and be willing to accept them.

Encumbrances include anything that limits or affects the title, such as mineral, timber, or water rights held by the seller or a third party; easement rights permitting others to cross the property; and restrictive covenants in the deed limiting what the property can be used for.

Liens are also encumbrances, but they arise only when a property becomes security for the payment of a debt. A lien is a legal claim against a property or a person to insure payment of a debt, and a lienholder has the right to go to court to sell your property if you don't pay off the debt. This claim against a property makes transferring title or selling a property impossible without first either paying off the debt or assuming it.

Liens may be voluntary (a mortgage or deed of trust), statutory (property taxes), or involuntary (a judgment affecting all the property an owner has or acquires during the legal life of the lien).

Statutory and involuntary liens fall into four main categories:

- *Property Tax Liens*—These are placed against a property when the property taxes are not paid on time; they are given precedence over all other claims; if they continue to be delinquent for five years, the property will be sold off to pay the taxes; whenever a property is foreclosed upon, taxes are always the first debts paid;

- *Judgment Liens*—These are general liens resulting when a person suing another person wins a judgment from a court for the sums owing and records an abstract of that judgment;

- *Mechanics' Liens*—These are recorded with the county by contractors, subcontractors, materials suppliers, or workers who wish to be paid for their delinquent bills covering labor or materials on new construction, land improvements, or remodeling projects; and

- *Federal or State Liens*—These result from unpaid federal or state taxes, personal and inheritance taxes being the most common.

The seller normally has to clear all liens from the property before he can sell and deliver clear title to the buyer. Any money used to satisfy these liens will be deducted from the seller's sales proceeds. Remember that special assessments, such as city assessments levied to repair a street; and recorded judgments, such as a mechanic's lien or unpaid bills resulting from a court action, will all have to be paid off in order to close escrow. If you're the seller in such a situation, be aware that these "hidden" liens will cost you money at closing time.

A COMMON MISUNDERSTANDING: Fred has sold his house, and it's due to close escrow in three weeks, but the property taxes have to be paid next week. He figures that the taxes should be the new owner's responsibility, so he decides not to pay them.

THE WAY THINGS REALLY ARE: In escrow Fred will have to pay all the property taxes and the property-tax penalties he owes. They will show up in the title search as a lien on the house, a lien which has to be paid in order for escrow to close. If he has the money available to pay them when they're due, he should pay them, and he will then avoid having to pay a penalty for late payment.

IS IT POSSIBLE TO TAKE TITLE SUBJECT TO CERTAIN EXCEPTIONS?

Yes, you may agree to take title subject to exceptions, such as current property taxes, easements, assumed liens, trust deeds, and CC & R's, but you should be absolutely certain you know what they are. Look at the numbered items on your title report. They are the exceptions for this particular property. Make a check list of these exceptions, verify them, and go over the following questions:

- Are there any unpaid special assessments for roads, sewers, or other major improvements?

- Are there any tax liens on the property?

- Are there any outstanding judgments (collection agency bills, etc.)?

- Is the current owner's name correct? Is ownership held by a trust, partnership, or corporation which might complicate the consummation of your transaction?

- Are there any mortgages or deeds of trust that are assumable? If there are, what is the amount and the interest rate?

- Who is the current lender, and will the new buyer be able to obtain financing from him? (This might save the seller from having to pay a prepayment penalty.)

- If there is any new construction involved, was a notice of completion recorded and if so, when? (If a notice was recorded, then the original contractor has 60 days from the recording date to file a lien, and all other persons must record their claims within 30 days. If a notice was not recorded, claimants have 90 days from the actual date of completion during which to file. Any lien resulting from land improvements prior to recording of a trust deed has precedence over the trust deed.)

- What are the current taxes and when was the last assessment year?

After you have read the preliminary report and checked off the exceptions, inform your escrow officer whether the existing loans will be paid off or whether you will be taking title subject to these liens. This information is vital to the smooth processing of your escrow, so vital, in fact, that it will be discussed in more detail later under the subject of assumptions.

WHAT IS AN ATTORNEY'S CERTIFICATE OF TITLE?

As mentioned before, the procedure used in tracing a chain of title is slightly different in some Eastern states, where an attorney rather than a title company is hired to examine all the recorded documents relating to the title. The attorney makes a report of his findings in what is called an abstract or certificate of title. This report details both what records were examined and what encumbrances currently exist against the title, and it is essentially the same as a title report. It is not insurance of marketable title nor does it insure against undisclosed defects, such as forgery, clerical errors, undisclosed heirs, improper interpretation of wills, and so on.

If the attorney makes a negligent mistake in his title search, naturally you may sue him for any losses you suffer due to his negligence just as you may sue a title company under the same circumstances.

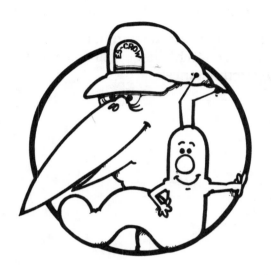

4
HOLDING TITLE

WHY SHOULD I BE CONCERNED ABOUT HOLDING TITLE?

One of the most important aspects of the entire escrow procedure is how you take title because it not only determines how you will be insured, it has significant legal and tax consequences as well. It can even create some unanticipated complications in the future when you decide to transfer the title to someone else. So much depends upon the precise way you hold title, in fact, that you should not rely on advice from a real estate agent, escrow officer, or friend when you are trying to determine how to hold title. You would be wise to consult your attorney or tax consultant about the best way for you to hold title in your particular circumstances.

A COMMON MISUNDERSTANDING: Bill and Judy are a married couple in their late twenties who have never given estate planning a second thought. They do their own income taxes and haven't yet needed an attorney for anything. They decide to take title to their first house the same way all their friends have, as joint tenants.

THE WAY THINGS REALLY ARE: Joint tenancy may not be the best way for Bill and Judy to take title. They have three small children and want the property to pass to their children in case they both die. Bill and Judy need to secure more information about holding title before they make up their minds.

WHAT ARE THE MOST COMMON WAYS TO HOLD TITLE?

There are four common ways to hold title to real property: joint tenancy,

tenancy-in-common, community property (also known in some states as tenancy by entirety), and sole-and-separate.

- *Joint Tenancy*—The main distinguishing characteristic of joint tenancy is the right of survivorship. If one of the joint tenants ("tenants" here means "owners," not "renters") dies, his interest passes automatically to the surviving party or parties instead of being tied up in lengthy probate proceedings. When two or more people own a property as joint tenants, they own an undivided equal interest in the property and have the same rights to the use of the entire property, that is, neither co-tenant can distinguish which portion of the land he owns. Once a joint tenancy has been created, no joint tenant can sell his interest without terminating the joint tenancy. If one does sell his interest, his buyer comes in as a tenant-in-common rather than as a joint tenant. For example, if Appleby, Baker, and Crabtree hold a piece of property as joint tenants and Crabtree sells his interest to Duffy, Duffy buys in as a tenant-in-common. If Duffy dies, his share goes to his heirs rather than to Appleby or Baker. Appleby and Baker remain joint tenants and each has the right of survivorship to the other's interest. Upon their death, their interest would never go to Duffy. If a joint tenant chooses to sell his interest, he may do so without the consent of the other owners, unless the owners specify otherwise in a contract among themselves. This situation sometimes occurs when a husband or wife wants to leave his or her interest by will. Remember that a joint tenant cannot leave his interest to anyone else but his fellow joint tenant(s) in his will, not even to his children.

- *Tenancy-in-Common*—When two or more persons buy property together, whether their shares are equal or unequal, they are said to hold the property as tenants-in-common. Tenancy-in-common is so standard as a form of ownership for unrelated buyers that it is generally presumed to be the way they hold title if nothing else appears to the contrary. The shares are also presumed to be equal unless they are listed otherwise on the deed, and each of the tenants has equal rights of possession. Each co-tenant owns an undivided interest, but unlike a joint tenancy, these interests need not be equal and may arise from different conveyances and at different times. There is no right of survivorship as in a joint tenancy so that if one of the tenants-in-common should happen to die, his interest would not revert automatically to the remaining tenants. Consequently, each tenant-in-common should note in his will the person or persons to whom his share will pass. Unrelated property buyers usually buy as tenants-in-common rather than as joint tenants because they want their property to go to their heirs and not to the surviving joint tenants. Each individual co-tenant can sell or mortgage his interest in the land, but he acts only for his own share and cannot bind anyone else's interest.

- *Community Property*—Holding title to real property as community property is a type of ownership available to married couples only. At present, there are nine states which are considered "community-property states": Arizona, California, Idaho, Louisiana, Nevada, New Mexico, Texas, Washington, and Wisconsin (the "Marital Property Act" defined Wisconsin as a community-property state, but individual circumstances will dictate how this act is interpreted; check with a knowledgeable expert if you need an interpretation). These states regard any property purchased during a marriage as community property. Both husband and wife have an equal right to possess the property during their marriage, and, in some states, upon the death of either spouse, the survivor automatically receives half of the community property and the other half passes to the lawful heirs. Neither holder of community property may sell the entire property without the consent of the other, yet either holder may sell his own share without notifying the other. If either one dies and leaves no will, the surviving holder may acquire the property, but unlike joint tenancy, either holder may will his half interest to others if he so chooses.

- *Sole and Separate Property*—Holding title as "sole and separate property" means that no one else has any interest in it. If you are married and want to take title this way, you may, but you should record a quitclaim deed from your spouse to yourself so that no community interest could be claimed at a later date (applies only in community-property states). The quitclaim deed transfers any interest or right you may have in a property, but it does not, remember, make any guarantees or warranties as to the condition of title.

As you have probably observed, these four ways of taking title offer extremely varied possibilities. In general, if you have children, or plan to, you will most likely want to consider taking title under community property or as tenants-in-common, since you will likely want your children to inherit your property, something which joint tenancy does not permit.

In California, property of a married person is either separate property or community property. Community property law presumes that all property acquired during marriage is community property or co-owned unless it is proven to be sole and separate property. If it is separate property, it may be held in severalty (sole and separate), in joint tenancy, in tenancy-in-common, or in partnership. If one spouse is to hold property in severalty, a quitclaim deed is required to release any interest of the other spouse. Whether the property of a husband and wife is separate property or community property may become extremely important whenever there are actions affecting community property, such as divorce or probate proceedings.

A COMMON MISUNDERSTANDING: Dick and Sam want to buy a property together as partners. Dick is married and living in a community-property state, while Sam is still single. Dick thinks that his wife won't approve of the partnership or of the property so he decides to take title to his half as his "sole and separate property." His wife, then, won't have any interest in the property.

THE WAY THINGS REALLY ARE: In a community-property state, Dick may indeed take title to half the partnership property as his "sole and separate property," but unless his wife signs a quitclaim deed specifically denying herself an interest in the property, she still does have an interest, whether she was named on the grant deed as an owner or not. He wouldn't have any difficulty acquiring the property by himself, but he would have some difficulty in divesting of it by himself.

STEP-BY-STEP PROCEDURE FOR COMPLETING AND RECORDING A QUITCLAIM DEED

1. Obtain a blank quitclaim deed form. Use the one in the back of this book or get one from an escrow or title company.

2. If you're the least bit fearful of making a mistake, make a photocopy of the form and follow steps three through nine below, using a pencil and making a "rough draft" of all the information you want to include on the recorded copy. Then transfer this information to the actual form you plan to record. Your recorded copy should be neat and legible, with a minimum of additions, corrections, and deletions.

3. Under "RECORDING REQUESTED BY," put your own name, unless, of course, you're filling out the deed for someone else who is making the request. Under "MAIL TAX STATEMENT TO," put "Same as Below," so the persons granted the property will receive the tax bills at the same address where they normally receive their mail.

4. Under "WHEN RECORDED MAIL TO," put the names and a single address of the persons to whom the deed should be mailed.

5. Put the word "None" on the line after "DOCUMENTARY TRANSFER TAX $." Because no money is changing hands, there is no liability for a transfer tax.

6. After "City of," put the name of the city or town where the property is located, and after "Tax Parcel No." put the same assessor's tax parcel number which appears on the property's tax bill, grant deed, or title insurance policy. Double-check this number. It's absolutely crucial. An incorrect number will make the quitclaim deed refer to another property entirely.

7. In the space before the words "FOR A VALUABLE CONSIDERATION," put the names of those who appear on the original grant deed, and be sure the names are exactly alike, middle initials and all. If you can't find the deed, check the title insurance policy. Then put the word "DO" in the space before "HEREBY" if more than one person is granting the quitclaim or "DOES" if there is only one person involved.

8. After the words "QUITCLAIM TO," enter the names of the persons who are receiving the title, along with the way they intend to hold that title.

9. After "County of" and "State of," include the county and state where the property is located, and then enter a legal description of the property. This description should correspond to the one given in the original grant deed or in the title insurance policy.

10. Date and sign the quitclaim deed in the presence of a notary. The notary will then acknowledge the signatures with his own and stamp the deed with his official seal.

11. Take the quitclaim deed to the county recorder's office and pay the recording fee. The recorder will stamp the deed with the date and time and index it in the county's official records.

Within two to three weeks, the deed will be returned to the address given in step four, and it will have become a part of the county's permanent records.

This same procedure may be used for changing the way you hold title, for deleting names from the grant deed, for adding new names, or, in community-property states, for granting one spouse the sole ownership of certain property.

RECORDING REQUESTED BY:

Bruce B. Buyer

MAIL TAX STATEMENT TO:

Bruce B. Buyer

WHEN RECORDED, MAIL TO:

Mr. & Mrs. Bruce B. Buyer
12 Allendale Ct.
Boonville, CA 11002

302211

RECEIVED OCT 1 3 1990

RECORDED AT REQUEST OF
SECURE TITLE CO.

AT 2 O'CLOCK *P.* M.
BARRETT COUNTY RECORDS

FEE $ 5⁵⁰   V. L. GRAVES
COUNTY RECORDER

Recorder's Use Only

302211

ORDER NO.

ESCROW NO.

QUITCLAIM DEED

DOCUMENTARY TRANSFER TAX $___NONE___
COMPUTED ON FULL VALUE OF PROPERTY CONVEYED, OR
COMPUTED ON FULL VALUE LESS LIENS & ENCUMBRANCES
REMAINING THEREON AT TIME OF SALE.
____Unincorporated Area____ City of __Boonville__
Tax Parcel No.____184-162-21____

BRUCE B. BUYER AND BARBARA A. BUYER, his wife as Joint Tenants

FOR A VALUABLE CONSIDERATION,   DO   HEREBY QUITCLAIM to:

BRUCE B. BUYER AND BARBARA A. BUYER, HIS WIFE AS COMMUNITY PROPERTY

the real property in the County of __Barrett__, State of __California__, described as:

LOT 142, as shown upon that certain map entitled "Map of Barrett
Bay Unit One, Boonville, California," filed for record September
22, 1960 in Volume 10 of Maps, at Page 78, Barrett County Records.

Witness my hand this __13__ day of __October__, 19_90_.

Bruce B. Buyer
BRUCE B. BUYER

Barbara A. Buyer
BARBARA A. BUYER

STATE OF California   )
) s.s.
COUNTY OF   Barrett   )

On _____October 13_____, 19_90_,
before me, the undersigned, a Notary Public in and for said County
and State, personally appeared

Bruce B. Buyer and
Barbara A. Buyer

WITNESS my hand and official seal:

Edna Edwards
Notary Public in and for said County and State

NOTARY SEAL

OFFICIAL SEAL
EDNA EDWARDS
Notary Public

proved to me on the basis of satisfactory evidence to be the person_s_
whose name_s_ is (are) subscribed to the within instrument and
acknowledged that __they__ executed the same.

MAIL TAX STATEMENT AS DIRECTED ABOVE

CONSEQUENCES OF HOW TITLE IS HELD

Agreement	Person	Property Split	Property Sale	Lease Expiration	Inheritors	Creditors	Federal Estate Tax
JOINT TENANCY WITH RIGHT OF SURVIVORSHIP	Two or more people (spouses or others)	Equal shares according to contract or money paid	No consent necessary	Depends on the agreement in the contract	Survivor becomes sole owner (property split evenly if more than one survivor); no will necessary	Levy a judgment	Full estate taxed (assumed that first to die provided all funds for property unless survivor proves otherwise); spouse can claim marital deduction
TENANCY IN COMMON	Two or more people	Equal or unequal shares	No consent necessary	When one person sells shares, others continue tenancy in common	Passed to person named in will; divided by state if no will	Subject to creditors' claims	Portion of estate taxed according to property split; spouse can claim marital deduction
COMMUNITY PROPERTY (TENANCY BY ENTIRETY)	Spouses only	Equal shares	With partner's consent	At divorce or by mutual consent	Survivor becomes sole owner; no will necessary	Safe from spouse's creditors	Half of estate taxed; spouse can claim marital deduction
SOLE PROPRIETORSHIP (SOLE AND SEPARATE PROPERTY)	One person	One undivided share	No consent necessary	When property is sold	Passed to person named in will; divided by state if no will	N/A	Full estate taxed

MAY I CHANGE THE WAY I HOLD TITLE AFTER ESCROW CLOSES?

Yes, you certainly may change the way you hold title after escrow closes. You may change the way you hold title at any time, generally without tax consequences, too (check with your attorney or tax consultant to find out how the change will affect your particular circumstances). You may effect the change yourself, or you may ask your escrow officer to help you do it when you're ready. You simply deed the property from yourself (yourselves) to yourself (yourselves) in the new manner in which you wish to hold title.

You may even change the way you hold title by simply making up a written agreement and putting it in a safe place. Should you change your mind later, you

merely tear up the agreement. That's all there is to it. You don't have to record this agreement if you don't want to, but you probably should record it unless you have some particular reason for not doing so.

On the next page, you'll find an agreement you might use yourself if you should ever want to change the way you hold title from joint tenancy to community property. And you'll find a blank agreement form in the back of this book.

AGREEMENT TO CHANGE TITLE FROM JOINT TENANCY TO COMMUNITY PROPERTY

1) PARTIES:

Parties to this agreement are ___Bruce B. Buyer_____
and __Barbara A. Buyer_____.

2) RECITALS:

a) The parties hereto are husband and wife, residing in the County of __Barrett_____
_____, State of __California_____.

b) They have heretofore held property in their common or separate names, and may hereafter do so.

c) They hold portions of their property in joint tenancy only as a matter of convenience of transfer.

d) This agreement is entered into with the full knowledge on the part of each party of the extent and probable value of all of the property and estate of the community, and of the separate and joint property of each other, ownership of which would be conferred by law on each of them in the event of the termination of their relationship by death or otherwise.

e) It is the express intent of the parties hereto that all their common properties are and shall be their community property.

3. AGREEMENT THAT ALL PROPERTY SHALL BE COMMUNITY:

Each party hereby releases all of his or her separate rights in and to any and all property, real or personal and wherever situated, which either party now owns or has an interest in, and each party agrees that all property or interest therein owned heretofore or presently or hereafter acquired by either from common funds shall be deemed to be community property of the parties hereto, whether held in their separate names, as joint tenants, as tenants in common, or in any other legal form. The parties understand that this agreement will automatically, without other formality, transfer to the other a one-half interest in any separate property now owned and that such transfer could constitute a taxable gift under Federal and State law.

4. AGREEMENT MODIFIABLE IN WRITING ONLY:

This agreement shall not be modified except in writing signed by both parties, or by the mutual written surrender or abandonment of their said community interest in accordance with the laws of said State pertaining to the management of community property, or by the termination of their marriage by death or otherwise.

DATED: ___October 13_____, 19_90_

Bruce B. Buyer
_____
Bruce B. Buyer

Barbara A. Buyer
_____
Barbara A. Buyer

WHAT OTHER WAYS ARE AVAILABLE FOR PEOPLE TO HOLD TITLE?

As real estate prices climb, some people are joining together with others to pool their resources and buy property together as a group. Although the two most frequently used forms of real estate co-ownership are tenancy-in-common and joint tenancy, you might want to consider such alternate methods of co-ownership as partnerships, joint ventures, or corporations.

- *Partnership*—An association of two or more persons who as co-owners carry on a business for profit is called a partnership. It is created by an agreement between two or more persons to take care of business jointly and share the profits. It may be a general partnership, where each partner is liable for the debts of the partnership, or a limited partnership, where each limited partner's liability is limited to the amount of his investment and he is not otherwise liable for the debts of the partnership. Holding title in partnership with others allows any number of partners to have an equal or an unequal interest in a property. Each partner has equal rights of possession but only according to the partnership agreement.

- *Joint Ventures*—Like a partnership, a joint venture is an agreement between two or more persons to conduct a business enterprise jointly for profit. Unlike a partnership, which may involve any number of different enterprises, a joint venture involves only a single enterprise.

- *Corporations*—A corporation involves each person's putting up a sum of money toward making the down payment for a property in return for shares of stock and becoming a shareholder in the corporation. The unique feature about a corporation is that it has all the legal aspects of a single person. Land owned by a corporation cannot be attached for personal debts or judgments rendered against any of its shareholders. A creditor can attach only the person's shares in the corporation. On the other hand, if the corporation cannot pay its debts, none of the shareholders can individually be forced to pay a creditor, although the corporation's assets, including its real property, can be reached and sold to pay a debt. To form a corporation, one need not have a New York Stock Exchange listing or even an income-producing business. One must, however, file certain papers with the state. The shareholders must draw up articles of incorporation, by-laws, and a shareholders' agreement. Each state has its own requirements regarding the proper legal form for these documents and for their filing with the secretary of the state where the corporation is to be located. You may consult an attorney to draw up articles of incorporation and other necessary paperwork. There are also several books available on forming your own corporation, which might be useful as reference material.

No matter which type of co-ownership or group ownership that you consider, you should discuss, and perhaps even write out in detail, the full terms of the co-ownership before making your final decision. The entire group should understand as completely as possible the intentions and desires of each person involved. Even the best intentioned people cannot possibly predict what will happen to them when they become co-owners of land with all the responsibilities it entails.

WHAT'S A LIVING TRUST? CAN I HOLD TITLE IN A LIVING TRUST?

A living trust, sometimes called an *inter-vivos* trust by attorneys, operates during one's lifetime and is revocable at any time before death. The person who creates the living trust, also known as the *settlor*, acts as his own trustee so long as he lives. He maintains full control of everything just as if there were no living trust. The difference is that in a living trust he doesn't hold title in his own name. The trust holds title, and the trustee then buys and sells property on behalf of the trust. When the settlor dies, the successor trustee takes immediate control and turns the property over to the beneficiary or beneficiaries without having to go through a lengthy probate or make the details of the estate public.

Naturally, a husband and wife may form a joint trusteeship if they so choose. When one of the co-owners dies, the survivor takes control.

Lest you think that living trusts are only for strange people in strange situations, you should know that there is a popular do-it-yourself book on living trusts called *How to Avoid Probate* by Norman Dacey. You should also know that one of the largest estates ever handled as a living trust was Bing Crosby's, a man of no small means.

Should you wish your living trust to hold title to the property you are buying, instruct the escrow officer to make out the papers referring to you as the trustee or trustees. The deed would read "Bruce B. Buyer and Barbara A. Buyer, Trustees under their Declaration of Trust dated xx/xx/xx."

Take the time to inform yourself more fully about living trusts by visiting with a knowledgeable attorney or by reading the Dacey book.

5
INSURING THE CONDITION OF THE BUILDING

WHAT IS A TERMITE INSPECTION AND WHAT PROTECTION DOES IT GIVE?

A termite inspection used to consist of an inspection for termites which was confined to the ground floor of a building and its underside only. Nowadays a termite inspection is much more comprehensive than that, and strictly speaking, it's no longer even called a termite inspection. It's called a structural pest control inspection, but most people still call it a termite inspection anyway because they're accustomed to the term.

Today's termite inspection involves checking for signs of wood damage and potential wood damage throughout a building, no matter what the cause. Termite inspectors now check for fungus, dry rot, faulty grade levels, earth-wood contacts, water leaks, scattered wood scraps and cellulose debris on the subsoil, and excessive moisture conditions. They also check for evidence of subterranean termites, dry-wood termites, dampwood termites, and other wood-destroying pests such as certain varieties of beetles.

A termite inspector's report shows two types of work to be performed:

- *Corrective* work to remedy current infestation, and

- *Preventive* work to inhibit future or threatened infestation.

STANDARD STRUCTURAL PEST CONTROL INSPECTION REPORT
(WOOD-DESTROYING PESTS OR ORGANISMS)
This is an inspection report only—not a Notice of Completion.

ADDRESS OF PROPERTY INSPECTED	BLDG. NO.	STREET	CITY	DATE OF INSPECTION
	12	Allendale Ct.	Boonville	July 5, 1990
			CO. CODE	

Affix stamp here on Board copy only
↓ A LICENSED PEST CONTROL OPER-↓
ATOR IS AN EXPERT IN HIS FIELD.
ANY QUESTIONS RELATIVE TO THIS
REPORT SHOULD BE REFERRED TO
HIM.

GETTEM TERMITE CONTROL COMPANY
612 Seventh St., Boonville, CA 11002   Telephone 423-7654

FIRM LICENSE NO. 1981	REPORT NO. 737	STAMP NUMBER 94936

Inspection Ordered by (Name and Address) Bruce B. Buyer, c/o Security Title
Report Sent to (Name and Address) Same as Above
Owner's Name and Address Samuel P. Seller, c/o property address
Name and Address of a Party in Interest

INSPECTED BY: Al Hart   LICENSE NO. 465   Original Report ☒   Supplemental Report ☐   Number of Pages

YES	CODE	SEE DIAGRAM BELOW	YES	CODE	SEE DIAGRAM BELOW	YES	CODE	SEE DIAGRAM BELOW	YES	CODE	SEE DIAGRAM BELOW
X	S—Subterranean Termites			B—Beetles—Other Wood Pests			Z—Dampwood Termites			EM—Excessive Moisture Condition	
X	K—Dry-Wood Termites			FG—Faulty Grade Levels			SL—Shower Leaks			IA—Inaccessible Areas	
X	F—Fungus or Dry Rot			EC—Earth-wood Contacts		X	CD—Cellulose Debris			FI—Further Inspection Recom.	

1. **SUBSTRUCTURE AREA** (soil conditions, accessibility, etc.)   100%   See 1
2. **Was Stall Shower water tested?** 1 O.K.   **Did floor coverings indicate leaks?** No
3. **FOUNDATIONS** (Type, Relation to Grade, etc.)   Concrete O.K.
4. **PORCHES . . . STEPS . . . PATIOS**   Concrete O.K.
5. **VENTILATION** (Amount, Relation to Grade, etc.)   Adequate
6. **ABUTMENTS . . . Stucco walls, columns, arches, etc.** None
7. **ATTIC SPACES** (accessibility, insulation, etc.)   Accessible   See 7
8. **GARAGES** (Type, accessibility, etc.)
9. **OTHER**   See 9

DIAGRAM AND EXPLANATION OF FINDINGS (This report is limited to structure or structures shown on diagram.)

General Description Two story stucco frame residence, furnished and occupied, composition roof and unimproved underarea.

There are areas of a building which we are not able to inspect. Although we make a visual examination, we do not deface or probe into window or door frames or decorative trim. The interiors of hollow walls are not inspected unless noted below and were not inspected at this time as they are inaccessible. We did not move built-ins, appliances, furniture, raise floor coverings or move storage unless otherwise specified within this report. These areas will be inspected if they are made accessible by the owner at his expense. Showers over finished ceilings are not water tested unless water stains are evident on the ceiling below in which case recommendations will be made for further testing. Detached wood fence or garden trellises are not part of this report. If the owner desires further information on the condition of the roof, we recommend a licensed roofing contractor be contacted. This inspection is only on the structures indicated on the diagram below.

1. SUBSTRUCTURE:
FINDING: 1. Cellulose debris and evidence of subterranean termites noted in the subarea as indicated on the diagram.

RECOMMENDATION: 1. Remove cellulose debris from the subarea and take away from the premises. Treat the entire subarea soil with registered chemicals for the control of subterranean termites.

2. ATTIC SPACES:
FINDING: 7. Evidence of drywood termites noted on rafters in the attic area as indicated on the diagram.

RECOMMENDATION: 7. Drill and chemically treat local drywood termite infested timbers in visible and accessible areas as indicated on the diagram.

3. OTHER:
FINDING: 9. Fungus infection noted in sub-floor as indicated on the diagram. Condition appears to be due to previous leak that has been repaired.

RECOMMENDATION: 9. Remove surface fungus and treat area (s) with a fungicide.

Estimated Cost:$ 250.00

Signature *Al Hart*

A COMMON MISUNDERSTANDING: The house looks terrific, all freshly painted. The yard is beautifully landscaped and cared for. Lisa won't need a termite or building inspection. She can see for herself that the place is in great shape.

THE WAY THINGS REALLY ARE: Looks can be very deceiving. Lisa may be dealing with a seller who painted over a water-damaged ceiling without repairing the leaky roof or who hung pictures over holes in the walls. Only a thorough inspection by someone who knows buildings well will give her the assurance she needs of the building's soundness.

In addition, the report will quote a price for having the inspector's company actually do the recommended work. With the report, termite companies generally include a work authorization form. They require an authorization, signed by the seller, before they will begin the work.

Pest control companies which do termite inspections are licensed and regulated by a state structural pest control board, and all of their inspection reports must be filed with this board. The board makes available to the public copies of any report filed on a building during the preceding two years.

Having inspected and cleared a building, the pest control company guarantees only that the building is structurally sound as of the inspection date and according to the specific limits given in the clearance. Those areas listed on the report as inaccessible or requiring further inspection, for example, would not be covered. The company does not guarantee that the building will continue to be structurally sound in the future, either. Conceivably, on the day after the inspection, termites could invade the

place and a toilet could begin to leak at its base, and these conditions could cause real structural problems next year. The damage they cause would not be covered by the inspector's company.

WHO REQUIRES THE TERMITE INSPECTION?

The termite inspection is generally required by buyer and lender. That's why the buyer, not the seller, usually pays for the inspection. The buyer wants to rest assured that the building is sound enough to outlast his ownership, and the lender wants to rest assured that the building is sound enough to outlast the mortgage. Neither the inspection nor clearance of the inspection is required by law.

WHO ORDERS THE TERMITE INSPECTION?

Just as any of those involved in a real estate transaction may open escrow, any of them may order a termite inspection. Generally the real estate agent, if instructed to do so, will order the inspection from a reputable pest control company, but if there is no agent involved, either the buyer or the seller may do it simply by calling a termite company and giving them the property address, the escrow company's name, and the escrow number.

WHY DO TERMITE REPORTS CAUSE PROBLEMS IN ESCROW?

Termite reports cause numerous problems in escrow, as many as any other single cause, for several reasons. One is that the company which inspects a building also submits an estimate for doing the work. In other words, the termite company is given the responsibility of determining the extent of the work to be done and the charges for doing it, and after the work is completed, the company also clears the report. If the inspector finds that some work needs to be done, he usually gets the job to do that work. If he doesn't find anything wrong with the structure, he doesn't get any work. Needless to say, he is rather thorough in his inspection. That's good to some extent, but it can be troublesome, too.

Another reason why termite reports cause problems is that the inspector determines *how* the corrective and preventive work is to be done. Frequently there are several ways to remedy a problem, but the inspector is inclined to indicate just one of those ways on his report, and often it's the most expensive one, the one which will yield him the most work. I know of a case where an inspector called for $4,000 worth of work which later was done satisfactorily in another way for $5. In another case, an inspector called for $500 worth of work which later was completed for $2.

The termite inspector can wield awesome power in real estate transactions because his clearance is frequently an essential element required for escrow to close. Because large sums of money are involved in most real estate transactions, many people overlook the savings which are possible. Like Las Vegas gamblers who have forgotten the value of a dollar, they pay out large sums for termite repairs which might be done for much less.

Even a relatively new house will often cause termite report problems in escrow. A new house might have wooden scraps on the subsoil left there by the builder, or it might have wooden forms for the concrete foundation still imbedded in the soil. These problems have to be remedied for clearance, and sellers become angry that they have to pay the cost of the remedy. Can you blame them?

HOW MIGHT I AS A SELLER PROTECT MYSELF FROM OUTLANDISH TERMITE REPAIR BILLS?

Actually there are several ways you might protect yourself from having to pay outlandish termite repair bills.

Obtain a termite report before you ever offer your property for sale. With this information available, you will know before negotiating a sales price exactly what your maximum liability for structural damage will be, and you will also have the option of having all the work performed before possibly scaring the buyer with the extent of the work required for clearance. If you do opt to obtain a termite report on your building before putting it up for sale, you will, of course, have to pay for the inspection fee yourself. The buyer could later accept this report or reject it and order another at his own expense.

Select an inspector who has a reputation for being fair and who will clear work that you or others have done. Because real estate agents deal with these companies all the time, they will have had enough experience to be able to make good recommendations. Tell an agent what your primary concerns are and ask for recommendations.

Set up the inspection appointment for a mutually convenient time so you are able to accompany the inspector. If possible, try to arrange an appointment with the firm's owner to do the inspection, even if it means waiting longer for him. Owners tend to be more disposed to explaining the work, suggesting inexpensive alternatives, and letting you do certain work yourself. Cooperate cheerfully, but ask for an explanation of the damage findings on the spot. If you can, get the inspector to itemize his estimate of repairs so you can determine how much each part of the total job costs.

Do not hesitate to get two or more termite reports if you feel the first estimate for work is excessive (sellers sometimes feel this way) or if you feel it doesn't show all the work that you think the property requires (buyers sometimes feel this way).

Once you get a written report, scrutinize it carefully. Try to understand all that it says. If the findings, recommendations, and estimates all seem reasonable, go ahead and hire the company to complete the work. If they seem unreasonable, discuss them with the inspector and see whether he will accept any alternatives. If he won't be reasonable, do the easiest work yourself in a way you deem best and ask a contractor or independent carpenter to bid on the balance (you won't have to pay for their bids). Look in your daily newspaper's service directory, and you will likely find independents who advertise that they specialize in doing termite work at 20-33% off the termite companies' estimates and also guarantee that their work will pass inspection. Be careful whenever you deal with independents, however. Check their references, and pay them in full only after the work has been completed *and* inspected.

Some termite companies will not issue a clearance unless they were hired to do the termite work, so you may have to pay another company to inspect the work completed by yourself and/or an independent contractor. For this reason, don't quibble with a termite company over anything less than a hundred dollars, because securing an inspection by another company will surely cost you that, and each termite company's estimate for the work it does itself also includes clearance of the report at no additional charge.

Because an institutional lender will generally require a current termite report before approving any new loan, it is often helpful to the lender and it will speed up your loan request if you submit a copy of the current termite report along with your loan application.

WHO PAYS FOR TERMITE CLEARANCE?

The buyer and seller should determine through negotiations who will be responsible to pay for the corrective and preventive work recommended by the inspector. In general, the seller agrees to pay for the repair work, or at least a portion of it, while the buyer pays for the termite report and any preventive work. Often the buyer will add a statement to the purchase agreement stating that he is willing to buy the property provided that the termite work does not exceed a certain sum. If the report lists a substantial amount of work to be completed, you might even want to take a second look at what you are buying or at the price you are paying for the property.

Who is to pay for the termite report and what termite work needs to be done should all be fully explained to your escrow officer because these bills are usually paid through escrow by the escrow holder.

WHAT HAPPENS WHEN THE TERMITE REPORT CAN'T BE CLEARED BEFORE THE CLOSE OF ESCROW?

Whenever the work necessary to clear a termite report cannot be completed prior to the close of escrow, the balance of funds due the termite company must then be held in escrow for release upon the buyer's and seller's written assurance that the work was done to their satisfaction. Include the conditions for release in your escrow instructions because, whereas the seller will most always agree that the work is satisfactory, the buyer won't necessarily agree, and the buyer must also approve the corrections made.

Be certain you verify your lender's policy regarding termite clearance, for some institutional lenders do not permit escrow to close before all of the termite work has been completed.

ARE THERE ANY OTHER INSPECTIONS ONE MIGHT ORDER?

In addition to a termite report, you as a buyer may want to order a complete building inspection made by a licensed building contractor or inspection service. Such people advertise in the Yellow Pages under "Building Inspection Service." For a nominal fee, around $150-200, a qualified contractor or inspector will give the building an overall structural inspection covering all major systems, such as foundation, plumbing, electrical, roof, and heating.

These inspections are generally well worth their cost, especially for those who are novices about building construction. Should you wish to have this option, whether you conduct the inspection yourself or have someone do it for you, be sure to include in your original purchase agreement the following statement: "Offer contingent upon buyer's full inspection (or inspection by a licensed contractor) and approval of the property within five business days after acceptance by the seller."

By adding this statement, you are free to negotiate the price and other terms of the house first, and then you may renegotiate the price after the inspection, or you may have an escape if your personal inspection isn't to your satisfaction.

Whenever you do choose a building contractor or an inspection service, be certain that the person you choose is licensed with the state as either a contractor or an inspector and that he will prepare a written report of the findings. Having this written report could be very useful later in case a lawsuit arose because of undisclosed structural damage.

CAN A BUYER GET INSURANCE COVERING OTHER POTENTIAL BUILDING PROBLEMS?

Yes, in most states a buyer can now get a home warranty insurance policy which insures against plumbing, electrical, heating, and major appliance problems for one year after escrow closes and is renewable annually thereafter.

This kind of policy has become quite popular because it offers welcome peace of mind at a reasonable price. It is especially attractive to buyers who have just emptied all of their savings accounts and piggy banks to make the large down payment required to buy a house, only to live in fear that they might encounter some unforeseen and expensive repair bills which might result in their either losing the house altogether or eating lots of beans. A policy costs approximately $295 for a house without air conditioning and $325 for one with air conditioning. Two companies offering this coverage are American Home Shield, 7950 Dublin Blvd., Dublin, CA 94566, (800) 642-2440 and Ticor Home Protection, 6300 Wilshire Blvd., Los Angeles, CA 90048, (800) 252-0638.

Read your policy carefully, for some contain exclusions which may be significant. Roofs and outside sprinkler systems, for example, are sometimes excluded.

Sellers forced to relocate before their house is sold are also fond of home warranties because coverage begins 10 to 15 days after they apply for it, and they don't even have to pay the premium until the house does sell, regardless of how many repairs the house requires once the warranty is in force.

A COMMON MISUNDERSTANDING: Margi and Fletcher didn't bother to apply for a home warranty plan when they moved from their lovely house in Maine because it was in perfect condition and they thought it would sell in no time.

THE WAY THINGS REALLY ARE: Margi and Fletcher's charming and historical house languished on the market for two years without attracting a buyer. In that time, pipes cracked, appliances rusted, and plumbing fixtures began to leak. They had to pay for all the repairs themselves. Had they applied for an all-inclusive home warranty policy, they wouldn't have had to pay a cent in premiums, and the policy would have covered all the mishaps.

PLEASE NOTE WELL

Responsibility for paying the premium on this policy, like many other escrow charges, is negotiable. No matter who pays it, though, be certain that the premium has been paid the day escrow closes, for often the buyer will have to use the policy the very next day, when he moves in and learns that the heater or air conditioner doesn't work.

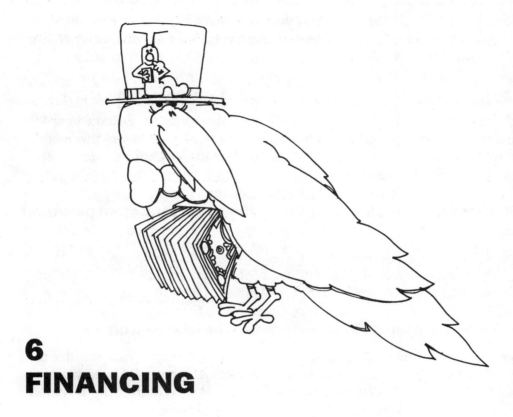

6
FINANCING

WHY IS FINANCING SO IMPORTANT?

The financing available to acquire a property will determine whether that property changes ownership or not. Unless you have just inherited a fortune, acquired some clandestine capital, or saved religiously for years, you will probably have to borrow most of the money you need to pay for your property. You'll have to get some financing, perhaps even a lot of financing.

Because the various costs involved in borrowing money will likely be the biggest expense in acquiring your property, the financing you get is extremely important, important enough for you to negotiate good terms with the seller and important enough for you to shop around as much as possible for conventional financing if needed.

Monthly Payment (Fully Amortized) — $80,000 for 30 Years at Varying Interest Rates

10%	10.5%	11%	11.5%	12%	12.5%	13%	13.5%	14%	14.5%
702.06	731.80	761.86	792.24	822.90	853.81	884.96	916.33	947.90	979.65

You will find when you shop around for conventional financing that types of loans, fees, and rates will all vary from lender to lender. Variances in the rates, for example, may appear at first to be small, 2% at most, but you will find that they have very direct and important consequences. Consider that, depending on the size of the loan, even a 1/2% difference in the interest rate may add an extra $30 or $40 to your monthly mortgage payments. Consequently, if you do shop around for the money you need, you'll be glad that you did during every month you own the property.

Besides considering the rate, consider also the length of your loan. Fifteen-year loans are becoming more and more common because they save borrowers thousands in interest costs and are paid off twice as fast as thirty-year loans. Contrary to what you might think, the payments on a fifteen-year loan are not twice what they would be on a thirty-year loan. They're only slightly higher because most of the payment during the first years of a loan goes toward interest; very little goes toward paying off the principal.

Here's an example. Let's say you get an $80,000 loan with a 12.5% interest rate, fully amortized over thirty years. After making monthly payments of $853.81 for fifteen years, you would still owe the lender almost $70,000. Had you been making payments of only $132.25 more every month for those same fifteen years, you wouldn't owe the lender anything. Your property would be fully paid off.

Some fifteen-year loans are not fully amortized. Be wary of them. They require a large balloon payment after you've made payments for fifteen years. Be sure you understand whether your loan is fully amortized or not, that is, whether the payments are structured to pay off the loan over a designated period of time.

One way to circumvent having to make a balloon payment on a loan which isn't fully amortized is to make higher payments, just as if the loan were fully amortized. In most cases, you may make higher payments based on an amortized schedule even though the loan calls for lower payments. If you choose to pay your loan off in this way, make sure you indicate clearly to the lender that you want the excess funds applied to the loan principal. Mark each check with the words "Apply Excess Funds to Principal Only."

WHAT IS AN INTEREST RATE?

Essentially an interest rate is the rent paid for borrowing money. Expressed another way, it's the lender's charge for lending money. Interest rates are generally given in percentages per year, and they are applied to the amount of money borrowed, not the original amount borrowed, but the amount currently outstanding, the principal.

Be aware that nowadays interest rates for conventional loans may be either fixed or variable. If it is fixed, the rate will remain constant over the entire life of the loan, be it 10, 15, 20, or 30 years. If it is variable, it will be adjusted periodically up or down according to the prevailing interest rate.

A COMMON MISUNDERSTANDING: Dennis learns that the seller of a certain piece of property will give him attractive terms. He doesn't know how he'll make the payments, but he'll figure that out later. He's always felt that getting a loan is the biggest problem in acquiring real estate.

THE WAY THINGS REALLY ARE: The very first thing Dennis should consider is how he's going to meet those payments he's obligating himself to make every month. People do lose their properties when they overextend themselves, and Dennis could, too.

HOW DOES A VARIABLE-RATE LOAN WORK?

With this type of loan, your interest rate is reviewed once each year and compared to the most recent Cost-of-Money Standard published by the Federal Home Loan Bank. This index, published twice a year, reflects up-and-down movements in the average rates paid for savings and other funds by insured savings and loan associations throughout the United States. If the index changes during the six months preceding your annual review, your interest rate may change. This would, of course, cause a change, up or down, in either the amount of your monthly payments or the total number of payments you will make over the life of your loan.

No matter how widely the index fluctuates, however, you are protected in two ways. First, your interest rate can never move up or down more than a half percent in any one year and then only at 6-month intervals. And second, throughout the entire life of the loan, your interest rate may never increase more than 2.5-3% above the original rate (check your variable-rate loan to be sure; some no longer have ceilings; if your lender quotes you a rate with a ceiling, get the quote in writing). For instance, if you originally obtain a loan at 10%, in most cases the rate could increase to no more than 12.5%, but it could decrease potentially by any amount.

While this type of loan has its uncertainties, it does offer some flexibility in dealing with those uncertainties. If the index bumps your payments upward, for example, but they're still comfortable for you, you simply make your payments at the new amount. If you are unable or unwilling to pay the new amount, you may exercise any of several options. To keep your payments down, you may opt to extend the loan by as much as one-third of the original term. A 30-year loan may thus become a 40-year loan if you want it to be. You may pay off the entire loan or any part of it without a prepayment charge if the new rate is higher than your original rate. You may even do both, extend the loan and pay off part of it.

Be sure you check the figures over carefully before you elect to extend your loan, though, for extending the life of a loan beyond fifteen or twenty years doesn't really decrease the payment very much. Check the figures.

Monthly Payment (Fully Amortized) — $80,000 at 11.5% for a Varying Number of Years

10	15	20	25	30	35	40
1,124.77	934.56	853.15	813.18	792.24	780.89	774.63

Your variable-rate lender will send you written notification of any rate adjustment at least one month before the new rate is to go into effect. This notification will tell you the old and new index rates and your current and new interest rates.

BESIDES FIXED-RATE LOANS AND VARIABLE-RATE LOANS, ARE THERE ANY OTHER FINANCING ARRANGEMENTS AVAILABLE THROUGH INSTITUTIONAL LENDERS?

With housing prices getting out of reach to all but the more affluent, institutional lenders are trying various new kinds of financing arrangements so that more and more people can qualify to buy. The whole idea behind them is to reduce the down payments and/or the monthly payments which would be required for old-style loans.

Adjustable-rate mortgage loans, shared-appreciation mortgage loans, and graduated-payment mortgage loans are just three of the more popular new financing arrangements being tried today. They serve to illustrate how lenders are changing their ways of doing business to accommodate changes in the marketplace.

Adjustable-rate mortgage (ARM) loans generally span a 15- or 30-year period and carry lower interest rates than fixed-rate loans. The interest-rate adjustment is tied to one or more of the following economic indices: U.S. One-Year Treasury Bill rates, current money-market rates, cost-of-funds rates, or the Federal Home Loan Bank Board's average of mortgage rates. One lender might use the 6-month Treasury Bill rate and add four points, while another might use the Eleventh District Cost of Funds rate and add three points. The interest rates on ARM loans may change semi-annually or, in some cases, even monthly, and they may change in a limited fashion, 1% at a time, or in an unlimited fashion. A good ARM loan will contain a "cap" of three or four points on the interest rate, so the borrower is not totally at the mercy of relentlessly rising economic indices.

Besides being adjustable, adjustable rate mortgages may be "negative" or "non-negative." If yours is negative, the interest rate may change on a monthly basis, but the monthly payment itself does not. Consequently, the payment may or may not be enough to pay the interest. If it is enough to pay the interest and there's something left over, the amount left over is *deducted* from the principal. If it is not enough to pay the interest, the shortage is *added* to the principal, and you could wind up owing more than you originally borrowed, even after you've made payments for a long period of time.

If yours is a non-negative adjustable rate mortgage, your payment will change whenever the interest rate changes so there is always enough to pay something on the principal.

Lenders using shared-appreciation mortgage (SAM) loans reduce the interest rate normally being charged in exchange for an equity interest in the house. The borrower pays the lender this equity interest at some time within a certain number of years when the house is either sold or refinanced. SAM's reduce the monthly payments considerably and enable buyers to qualify for buying a house which would be out of their reach otherwise.

Graduated-payment mortgage (GPM) loans have lower initial monthly payments than standard fixed-rate level-payment loans, but gradually their payments rise to a level which will amortize the principal balance over the remaining life of the loan. The objective of GPM's is to reduce the initial payments while the borrower's income is low, in the expectation that the borrower's income will increase later. GPM's enable a buyer to buy a house at today's prices and pay for it comfortably with smaller payments in the beginning and larger payments later, when he can afford them. If you are attracted to a GPM loan, be sure to get a listing of the fixed schedule of payments, so you'll know long in advance exactly when the payments are going to change.

A COMMON MISUNDERSTANDING: Christine and David, madly in love, are newlyweds who are anxious to buy their first home. They grab the first adjustable-rate mortgage loan offered to them, thinking that it must be similar to the variable-rate mortgage loan which their friends Virgie and Bud were most pleased with.

THE WAY THINGS REALLY ARE: Adjustable-rate mortgage loans differ significantly from variable-rate mortgage loans; they are generally more favorable to the lender than to the borrower. After six months of "honeymooning" in their dream home, Christine and David noticed that their payment had been increased by almost a hundred dollars and they got scared. When they looked more closely at their mortgage's terms, they found that it had no "cap" at all, that the interest rate could change every month after the first six months, and that the initial interest rate was nothing more than an inducement. It wasn't set according to the index which was going to determine the interest rate throughout the rest of the life of the loan. Chris-

tine and David learned their lesson the hard way. Now they're renters, but they came up with the following advice for anyone looking at an adjustable-rate mortgage: Ask 1) what the initial interest rate is based on; 2) what the interest rate after the first six months is based on; 3) how much and how frequently the interest rate can change in a year; 4) what the "cap" on the interest rate is over the life of the loan; and 5) how interest rate changes will affect the payments. Christine and David wish that somebody had warned them to ask about these "little things" before they ever got their loan.

Before choosing the loan you will be living with for the next 15, 20, or even 30 years, ask yourself some very important questions. What is the initial interest rate based upon? Is this basis going to change after the first six months? What is the cap on the interest rate? How will an interest rate change affect my monthly payments?

Try to determine what the worst-case scenario might be for the loan you're contemplating. You don't want to be surprised later and lose your property.

WHAT LOAN FEES DO LENDERS CHARGE?

The various fees charged by institutional lenders for making a loan vary considerably from lender to lender.

First, there's the loan fee which the lender charges to process your loan. Usually this is a set fee, say a flat $150, $1,000, or even $2,000. Whatever the amount happens to be, just keep in mind that this fee covers only the cost of processing your loan papers, nothing else.

Second, there is a charge called points, a charge to originate a loan based on the amount of the loan itself. Borrowers pay points only once, before they receive any loan proceeds. One point is 1% of the loan amount. Two points is 2%; three points, 3%; and so on. If your loan were, say $80,000, each point would equal $800. Four points on such a loan would be $3,200. Points may vary from one all the way up to six, depending on the money market, that is, the availability of money to loan. Determining who will pay the points is a matter for negotiation between buyer and seller. FHA loans stipulate that the buyer may not pay more than one point.

Third, there's a credit report fee, something charged to check out your credit and your employment. This fee is usually minimal, considering the other sums charged. It will range from $25 to $175.

Fourth, there's a tax service fee to cover what the lender has to pay an outside agency to keep informed as to the status of your property taxes. Your lender wants to be notified if you fail to pay your property taxes and the property comes into jeopardy of being sold for back taxes. But because no lender has time to check twice a year to see whether all of its borrowers have paid their property taxes, it hires an outside tax service agency to provide this information, and naturally it charges its borrowers for the service. Usually the charge will run between $20 and $30 over the life of the loan.

Fifth, there may be miscellaneous loan fees for processing and appraising.

Lumped together, the loan fee, points, credit report fee, tax service fee, and any miscellaneous fees, all may add up easily to hundreds and even thousands of dollars. More importantly, though, these fees are all paid in advance. You have to pay them before you can ever receive the actual loan proceeds. Either they are paid into escrow and turned over to the bank once you get your loan, or, more generally, they are deducted from the loan proceeds themselves. As a consequence, the loan fees are actually added to your down payment and must be paid "up-front."

So, you see, it is exceedingly important that you shop around for both a favorable interest rate and the best possible loan fees.

A COMMON MISUNDERSTANDING: Even though the loan fees turn out to be double what he thought they would be, Oliver figures that he had better go through with his loan anyway. Loans are hard to come by.

THE WAY THINGS REALLY ARE: Lenders all charge different loan fees. Oliver should shop around when he has the chance, and he should get an estimate of his loan fees in writing before deciding to go ahead with the loan.

HOW SHOULD I PREPARE TO GET A LOAN?

The first thing to do, even before you begin shopping around for a loan, is to determine what is the greatest monthly payment you can make. Although the property you are buying is itself security for the loan, you must be able to meet the monthly payments, or the lender will have the right to foreclose. To determine your ability to pay back a home loan, lenders generally use a ratio based upon your gross monthly income being so many times the amount of the monthly mortgage payments. The commonly accepted rule of thumb for this type of evaluation is that your gross monthly income must be three or four times the monthly payments. For example, if your monthly payment is $900, then your monthly income from wages, dividends, interest, and bonuses should be between $2,700 and $3,600. Naturally this rule of thumb will vary depending on inflation and on the lender's individual policy.

Of course, if you should be buying income property, something you intend to rent out, the income you can expect from the rents may be added to the rest of your monthly income in making a determination.

In addition to figuring out what you can afford to pay every month according to your income, you ought to think about setting aside some funds just in case you should suffer a financial setback sometime during the life of the loan. Many financial advisors recommend that borrowers set aside a three-month reserve of mortgage payments in a separate "peace-of-mind" savings account for use in case of "rainy days."

Next, you should know how lenders determine a loan, that is, how they figure the maximum amount they will lend on a property. Generally, they do it in one of two ways, as a percentage of the purchase price or as a percentage of the appraised value.

The property you intend to buy will always be appraised by the lending institution. They appraise it before they make a loan because they must protect their investors' money. They want to be sure that if you should stop making the payments on your loan that they can get their money back by reselling your property. Just remember that each lender's appraisal figure is somewhat arbitrary. There is no such thing as an exact property value. It is the lender's appraisal, however, on which they will base their loan commitment. One bank may consider your intended property as being located in an up-and-coming area and thus offer you a larger loan, which is, of course, to your advantage, but another lender may consider that same property as declining in value or as having no growth potential and thus they will offer you a much lower loan. Each lender has different self-imposed rules and regulations, but all of them base their appraisals on the probable market value of the property during the life of the loan.

Generally speaking, most loans are based on the purchase price, though occasionally a loan will be based on the appraisal figure alone. Some lenders follow a policy of giving a loan commitment on whichever is the lower figure, the appraised value or the purchase price.

HOW MUCH WILL A LENDER LEND ME?

Let's assume that your loan is customary, that is, based upon the purchase price. Lenders will lend you a percentage of that price, varying anywhere from 60% to 90%; generally it's 80%. Commercial property almost never exceeds 70% of the purchase price, while residential property, on the other hand, may secure a 90% loan. Also, much depends on whether you will live there or rent it out. Lenders invariably lend a higher percentage on owner-occupied property. For example, suppose you find a house you like for $100,000. A lender might offer you a loan of, say, 80% of $100,000 or

$80,000 if you were planning to occupy it yourself, and you would have to come up with a down payment of $20,000 plus the loan fees and other closing costs. If you were buying the same house strictly as an investment, and you were planning to rent it out, the lender would lend only 70% or 75% of the purchase price, and you would have to come up with a larger down payment.

Although loans based upon a percentage of the appraised value are not so common as those based on the purchase price, you should know that the FHA (Federal Housing Administration) and VA (Veterans Administration) base their loans solely on their appraisal figure. For example, if they appraise your $100,000 house at $80,000, they may want to offer only 80% of this $80,000, their appraisal figure, and that amounts to a loan offer of only $64,000.

Except for VA and FHA loans, a loan based on an appraisal figure rather than a purchase price figure generally indicates that the sales price is higher than what the banks consider the true value to be.

HOW SHOULD I GO ABOUT SHOPPING FOR A LOAN?

If we assume that there's no real estate agent involved, here's what you should do yourself to secure a loan:

- Pick up an interest rate "stat sheet" which some title and escrow companies prepare for their customers. These stat sheets list the prevailing interest rates and

SECURE TITLE COMPANY
1220 Oak Park Blvd.
Boonville, CA 11002
Telephone 423-4567

Interest rates for: _July 25, 1990_

LENDERS	TERMS						REMARKS
AMERICAN MORTGAGE	80% loan	12¼ %+	1½	Pts+$135	To 150,000		FHA AND VA
	80% w2nd	%+		Pts+	To		11½% 4 PTS.
	90% loan	12¼ %+	2½	Pts+$135	To 150,000		
BOONVILLE BANK	80% loan	11¾ %+	2	Pts+$150	To 95,000		CALL FOR QUOTES ON NON-
	80% w2nd	12 %+	2	Pts+	To 150,000		OWNER Single FAmily Dwelling
	90% loan	%+		Pts+	To		2-4 UNITS
HELPFUL FINANCIAL	80% loan	12 %+	1½	Pts+$100	To 93,750		2 NDS, Home Improvement
	80% w2nd	12 %+	2	Pts+$100	To 150,000		LOANS.
	90% loan	%+		Pts+	To		Also Commercial LOANS
W & W WRAP MTG.	80% loan	11½ %+	2	Pts+	To 250,000		WRAPS ONLY
	80% w2nd	11¾ %+	2	Pts+	To 200,000		APARTMENTS:
	90% loan	%+		Pts+	To		5-200 UNITS 12%

the loan fees for institutional lenders in the area.

- Call or visit several banks and/or savings and loan offices. Consider those where you normally bank first. Then consider any which have been recommended by relatives, friends, or acquaintances.

• Call several loan brokers. See what they have to offer. They sometimes have connections with out-of-town lenders who would otherwise be unknown to you. Be aware that there are some unscrupulous loan brokers who make promises and ask for up-front money from applicants; once they get it, they do nothing. Should the loan broker whom you contact ask for up-front money, do some checking into the broker's reputation. Under no circumstances should you ever give a loan broker more than $100 in up-front money. He should be paid for his services after he secures you a loan, not before.

• Ask about interest rates and loan fees (be sure to ask about all of the fees already mentioned).

• Compare the percentage each lender is offering, that is, compare whether yours would be a 70%, 80%, or 90% loan. Also, note whether the loan would be based

on the appraisal or on the purchase price.

• Ask how quickly the lender can make an appraisal of the property. This is important because generally you have a set time (negotiable between you and the seller, but it can be as short a time as fifteen days) in which to obtain financing or a loan commitment once you sign the purchase agreement with the seller, and if you cannot get a fairly quick appraisal, you might not be able to buy the property at all. If, for example, the lender is busy and says that no one can get out to appraise the property for two or three weeks, you will want to go elsewhere to find your loan.

- Ask what types of loans are available (conventional, FHA, or VA).

- Prepare a "Loan Shopper" (you'll find a blank copy of this form in the back of the book) side-by-side comparison of the terms being offered to you by the various lenders, and think carefully about which loan would be the best for your circumstances.

LOAN SHOPPER

	Lender One	Lender Two	Lender Three
Initial interest rate on note	9½	9¾	11½
Fixed, variable, graduated, other	variable	variable	fixed
Amortization due date	30 yrs.	20 yrs.	15 yrs.
Points and other fees (total)	1½	2	2½
Pre-payment penalty	no	no	yes
Assumability (specific requirements)	yes, one only	yes	no
Interest rate cap	4 pts.	5 pts.	—
Index used	U.S. Treasury Securities	11th District Cost of Funds	—
Interest rate adjustments	every 3 months	every 6 months	
Co-borrowers allowed	yes	yes	yes
Maximum negative amortization	none	none	—

Your chances of obtaining a loan depend to a great extent on whether money is "tight" or "easy" when you are making your purchase. Lenders change their loan policies constantly, depending upon conditions in the national and local money markets and the local real estate market as well. Whatever you do, don't give up. If you are denied a loan by one lender, try another and another and another until you finally find a willing lender. Every lender has its own needs and policies, and you will discover that you can get a loan if you keep trying. When the money market is tight, being turned down for a loan repeatedly can be very discouraging, but just as often persistence pays off. Keep at it. Even if people tell you money isn't available, keep trying. After all, lenders are in business to make money, and they can only make money by lending out their customers' deposits.

You might be surprised to learn that there are certain lenders who make loans on non-conforming properties for non-conforming borrowers. No, I'm not referring to loan sharks. I'm referring to legitimate lenders willing to take more risk in exchange for higher fees and interest rates. They will make loans on properties which have liens against them, and they will lend to applicants with bankruptcies in their past. Seek these lenders out if you keep getting negative responses to your loan inquiries.

A COMMON MISUNDERSTANDING: The Bank of Central California turns down Jack's application for a loan to acquire a new house. He figures that they rejected him because of a questionable credit rating and that there's no sense wasting any more time applying to other lenders.

THE WAY THINGS REALLY ARE: Each lender has its own credit requirements and its own supply of available money. Jack may have had the credit he needed to qualify, but that particular bank may not have had any money to lend on a long-term first mortgage right then. Jack may very well be able to get the money he needs from another lender.

If there is a real estate agent involved in your transaction, he or she will shop for the loan for you, asking all the right questions, and then bring you the information and the loan applications, and he or she will submit your completed loan application to the lender in question. This is a major advantage of having an agent. The agent provides a loan broker's services at no extra charge. Not only does he or she do the leg work, but the agent will probably have a better knowledge of the lending market and will probably know which lenders are more receptive to someone with your qualifications and needs.

When answering lenders' questions, be as truthful as possible. The computerization of bank and credit accounts is becoming so thorough that dishonest answers are likely to be uncovered when the lending institution does its independent investigation. If you have had some problems repaying debts in the past, you should explain this to the loan officer handling your case rather than misstate the facts and have the lender discover the truth from some other source.

WHAT INFORMATION DO INSTITUTIONAL LENDERS GENERALLY REQUIRE?

Institutional lenders will almost always ask the following questions:

• How much cash and what liquid assets do you have? The lender will request a copy of your bank balance, savings account balance, and an accounting of your stocks and bonds.

• What type of work do you do for a living, and what is your current income?

• How many current debts do you have? All current debts in your family will be considered as well as possible future debts, such as schooling and common necessities.

• What is your credit history? This involves an investigation of your entire past with regard to loans and buying on credit.

• Do you have adequate credit references? Borrowing from banks ranks higher

than borrowing from finance companies.

• What is your past banking experience? Your banks will be contacted for information regarding the size of your accounts, the length of time you have banked with them, and the average amount of money you have on hand in the accounts.

• How old are you, your spouse, and your children? Age is considered because your earning potential usually declines as you get older.

• How much do you wish to borrow, and what repayment schedule do you desire?

Lenders ask for all of this information and sometimes a whole lot more because they will often sell their loans to other lenders, such as Fannie Mae, insurance companies, and pension funds, both here and abroad. In order to make their loans marketable, lenders verify almost every asset on your loan application and check out every negative credit rating, no matter how insignificant. The more documentation you give a lender in the beginning, the faster your loan will be processed.

You may also speed up the loan processing by providing the lender with copies of your federal tax returns for the previous two years and a copy of the current fire insurance on the property (in refinancing situations).

WHAT TYPES OF LOANS ARE AVAILABLE FROM INSTITUTIONAL LENDERS?

The three most common types of real estate loans available from institutional lenders are these: 1) the conventional loan (remember that the conventional loan may have a fixed rate, a variable rate, shared appreciation, graduated payments, or some

combination of these variations), 2) the VA loan, and 3) the FHA loan.

The conventional loan, which is the one most often used, has several advantages over the other two. Although it may not always be assumable, it is much less hampered by federal restrictions and red tape than are the other two, and there is no set maximum amount which may be borrowed. Virtually anyone who has basic good credit can qualify for a conventional loan. In addition, this type of loan takes the least amount of time to obtain.

The newly originated VA loan, as opposed to one being assumed, is available to eligible armed services veterans only. This type of loan is backed by the Veterans Administration and involves a certain amount of governmental red tape. Hence, it takes longer to obtain. Technically, this loan does not require a down payment if the appraisal is the same as or higher than the purchase price, but since the government's appraisal is almost invariably lower than the purchase price, a down payment is almost always necessary, and the veteran has to come up with the difference, a sum which may not be borrowed commercially. The veteran may borrow from a friend or relative but not from an institutional lender. Moreover, not all banks, lending institutions, insurance companies, or mortgage companies offer VA secured loans. You must either shop around or write the VA for a list of those which do offer VA loans in your area. The address for the Veterans' Administration is simply Washington, D.C. 20420.

VA loans have three major advantages over conventional loans: 1) they usually carry lower interest rates; 2) they are assumable by either veterans or non-veterans; and 3) there is no prepayment penalty.

The major disadvantage of the VA loan is its long processing time and its abundant paperwork, both of which simply mean that more things can go wrong.

FHA loans are sponsored by the Federal Housing Administration, a federal agency whose main purpose is to encourage home ownership. This loan is similar to the VA loan, except that the FHA loan is open to anyone with good credit, not just to veterans, and it has a maximum limit which is revised upward periodically to compensate for inflation. The FHA loan, like the VA loan, is assumable and carries no prepayment penalty. Again, like the VA loan, an FHA down payment may not be borrowed commercially unless the buyer is at least 62 years old or unless the buyer is assuming an existing FHA loan. Because it is a government-sponsored loan, there is more paperwork and more red tape, and it takes longer to process than a conventional loan.

If you wish more detailed information on loans, consult one of the numerous books on the subject. Sylvia Porter's *New Money Book for the '80s* is one good example. This book and others like it are available in the real estate or personal finance sections of bookstores and libraries.

Keep in mind that we are concerned here with so-called primary or first loans only. Secondary loans will be covered later.

HERE ARE SOME HELPFUL HINTS TO CONSIDER WHEN TAKING OUT LOANS:

- Weigh the advantages and disadvantages of each different type of loan available to you: conventional (ask about the current types available), FHA, and VA.

- Be ever aware of the time limit you have in which to close escrow. You must know how soon you can get the loan.

- Ask your local banker or real estate agent for help if you don't understand something.

- Make sure that any special agreements with the lender are in writing. Take nothing for granted.

- Read the loan forms thoroughly.

- Understand that interest rates may vary from the time a lender quotes you a figure to the time your loan is actually processed.

- Get a loan commitment in writing from the loan officer, and be sure you know when the commitment will expire. Most commitments are good for thirty days. Do not, whatever you do, rely on verbal agreements.

- Request an extension well ahead of the expiration date if you think you will need one. Most lenders will honor this request although they may very well change the interest rate.

- Know the annual percentage rate. Know whether it is variable or fixed.

- Know exactly how much the lender will lend you.

- Know whether you need a co-signer or security other than the property you intend to buy.

- Know whether the lender will permit any secondary financing.

PLEASE NOTE WELL

Shop around to find the terms that will suit your individual needs. You will find that loan terms and costs vary considerably from lender to lender. Excessive loan fees can alter the purchase price and will be added to the amount you must pay at the close of escrow. Taking everything into account, determine how much it will cost you to borrow the money.

HOW DOES A LOAN APPROVAL PROCEED?

Upon receiving your loan application, the lender will order a credit report to verify your financial stability and your ability to make the loan payments. Only after your credit has met with the lender's approval, will the property itself be appraised. From this appraisal, the lender will tell you how much he is willing to lend on the property. As mentioned earlier, this may vary anywhere from 60% to 90% of either the purchase or the appraisal price. Loans given on commercial property, businesses, and so forth usually range between 60% and 70% of the purchase price. Again, as mentioned, the appraisal will take anywhere from two days to two weeks to complete. It is often helpful to give the lender a copy of your preliminary title report along with your credit or loan application so they can process your application more quickly. Your escrow officer will mail copies of this report for you if you will only tell her where you would like them to be sent.

When your application is accepted, the lender will issue you a letter of commitment detailing the terms of the loan. This commitment is usually good for thirty days.

HOW DO I KNOW WHETHER THE LENDER IS COMPUTING EVERYTHING ABOUT THE LOAN CORRECTLY?

After the loan commitment has been made in writing, the lending institution will furnish you with a "Federal Truth in Lending Statement" or, as it's frequently called, the "Regulation 'Z'" form. This form states the estimated costs you will incur in connection with your loan, and it must, by federal law, give you, the borrower, the following information:

- The schedule of payments

- The annual percentage rate (A.P.R.), also known as the annual interest rate, represents the total amount of interest to be paid over the life of a loan. All of these items are listed under "prepaid finance charge" on the Regulation "Z" form. (The annual percentage rate frequently confuses people, especially when it is different from the rate stated in the note accompanying the mortgage or deed of trust. Almost always it is different, too; it is higher than the note's stated rate; it is never lower. What difference there is can always be attributed to points, fees, and other credit costs being added to the interest rate over the life of the loan.)

- The finance charges (points, interest, and loan fees).

- The total amount of the loan.

- The method used for computing late charges.

- The prepayment penalty.

The Regulation "Z" form was designed to protect you, the buyer. Just as the government requires that the contents of packaged foods be itemized, so does it request that all the fees involved in a loan be disclosed. This disclosure protects the consumer from hidden loan costs. You are to sign this disclosure statement as proof that you saw it and approved of its contents. The signed document is the lending agency's proof that it complied with the Federal Truth in Lending Law. Study the statement carefully before signing to be sure it contains all of the terms you have agreed to.

Take note that if your property is to be a personal residence, you have the right to cancel the entire loan without penalty if you do so within three working days following the signing of the loan contract. This is called the right of recision and is another federal consumer protection requirement.

HOW MIGHT I CALCULATE HOW MUCH CASH I'LL NEED TO CLOSE MY ESCROW?

Complete the cash-to-close worksheet much like the sample given on the next page (there's a blank copy of this worksheet in the back of the book), and you'll have calculated how much cash you'll need to close your escrow.

CASH-TO-CLOSE WORKSHEET

ANALYSIS OF CASH TO CLOSE

Full purchase price of new house $ 100,000   A
Loan amount requested $ 80,000   B
Down payment needed (without closing costs) $ 20,000   C=A-B
Closing cost estimate (3-5% of loan amount) $ 2,400   D

TOTAL CASH NEEDED TO CLOSE $ 22,400   E=C+D

SOURCES OF CASH NEEDED TO CLOSE

Amount from sale of present house $ 10,000   F
Amount of cash deposit $ 1,000   G
Amount from savings & checking accounts $ 1,400   H
Amount from gifts $ _____   I
Amount from stocks or other securities $ _____   J
Amount from other sources (secondary $ 10,000   K
     financing, etc.)
     2ⁿᵈ Note & D.T. to Seller

TOTAL CASH AVAILABLE FOR CLOSING $ 22,400   L=F+G+
     H+I+J+K

NOTE: "L" must be equal to or greater than "E."

WHEN DOES THE LENDER SUBMIT ESCROW INSTRUCTIONS?

After you have chosen your type of loan, filled out your loan application, and received a commitment in writing, your lender will then submit instructions to your escrow officer. These instructions specify the conditions that must be met in order for the loan to be completed. Do your best to meet these conditions within the time limits set by the lender. Remember, lenders give a loan commitment for a specific period of time, usually no more than thirty days.

All lenders, whether institutional or private, will require that at least four conditions be met prior to the close of escrow:

- The loan documents must be executed by the buyer;
- The title insurance in the amount of the loan must be issued to insure the lender's interest;
- The title policy must show only those exceptions approved by the lender; and
- Fire insurance must be issued for at least the amount of the loan, with the lender named as loss payee.

Institutional lenders do not, as a rule, deposit their check along with these instructions. They will disburse their loan proceeds (the actual loan amount, less their fees and any prepaid interest) only at the close of escrow and upon notification that their deed of trust has been recorded. Interest will, of course, begin to accrue from the date when this loan proceeds check is disbursed to your escrow officer.

WITH THE FIRST LOAN APPROVED, WHERE MIGHT I OBTAIN ADDITIONAL NEEDED FINANCING?

Let's suppose now that you have succeeded in getting your first loan but that it's not quite enough for you to consummate the purchase. Money is tight, but you need to borrow more. You need to negotiate a second loan. Since you have already received the maximum first loan obtainable from an institutional lender, you most often cannot borrow more from them right away. They simply will not write a second loan on the same property because they are restricted by regulation from lending more than their allowable maximum. They cannot afford to take the chance either, for if you default, the holder of the first loan is always paid first from the proceeds of a foreclosure sale, while the holder of the second may lose out.

Even though the first-loan holder cannot provide you with any more money, you may apply for "secondary financing" through so-called "non-institutional lenders." These lenders include private parties (the actual seller, a friend of yours, a relative, etc.), mortgage companies, pension funds, trust funds, and so on. These non-institutional lenders are not regulated as heavily and usually do not have as rigid a credit investigation as the institutional lenders.

Regardless of the company or person, however, non-institutional lenders must stay within the usury laws which set a limit on the interest that anyone may charge. Usury laws vary from state to state, so be sure to verify the current allowable interest rates for your area, but make note that many types of lenders are exempt from usury laws as they now exist. Verify this with your escrow officer.

Because some institutional lenders will not permit secondary financing in conjunction with their first loan, be sure to ask the lender of your first loan whether they will permit secondary financing at all. Indeed, you would be wise to ask this question when you originally inquire about your first loan. If you didn't ask about secondary financing before, you can always call and ask your lender about it when the matter becomes an issue. Even if they do consent, they will insist that their loan be superior to all other loans or credit liens. If you have more than one loan on your property, one is always junior to the other, which means that under a foreclosure action, the senior lender collects first and then the junior lender. If you fail to make your payments either to the institutional lender or to the seller who is carrying a second, the loan will be foreclosed, and the institutional lender will get to collect its money first. Any money left over goes next to the seller holding the second loan up to the amount of his loan. If any money is left after that, it goes to you.

A COMMON MISUNDERSTANDING: Interest rates on new loans are so high that Robert assumes he would be wasting his time even to look for a house right now. He knows that without a bank loan he could never afford to buy any property. He can't possibly scrape up enough cash.

THE WAY THINGS REALLY ARE: Robert should be out looking for his house. When bank loans are not readily available, a seller will usually have to help finance the sale of a property if he wants to sell it at all. Then, too, many properties have existing financing which can be assumed by the buyers. There are very few buyers who have all the cash necessary to purchase a property, no matter what the market conditions happen to be.

Let's look at one example of secondary financing to learn more about how it works. The first, and most common, place to look for a secondary loan is the seller himself. After all, he wants to sell his property, and if he believes in you and thinks you're a good credit risk, he may be agreeable to becoming the secondary lender for a short-term loan. Most secondary loans are for a short term, usually from one to five years. The seller doesn't actually lend you cash, but he extends you credit; he "carries back" the note you promise to pay, and he doesn't receive that sum in cash which you would otherwise be paying him. Naturally, he will charge an interest fee for lending the money, just as any other lender would. This "carrying back of paper by the seller" occurs fairly frequently in real estate transactions. Those sellers who would otherwise bank this money are often pleased to extend credit to the buyer in this way, since the interest rates on these notes are generally higher than they could get if they put that money in a savings account.

Should a seller be willing to lend on a second promissory note secured by the property you're buying from him, you and he will have to negotiate the terms of this note. "Terms" mean interest rate, monthly payments, due date, and other conditions. Once you have settled on the terms, your escrow officer will draw up the note and deed of trust or mortgage deed in accordance with your agreement. Never rely on a friendly handshake to bind the agreement. Insist that a promissory note secured by a deed of trust or mortgage deed be drawn up to act as the legally binding contract between borrower and lender. Then have the deed of trust or mortgage deed recorded. Every lender, institutional or private, should receive a deed of trust or mortgage deed and should keep it together with the note until the buyer has paid off the loan in full.

The seller of a residential property (one to four units only) in California who intends to finance part of the purchase price must provide the buyer a "Seller Financing Disclosure Statement." This statement spells out all the terms and conditions of the note.

Be sure to check for mistakes before you sign any note, too, because you will be responsible for precisely the terms written on the note. Mistakes are sometimes made even in the serious business of drawing up loan papers, and these mistakes may be overlooked in the haste of signing a variety of documents. One instance I can remember involved the seemingly innocent substitution of a period for a comma. That little typing error turned this particular conventional note into a demand note, *due anytime on demand* of the lender! Read every word of any note you sign. Be certain everything is done exactly right and that the terms are correct according to your understanding and your prior agreement.

WHAT IS A NOTE?

A note used in real estate transactions is actually a promise to pay, a kind of I.O.U. which is both legal and binding. All real estate notes must be in writing, and they must state both the amount of the debt and the date when it falls due. You as the borrower or signer of a note which is secured by a deed of trust are called the trustor, or if the note is secured by a mortgage deed, you are called the mortgagor. In the note, you promise to pay a certain sum of money or a consideration to the beneficiary, the lender, and you make a conditional promise in writing to the lender that you will pay the loan according to a specified plan. Most notes are negotiable, which means that the holder of a note may sell or transfer it to another person and the borrower would then make all future payments to the new holder of the note. You can tell whether a note is negotiable by its wording. If it states that you are to "pay to the order of" some person or entity, it is negotiable.

Real estate notes come in two varieties, straight and installment, and they differ in only one respect—what their payments cover. Payments on straight notes cover interest only; the original amount of the loan itself is due in one lump sum upon a given expiration date. Payments on installment notes cover both interest and principal, and they may or may not be fully amortized. That is, installment notes may or may not be paid off in full at the due date.

Sometimes people set up installment notes according to a thirty-year amortized schedule, but they stipulate that the balance is all due and payable in ten years. Such a note would have lower monthly payments than one which is fully amortized in ten years, but it would require a large balloon payment on the due date.

Because the terms of all notes are negotiated between the parties involved, don't be afraid to set up terms that you can live with, monthly payments that are within your budget, and a due date that fits in with your long-range financial plans. Review your financial ability carefully. Don't rush into a "second" without confidence that you can meet the payments.

If you are a seller considering a second, consult an accountant or a tax advisor before negotiating the terms of the note with the buyer. You might want, for instance, to receive only so much in each year, depending on your tax situation. Review carefully the tax consequences for the length of the loan, 3 years, 5 years, or whatever other period suits you, and consider adding a prepayment penalty so you'll have enough money to pay your extra tax liability in case the buyer decides to pay off the note before it's due. No matter what the other terms are in any note you are carrying, be certain that one of them includes a late fee to penalize your borrower for paying late. Some can be notoriously slow at paying otherwise. Also, do be sure you check the buyer's credit thoroughly if you're going to be lending him some money. Don't assume that the buyer has a good credit rating. You don't want to be surprised by his bad payment habits sometime later and have to go through a painful foreclosure.

On the next several pages you'll find samples of straight and installment notes and a form for the assignment of a deed of trust, together with instructions for using the assignment form. Blank copies of these forms appear in the back of the book. They might come in handy sometime if you get involved in owner financing.

And here's something else which might come in handy in case you become an "owner-financier." It's a computer spreadsheet template which creates loan tables with ease. Below is a partial table created by one of the numerous spreadsheet templates included in *Landlording™ (The Forms Diskette)*, which ExPress has available (see order form). Besides creating the table, the template calculates the monthly payment.

```
==============================================================
        LOAN PAYMENT CALCULATOR & LOAN TABLE
   BORROWER: Dario Miglia
     LENDER: Charles Meade
   PROPERTY: 1012 Laurel Avenue, Tarrytown
==============================================================
   PRINCIPAL:      10,000.00
    INTEREST:      11.250%
 TERM (YEARS):        5
STARTING DATE:     12/30/89
==============================================================
 Calc'd Payment:      218.67
==============================================================
```

Date	Pmt. No.	Prin. Bal. Before Pmt.	Interest	Principal	Prin. Bal. After Pmt.	Cumulative Interest
12/30/89	1	10,000.00	93.75	124.92	9,875.08	93.75
1/30/90	2	9,875.08	92.58	126.09	9,748.99	186.33
2/28/90	3	9,748.99	91.40	127.27	9,621.72	277.73
3/30/90	4	9,621.72	90.20	128.47	9,493.25	367.93
4/30/90	5	9,493.25	89.00	129.67	9,363.58	456.93
5/30/90	6	9,363.58	87.78	130.89	9,232.69	544.71
6/30/90	7	9,232.69	86.56	132.11	9,100.58	631.27

STRAIGHT NOTE

$ __10,000.00__ _____ Boonville _____ (city),

_____ California _____ (state), _____ August 10 _____ , 19__90__ ,

__ On or before 1 (one) year _____ after date, for value received,

I promise to pay to ____ Samuel P. Seller, a married man _____

_____ , or order, at

_____ Place designated by payee _____

the sum of __ Ten Thousand and no/100ths------------------------------ DOLLARS,

with interest from ___ August 10, 1990 _____ , until paid at the

rate of __ 10% __ per cent per annum, payable ___ At Maturity. _____

_____

Principal and interest payable in lawful money of the United States of America. Should default be made in payment of interest when due, the whole sum of principal and interest shall become immediately due at the option of the holder of this note. If action be instituted on this note, I promise to pay such sum as the Court may fix as Attorney's fees. This note is secured by a Mortgage Deed of a Deed of Trust of even date herewith.

The Deed of Trust securing this note contains the following provision:

In the event Trustor, without the prior written consent of the Beneficiary, sells, agrees to sell, transfers or conveys its interest in the real property or any part thereof or any interest therein, Beneficiary may at its option declare all sums secured hereby immediately due and payable.

_____ *Bruce B. Buyer* _____   _____ *Barbara A. Buyer* _____
BRUCE B. BUYER   BARABARA A. BUYER

_____   _____

When paid, this Note, if secured by a Deed of Trust, must be surrendered to Trustee for cancellation before reconveyance will be made.

DO NOT DESTROY

INSTALLMENT NOTE
(Combined Principal and Interest in Equal Installments)

$ __10,000.00__ ____Boonville_____ (city),

_____California_____ (state), ____August 10____, 19_90_,

FOR VALUE RECEIVED, I promise to pay in lawful money of the United States of America to
____Samuel P. Seller, a married man_____

or order, at ____Place designated by payee_____

the principal sum of ____Ten Thousand and no/100ths----------------------- DOLLARS,

with interest in like lawful money from_____August 10_____, 19_90____

at __10__ per cent per annum on the amounts of principal sum remaining unpaid from time to time. Principal and

interest payable in installments of__Two Hundred Twelve & 48/100 ($212.48)__ DOLLARS, or more

each, on the ____10th____ day of each and every _month_____

beginning __September 10, 1990; and continuing for a period of Five (5)____
years from date hereof, at which time the entire principal balance
and interest due thereon shall become due and payable.

Each payment shall be credited first to the interest then due, and the remainder to the principal sum; and interest shall thereupon cease upon the amount so paid on said principal sum. AND I agree that in case of default in the payment of any installments when due, then the whole of said principal sum then remaining unpaid, together with the interest that shall have accrued thereon, shall forthwith become due and payable at the election of the holder of this note, without notice. AND I agree, if action be instituted on this note, to pay such sum as the Court may fix as Attorney's fees. This note is secured by a Mortgage Deed or a Deed of Trust of even date herewith.

In the event that any payment is not paid within ten days of due date, there shall be paid a late charge of $60.00 on said delinquent payment.

The Deed of Trust securing this note contains the following provision:

In the event Trustor, without the prior written consent of the Beneficiary, sells, agrees to sell, transfers or conveys its interest in the real property or any part thereof or any interest therein, Beneficiary may at its option declare all sums secured hereby immediately due and payable.

Bruce B. Buyer
BRUCE B. BUYER

Barbara A. Buyer
BARBARA A. BUYER

When paid, this Note, if secured by a Deed of Trust, must be surrendered to Trustee for cancellation before reconveyance will be made.

DO NOT DESTROY

INSTRUCTIONS FOR TRANSFERRING A PROMISSORY NOTE WHICH IS SECURED BY A DEED OF TRUST

With all the trafficking in owner financing nowadays, you may at some time be involved in acquiring or disposing of a promissory note, or you may be the owner of a property which secures a note being transferred from one holder to another. To make certain that everyone involved is treated fairly and squarely, each party involved should follow certain steps.

The seller of the note should—

1. Type the following on the back of the promissory note and fill in the blanks:

   FOR VALUE RECEIVED, I (WE) HEREBY TRANSFER AND ASSIGN TO
   _____
   ALL MY (OUR) RIGHT, TITLE, AND INTEREST TO THIS NOTE, SO FAR AS THE SAME PERTAINS TO SAID NOTE, WITHOUT RECOURSE.

   DATED: _____

   SIGNED: _____

   _____

2. Complete the "Assignment of Deed of Trust" form.

3. Record the Assignment form and have the recorder mail it directly to the buyer.

4. Exchange the assigned note for the money agreed upon.

The buyer of the note should—

1. Order a preliminary title report to verify the liens against the property.

2. Request that the note seller follow the steps above.

3. Exchange the money agreed upon for the assigned note.

The owner of the property affected by the note assignment should—

1. Request that the new holder of the note show evidence of the assignment.

2. If at all possible, contact the old holder of the note to verify the assignment.

RECORDING REQUESTED BY:

Samuel P. Seller

WHEN RECORDED, MAIL TO:

Mr. Colin Smith
148 Michele Circle
Norman, California 11005

RECEIVED DEC 11 1990

RECORDED AT REQUEST OF
SECURE TITLE CO.

AT 2 O'CLOCK P. M.
BARRETT COUNTY RECORDS

FEE $ 5⁰⁰   V. L. GRAVES
COUNTY RECORDER

Recorder's Use Only

ASSIGNMENT OF DEED OF TRUST

FOR A VALUABLE CONSIDERATION, the undersigned hereby grants, assigns, and transfers to:

COLIN SMITH, a single man

all beneficial interest under that certain Deed of Trust dated _____August 10_____, 19 90

executed by _Bruce B. Buyer and Barbara B. Buyer, his wife_, as Trustor,

to _Secure Title Company_, as Trustee,

and recorded as Instrument Number _302208_ on _August 10_, 19 90

in Book _2450_ at Page _36_

of Official Records, in the office of the County Recorder of _Barrett_
together with the Promissory Note secured by said Deed of Trust and also all rights accrued or to accrue under said Deed of Trust.

Witness my hand this _11_ day of _December_, 19 90.

Samuel P. Seller
SAMUEL P. SELLER

STATE OF   California   )
) s.s.
COUNTY OF   Barrett   )

On _____December 11_____, 19 90,
before me, the undersigned, a Notary Public in and for said County
and State, personally appeared

SAMUEL P. SELLER

WITNESS my hand and official seal:

Edna Edwards
Notary Public in and for said County and State

NOTARY SEAL

OFFICIAL SEAL
EDNA EDWARDS
Notary Public

proved to me on the basis of satisfactory evidence to be the person__
whose name__ is (are) subscribed to the within instrument and
acknowledged that ___he___ executed the same.

NOTE: This Assignment should be kept with the Note and Deed of Trust hereby assigned.

WHAT IS A DUE-ON-SALE CLAUSE?

This clause simply means that the entire note will be due at once if the owner sells or transfers his interest in the property. Since the lender, whether he be a bank or a private party, has established the loan with you as the buyer and has qualified you as a good credit risk, he will not readily accept a sale or transfer of your property to someone else without demanding complete payment of the loan at once. If a lender wants this protection, he inserts a "due-on-sale" clause into the note. The due-on-sale clause is also known as an "acceleration" or "alienation" clause because the due date is rushed forward, and any new buyer is kept from assuming the loan obligation. Most notes do contain this clause. The common exceptions are VA and FHA loans. These loans, therefore, are considered to be assumable, a real advantage which will be explained later under the subject of assumptions.

A COMMON MISUNDERSTANDING: Mike has a loan on his house with a federally chartered savings and loan. It's an old loan at 7% with a due-on-sale clause which would make the entire loan balance, half the current value of the house, payable in full when he sells. He decides to offer the house for sale with wraparound financing at 12%. His buyer will make one payment every month directly to him, and Mike will continue making the old payments to the savings and loan, pocketing the difference. Because the savings and loan won't know there has been a sale, it won't call the loan due.

THE WAY THINGS REALLY ARE: The savings and loan may not find out about the sale if Mike keeps making his payments regularly, but then again it may be tipped off inadvertently by something like the new fire insurance policy which shows new owners, and if it is, it could call the loan due.

A sample due-on-sale clause written into a note might read as follows: "In the event Trustor, without the prior written consent of the Beneficiary, sells, agrees to sell, transfers, or conveys its interest in the real property or any part thereof or any interest therein, the Beneficiary may, at its option, declare all sums secured immediately due and payable."

WHY IS A MORTGAGE DEED OR A DEED OF TRUST USED?

A note itself is a fairly straightforward promise to pay, but to secure collateral for a note, the lender or your escrow officer draws up either a mortgage deed or a deed of trust, depending upon which is used in your state. Both of them describe the property against which the loan is written and enable the lender to foreclose on the property held as collateral under certain conditions. The basic difference between them is the use of a third party (trustee) in a deed of trust, something lacking in a mortgage deed, which is a two-party agreement with the lender holding the mortgage deed until the loan is fully paid. The mortgage deed, most common in the Midwest and East, allows the borrower one year to make up back payments and always requires a court hearing for foreclosure. As we shall see, foreclosure on a deed of trust is a simpler proposition.

A deed of trust deeds the property over to a third party for him to hold until the loan is fully paid. Lest you feel uneasy about a third party holding the deed to your property, rest assured that the only power transferred to the trustee is the power to sell the property in the event of a default. That's all.

The trustee is usually a commercial institution such as a title company, a bank, or an escrow company. The trust is established in the following manner: the seller delivers title to you, the buyer, by giving you a deed to the land; if the seller is your creditor, you give him a down payment on the land and sign a deed of trust; if you borrow the money from a third party, you pay the seller the entire purchase price, using your own and the lender's funds, and sign a deed of trust for the lender; you then place the deed to the property with the trustee.

Your deed of trust is recorded at the county recorder's office, making it a matter of public record, and then it is returned to the lender, who keeps it and the original note until you, the borrower, have completely paid the amount of that loan on the property.

WHY SHOULD A REQUEST FOR NOTICE OF DEFAULT BE RECORDED?

Now let's suppose that you, the borrower, do not have sufficient funds over and above the first loan to meet the purchase price, so you have taken out a second loan from the seller, who has agreed that he'll lend you the difference, so long as he gets some security in exchange. For his protection, he requires that a second mortgage deed or deed of trust be drawn up and recorded, and you agree. The seller, who has given you the second loan, then receives this second mortgage deed or deed of trust, which he holds as does the institutional lender who holds the first loan until you have paid him off completely.

Should something occur later so that you cannot make your payments, perhaps you cannot even pay the monthly installments to the bank, much less to the holder of the second loan, the bank will foreclose and sell your property to recoup its original investment. If this were to happen, it would leave the seller, who might be out of the country and unaware of your problems, with a total loss. He'd be unable to get his money back for the loan, because the first loan gets first claim in any default proceedings.

To protect himself, the holder of the second wants to be certain he is notified in case of any default on the first so he can take over the payments, if necessary, and not lose most or all of the collateral for the loan. In order to be notified promptly of such a possibility, he has the escrow officer prepare a REQUEST FOR NOTICE OF DEFAULT on the first. This form requests the trustee or mortgagee to inform the holder of the second when there is a default in payments or any other breach of the first note which might cause the lender to begin foreclosure proceedings. The trustee or mortgagee notifies the holder of the second within ten days after the notice of default is recorded. If no REQUEST FOR NOTICE OF DEFAULT has been recorded, the trustee need notify the note holder only within thirty days following the recording of a NOTICE OF DEFAULT. The law allows the holder of the second to cure any default on the first in order to protect his interests, and he can then proceed to foreclose to get his money back if he chooses

RECORDING REQUESTED BY

Secure Title Company

AND WHEN RECORDED MAIL TO

302207

RECEIVED AUG 1 0 1990

RECORDED AT REQUEST OF
SECURE TITLE CO.

AT 8 O'CLOCK *A.* M.
BARRETT COUNTY RECORDS

FEE $ 4

V. L. GRAVES
COUNTY RECORDER

302207

Name Mr. Samuel P. Seller
Street
Address 4 Evelyn Court
City &
State Sydney, Ill. 00010

——— SPACE ABOVE THIS LINE FOR RECORDER'S USE ———

SHORT FORM DEED OF TRUST AND ASSIGNMENT OF RENTS   A.P.N.

This Deed of Trust, made this   10th   day of   August   , between

Bruce B. Buyer and Barbara A. Buyer, his wife as Joint Tenants

, herein called TRUSTOR,

whose address is   12 Allendale Ct.,   Boonville,   Ca   11002   ,
(number and street)   (city)   (state)   (zip)

Secure Title Company, a California corporation, herein called TRUSTEE, and

Samuel P. Seller, a married man as his sole and
separate property   , herein called BENEFICIARY,

Witnesseth: That Trustor IRREVOCABLY GRANTS, TRANSFERS AND ASSIGNS to TRUSTEE IN TRUST, WITH POWER OF SALE,
that property in   Barrett   County, California, described as:

Lot 142, as shown upon that certain map entitled, "Map of Barrett Bay
Unit One, Boonville, California," filed for record September 22, 1960
in Volume 10 of Maps, at Page 78, Barrett County Records.

In the event the real property herein above described is sold or transferred by Trustor herein, the promissory note secured by the within deed
of trust shall become immediately due and payable at the option of the
payee.

TOGETHER WITH the rents, issues and profits thereof, SUBJECT, HOWEVER, to the right, power and authority given to and conferred
upon Beneficiary by paragraph (10) of the provisions incorporated herein by reference to collect and apply such rents, issues and profits.

For the Purpose of Securing: 1. Performance of each agreement of Trustor incorporated by reference or contained herein. 2. Payment
of the indebtedness evidenced by one promissory note of even date herewith, and any extension or renewal thereof, in the principal sum
of $ 10,000.00 executed by Trustor in favor of Beneficiary or order. 3. Payment of such further sums as the then record owner of
said property hereafter may borrow from Beneficiary, when evidenced by another note (or notes) reciting it is so secured.

To Protect the Security of This Deed of Trust, Trustor Agrees: By the execution and delivery of this Deed of Trust and the
note secured hereby, that provisions (1) to (14), inclusive, of the fictitious deed of trust recorded in Santa Barbara County and Sonoma
County October 18, 1961, and in all other counties October 23, 1961, in the book and at the page of Official Records in the office of the
county recorder of the county where said property is located, noted below opposite the name of such county, viz.:

COUNTY	BOOK	PAGE	COUNTY	BOOK	PAGE	COUNTY	BOOK	PAGE	COUNTY	BOOK	PAGE
Alameda	435	684	Kings	792	833	Placer	895	301	Sierra	29	335
Alpine	1	250	Lake	362	39	Plumas	151	5	Siskiyou	468	181
Amador	104	348	Lassen	171	471	Riverside	3005	523	Solano	1105	182
Butte	1145	1	Los Angeles	T2055	899	Sacramento	4331	62	Sonoma	1851	689
Calaveras	145	152	Madera	810	170	San Benito	271	383	Stanislaus	1715	456
Colusa	296	617	Marin	1508	339	San Bernardino	5567	61	Sutter	572	297
Contra Costa	3978	47	Mariposa	77	292	San Francisco	A332	905	Tehama	401	289
Del Norte	78	414	Mendocino	579	530	San Joaquin	2470	311	Trinity	93	366
El Dorado	568	456	Merced	1547	538	San Luis Obispo	1151	12	Tulare	2294	275
Fresno	4626	572	Modoc	184	851	San Mateo	4078	420	Tuolumne	135	47
Glenn	422	184	Mono	52	429	Santa Barbara	1878	860	Ventura	2062	386
Humboldt	657	527	Monterey	2194	538	Santa Clara	5336	341	Yolo	653	245
Imperial	1091	501	Napa	639	86	Santa Cruz	1431	494	Yuba	334	486
Inyo	147	598	Nevada	305	320	Shasta	684	528			
Kern	3427	60	Orange	5889	611	San Diego	Series 2 Book 1961, Page 183887				

(which provisions, identical in all counties, are printed on the reverse hereof) hereby are adopted and incorporated herein and made a part
hereof as fully as though set forth herein at length; that he will observe and perform said provisions; and that the references to property,
obligations, and parties in said provisions shall be construed to refer to the property, obligations, and parties set forth in this Deed of Trust.

The undersigned Trustor requests that a copy of any Notice of Default and of any Notice of Sale hereunder be mailed to him at his address
hereinbefore set forth.

STATE OF CALIFORNIA,

COUNTY OF Barrett } SS.

On August 10, 1990 before me, the under-
signed, a Notary Public in and for said State, personally appeared
Bruce B. Buyer and

Barbara A. Buyer

——————————————, known to me
to be the person S whose name are subscribed to the within
instrument and acknowledged that they executed the same.
WITNESS my hand and official seal.

Signature *Edna Edwards*

EDNA EDWARDS

Title Order No.

Escrow or Loan No. 1. 12345

SPT-1   2/78

Signature of Trustor

Bruce B. Buyer
BRUCE B. BUYER
Barbara A. Buyer
BARBARA A. BUYER

OFFICIAL SEAL
EDNA EDWARDS
Notary Public

(This area for official notarial seal)

RECORDING REQUESTED BY

Secure Title Company
ORDER NO.
ESCROW NO. 12345

WHEN RECORDED MAIL TO

Name
Street Address
City State Zip

Samuel P. Seller
4 Evelyn Ct.
Sydney, Ill. 00010

RECEIVED AUG 10 1990

302208

RECORDED AT REQUEST OF
SECURE TITLE CO.
AT 8 O'CLOCK A. M.
BARRETT COUNTY RECORDS
FEE $ 5.00   V. L. GRAVES
COUNTY RECORDER

302208

——— RECORDERS USE ONLY ———

REQUEST FOR COPY OF NOTICE OF DEFAULT

In accordance with Section 2924b, Civil Code, request is hereby made that a copy of any Notice of Default and a copy of any Notice of Sale under the Deed of Trust recorded _____ August 10 _____, 19 90

as Instrument No. 302206 , in book 3502 at Page 45 _____

_____ , Official Records of Barrett _____ County, California,

executed by   BRUCE B. BUYER AND BARBARA A. BUYER, HIS WIFE

, as Trustor,

to   Independent Trustee Company _____ as Trustee,

in which   FIRST SAVINGS AND TRUST COMPANY

is named as Beneficiary,

be mailed to: Samuel P. Seller _____

at   4 Evelyn Ct.   Sydney   Ill.   00010
       (Street and Number)   (City)   (State)   (Zip)

Dated: August 10, 1990

Samuel P. Seller
Samuel P. Seller

(If Assignment is executed by a corporation, the following corporation form of Acknowlegment must be used.)

STATE OF CALIFORNIA
COUNTY OF } ss.

On _____ , 19 ___
before me, the undersigned, a Notary Public in and for said County and State, personally appeared _____

known to me to be the _____ President, and

known to me to be the _____ Secretary of the corporation that executed the within instrument, and known to me to be the persons who executed the within instrument on behalf of the corporation therein named, and acknowledged to me that such corporation executed the within instrument pursuant to its By-Laws or a Resolution of its Board of Directors.
WITNESS my hand and official seal.

_____
Notary Public in and for said County and State.

—Notary Seal—

STATE OF CALIFORNIA
COUNTY OF Barrett } ss.

On August 10 , 19 90
before me, the undersigned, a Notary Public in and for said County and State, personally appeared

Samuel P. Seller

known to me to be the person___ whose name___ is subscribed to the within instrument and acknowledged that he _____ executed the same.

WITNESS my hand and official seal.

Edna Edwards
Notary Public in and for said County and State.

—Notary Seal—

OFFICIAL SEAL
EDNA EDWARDS
Notary Public

SPF-1   2/78

to do so.

The holder of the second loan must himself either ask the escrow officer or trustee to prepare and record a REQUEST FOR NOTICE OF DEFAULT or he must do it himself. It is not done automatically. If one is not prepared during escrow, the holder of the second can prepare and record one after escrow closes simply by giving the escrow officer the pertinent information and the fee for recording.

HOW DOES A FORECLOSURE WORK?

When you, the borrower, fail to meet your payments on a note, the lender has every right to sell the property given as collateral for the original loan and use that money to reimburse himself for what you still owe. The deed of trust or mortgage deed he holds spells out this right of foreclosure.

Although the term "foreclosure" carries an ominous connotation of unfairness about it, it's hardly unfair at all because the borrower actually has quite a bit of time, almost four months in California, in which to make up his back payments. Foreclosures don't happen overnight.

Let's look at the basic outline of a foreclosure under a deed of trust in California. Because consumer-oriented changes in foreclosure law are occurring regularly, you should consult your attorney or escrow company for the specific procedure practiced in your particular area. (You'll find some information about how other states handle foreclosures in the Appendix.)

- The lender gives the trustee (title company or trust company) written notice that you have defaulted, along with the note and deed of trust and a statement of the account.

- The trustee prepares a declaration of default and records this form in the recorder's office of the county where the property is situated.

- Within ten days from recording the notice of default, the trustee notifies by certified mail the borrower and any subsequent buyers and lenders to whom mandatory notice must be sent, that the lender wishes to sell the property to recover his debt and that a declaration of default has been recorded.

- The trustor or junior lienholder has three months in which to pay all sums due and cure the default. A notice of sale is recorded at the county recorder's office and then published in a local newspaper giving the time and place of the foreclosure sale. This may be done only after three calendar months have elapsed from the date of recording the declaration of default. This notice of sale must be published in a newspaper in the city where the property is located at least once a week for three consecutive weeks. At least twenty days before the sale, a copy of the notice of sale will be mailed to all parties who were sent copies of the notice of default.

- The foreclosure sale must be set at least twenty days after the day this advertisement first appears in the local newspaper.

- At least twenty days before the sale, a copy of the notice of sale must be posted on the property and in one public place.

- After the proper time has elapsed and the borrower still hasn't cured his default nor has any junior creditor done so, the property is then sold to the highest bidder. The sale itself often takes place in the lobby of the title company or on the courthouse steps.

- The minimum bid set by the trustee is the balance owing the lender on the note, plus all costs that have accumulated to process the foreclosure. Bids must be in cash or its equivalent.

- The trustee is reimbursed first for his costs, fees, and expenses, and then the

holder of the note is paid the monies owed to him. If there is any surplus of funds, subordinate lienholders may make claims for the sums owing them.

- A trustee's deed is given to the highest responsible bidder. The title passes to the new buyer without any right or period of redemption. The sale is final. Some states allow a period after the sale during which the borrower can still redeem the property.

Note that the holder of a deed of trust does not have to use an attorney to begin foreclosure proceedings. A foreclosure may be initiated merely by giving the trustee written notice and then letting the trustee handle the matter.

Every step of a foreclosure must be strictly complied with. Failure to publish notices properly, for example, could invalidate the sale. Should you be involved in a foreclosure, be sure to consult your title company or an attorney for the most up-to-date procedures.

A lot depends on whether the default occurs in a state using the "mortgage deed" system of real estate borrowing, or the "deed of trust" system. If you have a mortgage deed, rather than a deed of trust, you as the mortgagee have two choices:

- Petition an equity court to sell the property to recover the money loaned; or

- Sue the mortgagor in a court of law and obtain a judgment which may be used to force the sale of the property.

As you can see from the outline here, foreclosure does give the borrower ample time in which to come up with the money, anywhere from four months to two years, depending upon state laws. Most lenders do not like to foreclose on property, though, because it costs them time and money. They generally will make every effort to contact the borrower and determine the cause of nonpayment. In addition, the trustee makes every effort to notify all of those who might possibly have an interest in the property to see whether they might want to take over the property.

Sometimes the lender has the right to sue the borrower to get a deficiency judgment if an insufficient amount of money is obtained from a foreclosure sale to make up the amount of money due him. However, most states and courts will not permit a deficiency judgment when the loan is made for the purchase of one's own home.

As a result of 1986 legislation, the interest rate on any foreclosure property loan reverts to 10% during the foreclosure period. Lenders may request a title insurance endorsement to cover this situation.

For further information on foreclosure procedures and on acquiring foreclosure properties, consult *Goldmining in Foreclosure Properties* by Val Cabot and *How to Stop Foreclosure* by Hal Morris.

ARE THERE ANY OTHER WAYS TO FINANCE A PROPERTY PURCHASE?

Believe it or not, there are over a hundred ways to structure the financing of a real estate transaction, depending upon the cash position of the buyer and seller and what each needs. Many of these methods are commonly called "creative financing." Creative financing involves working in conjunction with the existing financing to create a financing package to enable the buyer to purchase the property with better interest rates or terms than conventional lenders are offering.

The creative financing approach is based on the ability of a buyer and seller to structure an arrangement which is acceptable to both. The structuring is often done by real estate agents who are knowledgeable about financing.

These are the four most commonly used creative financing methods: assumptions,

subject to's, wrap arounds, and land contracts.

HOW DO ASSUMPTIONS WORK?

An assumption occurs when you, the buyer, take over the seller's existing loan. Because a house in the United States sells on the average of every three to five years, the homeowner still normally owes a sizable sum of money on his first loan when he is ready to sell, but the interest rate on that loan is likely to be lower than what a new buyer's would be. Now, if the money market is tight and lenders aren't lending very readily, if you simply cannot obtain a loan even though your credit is good, or if you have enough cash available and you don't want to take out a high-interest loan, you may work out an agreement with the seller whereby you assume his loan. You take over his liability.

Lenders have the right both to charge an assumption fee and to raise the interest rate if there is a due-on-sale clause in the original loan. If there is none, they cannot charge any additional fees, nor can they increase the interest rate. An assumption of a loan without a due-on-sale clause is most often beneficial to you as a buyer, for you may avoid both the current interest rates and the many costly closing and loan fees.

If you can arrange an assumption, you will need to sign an "Assumption Agreement" with the lender. Later your escrow officer will record a "Substitution of Liability" form at the county recorder's office, and with that you will have formally assumed the seller's loan.

Remember that your escrow officer is available to help you sort out the details about assumptions and about your lender's particular policy regarding assumptions, too. Once you have determined that an assumption is available, she will write the lender and ask for a "Statement of Condition" (also known as a Beneficiary's Statement) of the loan, to include the remaining balance, the interest rate, monthly payments, and any delinquencies. You, the buyer, generally pay a small fee ($65-150) to obtain this Statement of Condition.

Note that with a new loan there is usually a thirty-day grace period before the first payment is due, but there may be no grace period at all when there's an assumption. Be sure to ask your escrow officer when the first payment will be due after you assume a loan.

WHAT IS "SUBJECT-TO" FINANCING?

Taking title "subject to" an existing loan means quite basically that you agree to take over the payments while the loan remains in the seller's name. There are no documents or agreements with the lender. You receive the grant deed and make the payments.

This method of financing greatly benefits you as the buyer because you assume the loan at the old interest rate and without having to pay any new loan fees (occasionally there may be a loan transfer fee of $60-100). It does mean, however, that you will normally have to make a larger cash down payment to pay the difference between the sales price and the loan balance, although you may, of course, take out a second loan.

Subject-to financing may be used only with a loan which has no due-on-sale clause in the original agreement, that is, unless the parties involved wish to take the risk upon themselves that the loan won't be called due. If there is a due-on-sale clause in the original agreement, the loan probably won't be called due so long as the lender has no knowledge that there has been a transfer of ownership, but there is always the possibility that the lender will discover the "sale" and call the loan due. In this kind of financing, the buyer is dealing strictly with the seller, not with the lender.

HOW DOES AN ASSUMPTION DIFFER FROM A "SUBJECT-TO"?

Here's a quick comparison of the differences between the two:

ASSUMPTION

- Old borrower (seller) is released from any liability for the loan.

- A "Substitution of Liability" is recorded, thereby releasing the original borrower from any responsibility for the debt.

- New borrower makes the monthly payments.

- Interest rate may be changed by the lender.

- Lender may charge an assumption fee.

• If there is a due-on-sale clause in the original note, the consent of the lender is required. If there is no such clause, consent is not required.

SUBJECT-TO

• Old borrower (seller) retains ultimate liability for the loan.

• No document is recorded, and no recorded agreement is made between the lender and the new buyer.

• New borrower makes the monthly payments.

• Neither the interest rate nor the other terms of the note are changed.

• There are no costly loan fees.

• There should be no due-on-sale clause in the original note.

WHAT IS A WRAPAROUND LOAN?

Essentially a wraparound is a loan which incorporates an old, existing loan with a new loan made by the seller of a property. The buyer makes one payment to the seller, and the seller continues paying any old loans on their original terms. The wraparound gains popularity whenever there are high interest rates and whenever institutional financing becomes difficult to obtain. During those times, people still have to buy and sell property so they turn to wraparounds as a means of financing.

Here's how a wraparound works. Suppose that you have good credit and a good job, but you don't have enough of a cash down payment available for a property purchase right now. You come across a house which you like very much and which the seller wants very much to sell. Let's say that he doesn't want all cash for his equity because he doesn't want to pay excess taxes that year. You explain your circumstances to him. He checks your credit and learns that it's good, so you and he work out what's called a wraparound loan.

The existing first loan remains in the seller's name as it does in a subject-to situation, and he agrees to give you a second loan, that is, to carry whatever you could not make as down payment. He does this for a rate of interest at the current level on both his old loan and the new loan he is offering you. Say, for example, that the selling price is $100,000. The existing first loan is now at $60,000, but you, the buyer, can come up with only $10,000 for a down payment. This leaves $30,000 more to be financed. The seller gives you, the buyer, a loan for $90,000, incorporating the $60,000 of the original loan and the difference between that and your cash down payment, or $30,000, and the seller gives you this loan using one interest rate for the entire amount. Hence, the term "wraparound" was coined, a packaged loan, also sometimes called an "all-inclusive note and deed of trust" because the new loan includes the original loan(s).

WHY HAVEN'T LENDERS CHALLENGED THE USE OF WRAPAROUNDS?

That's a good question. After all, wraparounds eliminate lenders' opportunities to charge higher interest rates as well as new loan fees on renegotiated loans. The answer is that lenders *have* challenged this practice.

On August 25, 1978, the California State Supreme Court ruled that a state-chartered bank or savings and loan could not call its loan due, nor could it keep a new buyer from assuming a loan, unless it (the lender) could prove that the new borrower's (buyer's) credit was worse than the original borrower's (seller's) credit or that the property had decreased in value [*Wellenkamp v Bank of America*].

This case, believe it or not, was over a mere $16 per month additional interest, but the consequences were dire for state-chartered lenders. The decision virtually stopped them from enforcing their due-on-sale clauses.

WHAT'S HAPPENED ON THE DUE-ON-SALE FRONT SINCE WELLENKAMP?

Because *Wellenkamp* was a state decision, it did not apply to federally chartered banks or savings and loans or to states other than California, but sixteen other states followed in one way or another (Arizona, Arkansas, Colorado, Florida, Georgia, Illinois, Iowa, Michigan, Minnesota, Mississippi, New Mexico, New York, Ohio, Oklahoma, South Carolina, and Washington), and lenders in the other 33 were holding their collective breath. Finally, on June 28, 1982, the *de la Cuesta* decision took the heat off federally chartered savings and loans by excluding them specifically from the terms of *Wellenkamp*. Then, on October 15, 1982, the President signed into law the Garn-St. Germain Bill, which made fully enforceable all due-on-sale clauses originated after that date for both institutional and private lenders.

Since there are some situations which were never meant to trigger a due-on-sale clause anyway, the Garn Bill spells out certain exceptions to its provisions. The following situations would *not* give a lender the right to exercise a due-on-sale clause: 1) transfer to a joint tenant upon the death of another joint tenant; 2) creation of a junior loan; 3) creation of a lease which is three years or shorter in duration and does not contain an option to purchase; 4) transfer to an heir; 5) transfer in a divorce settlement where a spouse becomes the owner; 6) transfer where the spouse or children become the owner; and 7) a transfer into an *inter vivos* trust in which the borrower is the beneficiary.

Although the main provisions of the Garn Bill affect only those loans created after October 15, 1982, Congress did make special provisions for loans either originated, acquired subject to existing financing, or assumed during the "window period" between the *Wellenkamp* decision and the Garn Bill. These loans continued to be assumable, as they were under *Wellenkamp*, until October 14, 1985.

To add to all this seeming confusion, I must note here that the governing body for each particular category of lender may deal with matters itself as well. The Office of the Comptroller of the Currency, which regulates national banks such as Wells Fargo, ruled that its banks may enforce their due-on-sale clauses on all loans beginning April 15, 1984. And the National Credit Union Administration, which regulates federal credit unions, ruled that its credit unions may enforce their due-on-sale clauses beginning December 8, 1982.

Remember that these rulings and legislation concerning due-on-sale matters may be changed at any time by further rulings and legislation, so be sure you verify the current status of assumptions and wraparounds with your attorney, tax adviser, or a well-informed real estate agent before you get involved in any financing which involves a due-on-sale clause.

HOW CAN I TELL WHETHER A LOAN IS ASSUMABLE?

You can tell whether a loan is assumable or not by considering these factors: 1) whether there actually is a due-on-sale clause in the original note (some notes have no due-on-sale clauses at all; look carefully); 2) what the wording of the due-on-sale clause happens to be (some notes have clauses as airtight as a vacuum bottle, prohibiting sales and transfers of every variety, and some have clauses as holey as balloon bread which enable creative buyers to structure transfers to circumvent the strict wording of the clauses); 3) where the property is located (if the property is not in one of the seventeen states listed above, then the due-on-sale clause is enforceable; if it is in one of these seventeen, then, depending upon certain other factors, the clause may or may not be enforceable); 4) who the lender is (if the noteholder is a federal savings and loan, the due-on-sale clause is enforceable; if it's a state-chartered savings and loan in one of the seventeen states, it may be enforceable; etc.); and 5) when the loan originated (if the loan originated after October 15, 1982, its due-on-sale clause is enforceable, no matter what; if it originated during a window period in one of the seventeen states and with certain lenders, it may not be enforceable).

All of these factors and dates may sound confusing. They are. But they are extremely important to anyone assuming a loan. If you're involved in an assumption, consult current source material and/or an attorney and satisfy yourself that you're on safe ground before you go ahead with the transaction.

ARE LAND CONTRACTS "CREATIVE FINANCING"?

Yes, they are. They are a fourth alternative to traditional financing, and they offer one effective way of getting around due-on-sale clauses. They rely on the principle of "buying on contract." A "Contract of Sale," "Installment Sales Contract," "Agreement to Convey," or "Contract for Deed" (they all mean pretty much the same thing) is a type of contract used in connection with the sale of real property where the seller retains legal title to the property until some future date, usually when the full purchase price has been paid.

The installment land contract is most often used as a security device just like the deed of trust. The seller lends the buyer a certain sum of money for buying real property, but unlike in a conventional sale, little or no money is transferred by the buyer to the seller at the time of sale, and the seller does not convey title to the property until the full obligation has been paid. The buyer is able to take possession of the property, to move in and use it as if he were the vested owner, but no deed is recorded, and the seller holds the deed until the full obligation has been satisfied. The buyer usually puts up a relatively small down payment and acquires an equity interest after making periodic payments. When he finally fulfills the contract, he acquires the fee title.

The two main advantages to the buyer using a land contract are that it provides a means to circumvent the due-on-sale clause found in the existing loan, and it offers the possibility that any money paid to the seller will be returned in case of default. When a deed of trust is foreclosed, the borrower is not entitled to the money he had already paid the beneficiary unless there are surplus funds generated by the foreclosure sale. In other words, he forfeits all his prior payments. In the event of a default under a land contract, however, the borrower is entitled to recover the money he has already paid toward the principal.

Naturally there are disadvantages to buying property under a land contract, too. These are the primary ones:

- Although he is limited by law as to the amount he can borrow after the execution of a land contract, the seller could still create new liens against the property, or he may have a judgment filed against him which would further encumber the property. In order to place his contract before all other encumbrances against the property, the buyer should record his contract with the county recorder.

- Circumstances may arise in the future, such as the seller's becoming bankrupt or incompetent or actually dying, which would prevent the buyer from obtaining legal title without court proceedings. The buyer would also lose the land if the seller fails to make his payments and his loan is foreclosed. If the buyer goes to court at that time, he may get his payments back, but it is very unlikely he will get the property since the seller no longer has it. The situation is similar if the seller goes bankrupt or dies and passes title to his heirs.

- Some due-on-sale clauses prohibit contract sales specifically. Should a lender discover that one has occurred, he may call the loan due.

- The seller may not have held legal title at the time the land contract was executed. The buyer should obtain title insurance to protect himself from this and other matters.

The advantage of the land contract to the seller is the ease with which he can eliminate the buyer's interest in case of default. If the contract is not recorded and the buyer defaults, the seller may prepare a notice of termination and regain possession in less time than he could if he were foreclosing on a deed of trust. Since he already has title to the land, he does not have to go through a regular court foreclosure.

If the land contract is recorded at the county recorder's office, however, clearing the title of record may become involved and expensive, especially if difficulties arise because the buyer has created liens, subcontracts, or other encumbrances of interest in favor of third parties, or if the buyer simply disappears. If a land contract is recorded, the seller cannot sell the property to anyone else without first obtaining a release from the buyer.

The rules for issuing title insurance on land contracts vary from state to state. The contract buyer's interest can be insured, and if requested, the contract seller's interest can be insured as well, but title insurance companies will insure recorded contracts only.

Any land contract should be drawn up carefully by someone knowledgeable about them. Such a contract should specify, among other things, the exact amount of the obligation, the method of payment, the interest rate, and the monthly payment schedule.

ARE THERE ANY GUIDELINES FOR A LAND CONTRACT?

There are indeed. As further safeguards, you as a buyer employing a land contract should follow these guidelines:

- Draw up a contract which states that the seller is to put the title to the land in trust with an escrow holder, or third party trustee, until you complete your payments or default on them.

- Require that the land contract be recorded immediately with the county recorder.

- Have the seller sign a deed to you and deliver it to the trustee together with instructions to give it to you upon completion of your payments. This will prevent him from selling or encumbering the title to the land before you receive it.

- Try to get the best financing arrangement possible. Because of the somewhat risky nature of land contracts, sellers often will agree to an extremely small down payment and low monthly payments.

- Specifically forbid the seller from encumbering the title in any way. He should not be allowed to bequeath the title to a beneficiary in his will. If he dies while you are still making payments, the land should remain under the care of his executor until you have either made all of your payments or defaulted.

- Never allow the seller to put a prepayment penalty clause into the contract penalizing you for paying off the balance at an earlier date than scheduled. For example, if your payments are to be $600 a month, you should be permitted to pay $600 a month "or more."

- Be required to keep the property in good repair and to pay for fire and hazard insurance on the property under terms to be approved by the seller. Be sure you and the seller are both beneficiaries under the policy.

- Have the seller state, in detail, the conditions under which he can force you off the land. Make sure you understand them.

- Get the seller to include a clause in which he promises to convey all or part of the title to you after you have completed a certain amount of the total payments. For example, after you have made half of the payments, he will give you full title to the land and you can give him back a mortgage or trust deed for the remaining amount due.

- Give a trustee or third party the responsibility of keeping track of the payments made and the current balances. Over the life of a loan—10, 15, 20, or 30 years—people move, change jobs, and disappear. I remember one instance in which the trustee, a title company, had changed hands; the original employees were gone; and the land contract was coming due. The seller said one amount was left owing, the buyer said quite another. The title company's file on the transaction was supposed to have contained the documentation for the original deposits, monthly payments, etc., but they were nowhere to be found, and there was nothing in the file to prove anything specific. The buyer eventually paid the seller what he felt was due, and the seller turned around and sued the title company for the balance (in this case $5,000) that he felt was owing. The problem was that no one could remember whether a $5,000 deposit had been made on the initial contract.

While not the most desirable of the creative financing techniques, the land contract does offer an alternative when other means of financing won't work for some reason or other. At times this becomes the only way one can buy a piece of property.

Amid all the wheeling, dealing, and financial razzle-dazzle of creative financing, both buyer and seller should be cautious. Beware of misinformation, risks, and liabilities. Be certain your real estate agent is well informed, and review any advice you are given with an attorney.

WHEN I PAY OFF A LOAN, WHAT FEES MUST I PAY?

When you want to pay off a loan, you will be responsible for paying quite a few fees. Here they are:

- *Reconveyance Fee*—The lender or escrow company charges a fee for drawing up a "Deed of Reconveyance," an instrument used to prove that the old deed of trust is indeed paid in full. Ordinarily, the lender will forward a release of claim on the property, and the escrow officer will see that it's recorded at the county recorder's office. This, of course, happens only at the close of escrow, when the loan has been paid off. The payoff and the deed of reconveyance clear the title and release the original borrower from the original loan. The fee for this service runs around $75 and is paid by the borrower (seller).

- *Recording Fee*—Through escrow, the seller pays about $5 to the county to record the deed of reconveyance.

- *Forwarding Fee*—To close out their loans, some lenders collect a "forwarding" or "processing" fee, varying from $40 to $100.

• *Prepayment Penalty*—Most people sell a property before it is completely paid off according to the terms of the original loan. The holder of the original loan is then faced with receiving a large cash sum and no further interest on that money. If the interest rates are currently higher than what was specified in the original note, this is a blessing to the lender, but if they are lower or about the same, it's a curse. Regardless of which it is, the lender will have to recommit those funds, that is, lend them to someone else, something which cannot be accomplished immediately. Because the lender will likely lose some interest on the sum paid off, the lender may charge a prepayment penalty to recover part of the interest lost on the money.

IS THERE ANYTHING I CAN DO TO AVOID PAYING THE RECONVEYANCE FEE?

When you're in escrow, you ought to let the escrow officer handle all the papers involved in the payoff and reconveyance of the loans which are being paid off by funds from new loans. The escrow officer will expedite matters and save you time thereby insuring that your escrow will close promptly.

When you're not in escrow and you have paid off a loan, either by making all the payments as called for in the note or by making a lump sum payoff out of some windfall, you can avoid paying a reconveyance fee by handling the paperwork yourself. It's

RECORDING REQUESTED BY:

Bruce B. Buyer

WHEN RECORDED, MAIL TO:

Bruce B. Buyer and
Barbara A. Buyer
12 Allendale Ct.
Boonville, CA 11002

RECEIVED AUG 1 0 1993

RECORDED AT REQUEST OF
SECURE TITLE CO.

AT __2__ O'CLOCK __P__ M.
BARRETT COUNTY RECORDS

FEE $ __5__   V. L. GRAVES
                   COUNTY RECORDER

Recorder's Use Only

SUBSTITUTION OF TRUSTEE AND FULL RECONVEYANCE

THE UNDERSIGNED, PRESENT BENEFICIARY under that certain Deed of Trust executed by:

Bruce B. Buyer and Barbara A. Buyer, his wife as Joint Tenants , as Trustor,

Secure Title Company , as Original Trustee,

and recorded as Instrument Number ___302207___ on ___August 10___, 19_90_

in Book ___12___ at Page ___459___ of Official Records, in the office of the County

Recorder of ___Barrett___ County, State of ___California___,
hereby appoints and SUBSTITUTES the Undersigned as the new and substituted Trustee thereunder in accordance with the terms and provisions contained therein; AND

as such duly appointed and substituted Trustee thereunder, the Undersigned DOES HEREBY RECONVEY to the person or persons legally entitled thereto, without warranty, all the estate, title, and interest acquired by the Original Trustee and by the Undersigned as the said substituted Trustee under said Deed of Trust.

Wherever the text of this document so requires, the singular includes the plural.

Witness my hand this _12th_ day of ___August___, 19_93_.

Beneficiary and Substituted Trustee:

Samuel P. Seller

STATE OF   CALIFORNIA   )
) s.s.
COUNTY OF   BARRETT   )

On ___August 12___, 19_93_,
before me, the undersigned, a Notary Public in and for said County
and State, personally appeared

Samuel P. Seller

proved to me on the basis of satisfactory evidence to be the person__
whose name__ is (are) subscribed to the within instrument and
acknowledged that ___he___ executed the same.

WITNESS my hand and official seal:

Edna Edwards
Notary Public in and for said County and State

NOTARY SEAL

OFFICIAL SEAL
EDNA EDWARDS
Notary Public

quite easy, especially because the money has already been paid, and no lender has to worry about signing papers before the money has all been paid. There's only one form you need to bother with, too, and it will cost only the amount required to have the form notarized ($5, more or less) and recorded ($5).

Here's what you do:

1. Find a copy of your original DEED OF TRUST, and note the names of the beneficiary (the lender), the trustor (the borrower), and the trustee (usually an escrow or title insurance company or a bank) as they are written there. If there has been an assignment of the deed of trust, then find the ASSIGNMENT OF DEED OF TRUST form as well.

2. Make a copy of the SUBSTITUTION OF TRUSTEE AND FULL RECONVEYANCE form in the back of this book.

3. Type your name beneath the words "RECORDING REQUESTED BY:" and then type your name and address beneath the words "WHEN RECORDED, MAIL TO:"

4. Type the name of the trustor on the first line and the name of the trustee on the second line where indicated. They should be *exactly* as shown on the original DEED OF TRUST or on a subsequently recorded assignment.

5. Type the recording information on the lines where indicated. You will find this information somewhere on the DEED OF TRUST. If any of it is missing, call the county recorder's office and ask someone there for help in identifying your particular DEED OF TRUST.

6. Then contact the beneficiary directly and ask for some cooperation in completing the balance of the form in the presence of a notary public. Offer to pay the notary's fees. Also ask the beneficiary to return to you the NOTE which is secured by this particular DEED OF TRUST with "paid in full" and the beneficiary's signature written on it.

7. Take the completed SUBSTITUTION OF TRUSTEE AND FULL RECONVEYANCE form to the recorder's office, pay the recording fee, and leave the form there to be recorded in the county's official records. Within two to three weeks, it will be returned to you, and you as the borrower will have official proof that the loan has been paid off.

Above all, remember to secure a reconveyance whenever you pay off a loan, whether you do it yourself or seek assistance. Many people forget about it, only to find out later when they want to dispose of the property, that they face delays and difficulties because the former noteholder has died or can't be found.

IS THERE ANYTHING I CAN DO TO AVOID PAYING A PREPAYMENT PENALTY?

As a matter of fact, there are some things you can do to avoid paying a prepayment penalty. Insist as a seller that your buyer obtain a loan from the same lender you used for your loan. In that case, the lender will usually waive the penalty. If you have a government-insured FHA or VA loan, this penalty is now automatically waived by a recent federal law covering prepayments.

If a prepayment penalty is written into your mortgage and the lender insists that you pay it, you cannot simply refuse. If you do, the lender will not allow the mortgage to be cleared from the title to your property, and you will not be able to give clear title to your buyer.

Almost all lending institutions will waive the penalty if you obtain a new loan at a higher interest rate. For example, when you want to borrow additional money from the same lender, "refinance" your loan, and the rate on your old loan is 8% while the interest rate on your new loan will be 10%, your lender will most likely forgo the prepayment penalty.

Also, remember that whenever the rate is revised upward on a variable-rate loan, the borrower has the option to pay off the loan in full without having to pay a prepayment penalty.

Avoiding a prepayment penalty is definitely to the seller's advantage because it could amount to $1,000 or more. The penalty is generally computed as a percentage of the remaining loan amount. Some lenders charge 3-5% of the balance while others charge an amount equal to six month's interest. On a loan with a principal balance of $80,000, this penalty could amount to quite a bit of money. For example, 3% of $80,000 is $2,400; six month's interest at 10% would be $4,000; either way it's calculated, it's no small sum. Generally, through the first five years of the loan, no more than 20% of the principal may be paid in any one year without incurring a prepayment penalty. In other words, on an $80,000 loan, you could make only a $16,000 principal payment in any one year without penalty.

Prepayment penalties are burdensome enough for borrowers, but when lenders enforce due-on-sale provisions *and* charge prepayment penalties besides, they're really being greedy. Because some lenders had been hitting certain borrowers with this "double whammy," the Federal Home Loan Bank Board finally issued a new regulation prohibiting the practice as of December 13, 1985. The regulation prohibits lenders from imposing prepayment penalties whenever a loan has to be paid off because of a sale or transfer. The regulation applies to all lenders, state and federal, institutional and private, but it applies only to loans secured by owner-occupied, one-to-four-unit residential property. Other loans are governed by whatever state laws there are on the subject.

WHAT DOES A PREPAYMENT CLAUSE LOOK LIKE?

Here's an example of how a prepayment clause might look in a note: "The indebtedness created hereby may be prepaid at any time, provided, that if the aggregate amount prepaid in any twelve-month period exceeds 20% of the original amount of this note, I agree to pay the holder hereof an amount equal to six month's advance interest, at the interest rate then in effect, on the amount prepaid in excess of 20% of the original principal amount. However, the charges and limitations contained in this paragraph are not applicable to any prepayment made more than five years after the date of execution of the deed of trust securing this note if the real property covered by said deed of trust is a single-family, owner-occupied dwelling."

HOW DO I GET THE PAYOFF INFORMATION?

To obtain the information necessary to compute all the sums owing on your old loan, your escrow officer will write your lender a "Demand Letter" and ask for a "Demand Statement." The lender will in turn send her a "Payoff or Beneficiary's Demand Statement," giving her all the information she needs to pay off your loan in full, together with documents necessary for reconveyance. Your escrow officer must allow ample time for the lender to furnish her with this information. If you're the seller, be sure to tell her as soon as possible whether the old loan will be paid off, or if you're the new buyer, whether you will be assuming it. This payoff, or Demand Request Letter, should be written at least ten days prior to the close of escrow.

If you as buyer are to assume the existing loan, your escrow officer will write the lender a "Request for Statement of Condition" or "Beneficiary's Statement" letter. In this, she requests the current status of the loan, the sums left owing, the interest rate, any delinquencies, etc. Because lenders are very sensitive about subject-to agreements and might try to prevent the takeover or raise the interest rate or make the new buyer qualify as if seeking a new loan or even call the loan due if a due-on-sale clause exists, your escrow officer must be quite careful to write for a request only and not for a demand payoff statement.

HOW MAY I OBTAIN "SHORT-TERM" FINANCING TO HELP ME THROUGH ESCROW?

Whenever you're faced with a situation where you've had to buy a new home before you've been able to sell the old one, you'll probably need to arrange some short-term financing. You need what's called a "swing loan," nothing more really than another mortgage placed on your old home for as long as 36 months.

Usually you can borrow up to 80% of the appraised value of your old home with a swing loan. If your old first mortgage is the only mortgage you have on the house, for example, and it equals 50% of the appraised value, then you should be able to get a swing loan equal to 30%, for a total indebtedness of 80% of the appraised value.

Another short-term financing arrangement, the "assignment loan," may come in handy when you have sold your old home and haven't been able to get enough cash out of it to purchase a new home because you had to carry back a note to get the old home sold. In that situation, you could ask a lender for an assignment loan, a loan usually written for 70% of the face value of the note you carried back. That note and its mortgage or deed of trust would be the collateral for the assignment loan which would then give you the cash you need to buy a new home.

HOW MAY I PAY OFF MY EXISTING HIGH-INTEREST LOAN AND OBTAIN A NEWER LOW-INTEREST LOAN?

If you want to pay off an existing high-interest loan and get one at a lower rate when available, you have to refinance your property, that is, secure a new loan to replace an old one or two or three, a common practice. Generally, people refinance their properties in order to take advantage of lower interest rates, pull cash out for other uses, reduce their payments, or do all three. They don't refinance to reduce their loan balance. In fact, unless they put out-of-pocket money into their refinancing, they will wind up owing more money to a lender after they refinance than before. Why? They'll owe more because there are so many fees involved in paying off the old loan and obtaining the new one, and these fees are usually paid out of the sum borrowed. Refinancing charges generally amount to 3% of the principal, though they may be as much as 5 or 6%, depending on the loan fees.

When you refinance a property, you start from scratch just as if you were buying the property initially. You work your way through the entire loan qualification procedure, filling out an application, a financial statement, and the usual forms required by the lender. That done and approval obtained, you pay the sundry fees and ultimately, after weeks and sometimes months of waiting, meet your objective.

As a rule, refinancing is worthwhile if you can reduce your interest rate by 2% or more and repay the refinancing costs within three years. To estimate how long the repayment of costs will take, divide the total cost of refinancing by the reduction in your monthly payment. The result will be the payback period in months, without taking any tax consequences into consideration.

Here's a table which shows payback periods for various interest rates, assuming that loan origination charges are 3% and that the loans are at fixed rates for 30 years.

Current Rate:	New Rate (%):				
12%	8.64	10.35	10.91	11.18	11.35
13%	9.71	11.38	11.93	12.20	12.36
14%	10.77	12.40	12.94	13.21	13.37
15%	11.49	13.09	13.60	13.85	14.19
	Payback period will be:				
	1 yr.	2 yrs.	3 yrs.	4 yrs.	5 yrs.

Don't overlook the tax considerations involved in refinancing. Lender's points are prepaid interest and thus tax-deductible, but note this: If you pay points by check instead of having them deducted from the loan proceeds, you should be able to deduct them all in the same year you refinance instead of having to amortize them over the life of the loan. So, if you pay $3,000 in points on a 30-year mortgage, you'll get a $3,000 one-time deduction by paying with your own check or you'll get a

$100-per-year deduction over 30 years if you have the points deducted. Prepayment penalties are considered interest payments, and as such, they're deductible when paid.

Before you go about refinancing your home to save on interest, consider how long you intend to live there. If you think you might be moving within a few years, try to get an assumable loan. It would make your home easier to sell, especially during times of rising interest rates. Also, if you think you might be moving soon, try to get a loan with lower loan costs and slightly higher monthly payments; in that way you'll shorten the time necessary to recoup the refinancing costs.

Cutting Closing Costs

- Look to your present lender first.
- Shop around for the best price on the title search and title insurance.
- Shop around for reasonable attorney's fees.
- Try to avoid having to pay mortgage insurance.
- Do some bargaining with the lender.

Here's one example of how refinancing might benefit homeowners who want to lower their monthly payments and pull some cash out of their property. After making $948.75 payments for three years on their home, the Tullys have managed to reduce the principal on their $75,000 loan (15%, 30 years) to $74,475. Today the home is appraised at $110,000, and they decide to borrow 80% of that amount, or $88,000, which is offered to them at 12% interest for 30 years. Their new payment is $905.52, a savings of $43.23 per month, but that's not all. Once they pay off their old loan and the closing costs of $2,600, they find that there's $10,925 left over, just what they need to pay off their kids' accumulated orthodontist bills and take a trip to Hawaii. They and their kids are smiling. That lower interest rate made all the difference.

7
TITLE INSURANCE

WHAT IS TITLE INSURANCE?

Title insurance is a guarantee that you are getting something for your money when you buy real property. Title insurance guarantees that the ownership of the property you are buying is just as it's stated in recorded documents.

Whenever you buy any real property, you expect to acquire use of the property as well as its "title" or legal ownership, and you want to be absolutely certain that the owner had clear title to it in the first place and consequently was legally entitled to sell it to you. He might say that he owns the Brooklyn Bridge and you might want to buy it from him on his terms, but unless you determine that he has clear title to it and unless you secure a title insurance policy to protect yourself, you will be giving him money for nothing, and he will have the last laugh.

A COMMON MISUNDERSTANDING: Donald is buying a house directly from an honest, reputable friend. The preliminary title report which he orders gives no evidence of title problems, so Donald decides not to waste any money on title insurance.

THE WAY THINGS REALLY ARE: Donald's friend may be honest and may have told Donald everything he knows about the house, but what about the previous owners? Did they have a valid claim to the property?

Many kinds of title defects are so serious that they can render a title unmarketable. It is the title insurance you purchase when you acquire real property which protects you against most of these defects.

"Real property," by the way, refers to land and all the things that are either attached to it or considered as part of it, including such things as buildings and minerals below the surface. Title insurance does not cover personal property, including movables like furniture, draperies, washers, or refrigerators.

Title insurance protects the buyer and lender involved in a real property transaction against incompetent past action, clerical errors, someone insane's having signed off an earlier deed, incorrect marital status, undisclosed heirs, improper interpretation of wills, signing by anyone without authority, a minor's signing, or any possible forgery in the entire past chain of title signatures.

In sum, it insures against claims made by third parties against the title. Like other types of insurance policies, title insurance affords protection to the insured by guaranteeing that the insurer, that is, the title insurance company, will reimburse him for actual loss or damage under the conditions specified in the policy. Unlike other insurance policies, title insurance insures against conditions that already existed rather than against those which may occur in the future.

WHY SHOULD I BUY TITLE INSURANCE?

The property you are buying may have a past fraught with shady dealings, forgeries, divorce claims, or other peculiarities. There's no way you can be absolutely certain that this seller or any of the previous sellers ever held clear title to the property and could legally transfer it over to you, for even though an owner has a deed and the right to possess the land, he might not have clear title because there may be a defect or cloud on the title that even he doesn't know about. To protect yourself from many such claims out of the past, you should secure title insurance, something which is available in every state except Iowa and for almost every conceivable kind of interest in real estate, including leaseholds, rights under a contract of sale, airspace, rights and easements, and mineral rights.

In addition, you must have title insurance if you intend to borrow any money on your property. Your lender, wanting to protect his interest in the property which secures his loan to you, will require a policy for his own protection, to insure himself against any previous claims made on the property by legitimate or illegitimate claimants. You need a policy to protect yourself, too. You don't want to learn after the sale that you have no rights to the property at all, that you have, in effect, bought the Brooklyn Bridge in disguise, and neither does your lender. He knows that you won't repay the money he has lent you to buy a property unless you are legally entitled to that property.

But even if your real estate transaction is an all-cash deal, you should obtain title insurance, for a grant deed by itself does not necessarily give clear title to a property. There may be outstanding claims and rights which cannot possibly be determined from the deed alone.

Remember, too, that although you are protected under your purchase agreement against certain damages, only the seller is liable to you for those damages, whereas under a title insurance policy, the title company assumes that liability. If you are not insured and you have to proceed against the seller for any defect in title or any breach of the purchase agreement, you yourself will have to pay the legal expenses prior to a judgment, and even if you do win a judgment, you might not be able to collect it, for you might not be able to locate the seller or he might not have the money to pay you. You could be left holding worthless paper. If, on the other hand, you have a title insurance policy, it will pay your legal costs and provide you with coverage for any losses included in the policy. Such insurance is essential to you as a property buyer.

If you were really determined to do so, however, you could insure yourself. In that case, you'd certainly want to try to trace your property's ownership and complete chain of title to get some idea about whether the seller had clear title. When you did, you'd find soon enough that a title search is both a time-consuming and a tedious task. Were you to make the same investigation as the title examiner, you would have to gather and review information from the following sources:

• Public records at the county recorder's office (in San Francisco County last year alone, there were over 120,000 documents recorded. In Los Angeles County, there are some 9,000 instruments recorded every day. Searching through just those records for one year would take a long time, and you'd have to go back through many years to be safe, to the original land grants in some cases. In Los Angeles County, for instance, land can be traced back to the rancho days in 1850, when the Los Angeles Recorder's Office first opened);

- Certain taxing authorities which levy taxes and assess real property;

- Documents in the general index (bankruptcy, divorce, name changes, judgments, trust agreements, probate proceedings, etc.); and

- Bankruptcy proceedings of the United States District Court.

Moreover, after going through all those records, you'd have to interpret the effects of such information on ownership. You might have to request documents and additional information. You might even have to initiate court proceedings to clear the title in order to be relatively certain that it was indeed clear. Even if you or your attorney did feel qualified to make a title search, examine the records, and evaluate the effects of those records, a prudent buyer or lender would still want assurance to protect himself against loss or damage in the event of an error because overlooking just one judgment or lien could be very costly.

The cost of title insurance is minimal when you consider the protection it provides. A title insurance policy for a $100,000 property, for example, costs less than $600.

HOW LONG DOES TITLE INSURANCE REMAIN IN EFFECT?

The protection provided by an owner's policy continues until the interest of the insured is transferred, that is, as long as you own the property. Even when an insured dies, his heirs or devisees remain protected under the terms of the policy. A title policy is not assignable or transferable to subsequent purchasers of the property, however. For instance, a seller cannot transfer his policy to you. Each new buyer must purchase a completely new policy regardless of how recently the seller had a title search conducted.

WHO OBTAINS TITLE INSURANCE?

Either the buyer or the lender or both of them may obtain title insurance. In many states, both the buyer and the lender are covered in one policy. In California, there are five distinct title insurance possibilities: The California Land Title Association (CLTA) Standard Owner's Policy, the CLTA Owner's and Lender's Joint Protection Policy, the CLTA Lender's Policy, the American Land Title Association (ALTA) Lender's Policy, and the ALTA Owner's Policy.

Most often, the buyer pays for the policies. In some areas, however, the seller pays for the owner's policy, and the buyer pays for the lender's policy. Your escrow officer can tell you who pays the various premiums in your area (also see Appendix). You may, of course, negotiate splitting the costs with the seller because it is only local practice which determines who pays the premiums and not local laws.

You might like to know, in addition, just in case you ever carry back a loan on a property you're selling, that a lender's policy is for the benefit not only of the lender who was insured originally, but also of anyone who might acquire the note at a later time. Liability under the policy doesn't end until the loan is finally paid off.

HOW MUCH INSURANCE WILL I NEED?

You, the buyer, should have a policy for the full amount of the purchase price, whereas the lender needs a policy only for the amount of the loan. In other words, the buyer and lender need enough insurance to cover their individual financial commitments on the property.

Where a multi-policy insurance system is available, your lender will require you to obtain for them an ALTA policy for the amount of their loan, and you as buyer should obtain a CLTA policy for the amount of the purchase price of the property. If the purchase price were $100,000 and the loan amount were $80,000, then you would want a CLTA policy based on your purchase price of $100,000 and an ALTA policy based on your loan of $80,000. If the title company should later have to defend you in a court action, it will be responsible for bearing costs up to the amount paid for the property plus the allowable inflation percentages provided for in the policy.

A COMMON MISUNDERSTANDING: The Hatfields bought a house for $100,000 and made a down payment of $20,000. Their lender required them to get a title insurance policy for $80,000, which they dutifully bought, but they decided against getting any more coverage than that because they were trying to save some money and thought they'd never need title insurance for themselves anyway.

THE WAY THINGS REALLY ARE: When a relative of the previous owner showed up and presented a valid claim to their house only a month after the Hatfields moved in, the title company had to reimburse the lender for its loss. In the aftermath, the lender delivered the mortgage note to the title company, and the Hatfields lost both their home and their equity, and because they hadn't covered themselves for the loss, they still owed the mortgage holder $80,000.

HOW ARE TITLE INSURANCE PREMIUMS DETERMINED AND HOW FREQUENTLY IS THE PREMIUM PAID?

Title insurance premiums are based strictly on the amount of coverage provided. The premium is paid only once, at the time the property is purchased or when its mortgage is refinanced.

ARE ALL RATES ALIKE?

Title insurance fees are not set by law, so they do vary somewhat. After the title company has set its own fees and has filed them with the state insurance commissioner, those fees must be adhered to. You will find by shopping around and making comparisons that fees vary up to $150 from company to company, county to county, and state to state. Most buyers don't bother to shop for the best title insurance rates, however, because they are too busy shopping around for a favorable loan, rearranging their personal finances, or worrying about termite repairs. They don't even think about looking for a better title insurance rate. Try comparing rates yourself the next time you have to pay for title insurance, and you'll be amazed at the savings which are possible.

   You should also be aware that most title insurance companies offer a discounted rate (usually 20%) on property that has been sold or been insured within the previous two to five years. Check with your escrow officer to see if your property qualifies for this discounted or "short-term" rate. If, for example, the basic rate for your title insurance is $550, the short-term, discounted rate would be $440, a savings of $110, almost enough for a night on the town.

IS THERE ANY OTHER WAY TO SAVE ON TITLE INSURANCE?

   There is still another way to save on title insurance which you ought to know about. If you expect to resell your property within a few years following your purchase, you may have the entire CLTA title insurance premium refunded to you, so long as you choose to buy a binder policy of title insurance when you first buy the property. The cost of this binder policy is 10% of the basic title insurance rate, but you will have to pay for both the binder and the standard policy when you buy the property, and if you fail to sell within the time limit specified in the binder, usually two to five years, you will lose the amount you have paid for the binder.

   If the basic title insurance premium for a property were $550, for example, you would have to pay an extra $55 for the binder, or a total of $605. You would then receive a refund of $550 when you sold the property, and the title insurance company would keep only the $55. Should you keep the property longer than the binder period, though, you would not qualify for a refund, but you would lose only 10% of the amount of the title insurance policy, whereas you would stand to gain 100% of the amount of the policy, a pretty good gamble if you think you would qualify.

Use of a binder does not dilute the policy in any way, but your buyer would have to buy a title insurance policy from the same company you used.

WHAT IS A CLTA TITLE INSURANCE POLICY?

The California Land Title Association Policy, as the name implies, was issued initially only in California, but other states, notably Nevada and Arizona, have now adopted it. Also referred to as the "Standard Coverage Policy," it insures owners and/or lenders. It is a limited policy because it will insure against only those matters which are disclosed in public records and will not cover any defects which are concealed from the title company. "Off-record" items such as an encroachment, an unrecorded easement, a discrepancy in boundary lines, or an interest of parties in possession of the property, which are discovered only by a survey or inspection of the property itself, are not covered by a CLTA Standard Policy.

When issued to insure a lender, a CLTA policy provides coverage against a loss sustained because the deed of trust proved to be invalid (there are some exceptions), because the deed of trust proved to be in a worse position than shown, or because an assignment in the policy proved to be invalid.

A CLTA policy may be issued in any of these three ways:

- An owner's policy, covering the owner only;

- A non-institutional lender's policy, covering the private lender only or an institutional lender if he wants it (institutional lenders generally prefer the broader coverage of an ALTA policy); and

- A joint-protection policy, covering both the owner and the lender in the same policy (used most often when a seller takes back a second note and deed of trust and wants to be named as an additional insured party).

In order to obtain insurance coverage on the items not covered in the standard policy, you may order added endorsements. Two of these owner's endorsements are included by most title insurers as a matter of course. The inflation endorsement, which is issued automatically at no additional charge, makes an upward adjustment in the amount of insurance provided in an owner's policy. In other words, if your $100,000 house is worth $110,000 next year, and there's a claim against the title, your title insurance policy will cover the inflated price of the house rather than just the original sales price.

The homeowner's endorsement, issued only on owner-occupied dwellings with four or fewer units (fourplex or smaller), insures against limited off-record risks involving certain matters related to access, encroachments, restrictions, zoning, taxes, mechanics' and material suppliers' liens, as well as the exercise of the right to take minerals. If these are not included in your policy of title insurance, you may order them for a nominal fee so long as the title company will make such endorsements. Your escrow officer will tell you which endorsements are available.

SECURE TITLE   Policy No.: CAS-223346

SUBJECT TO THE EXCLUSIONS FROM COVERAGE, THE EXCEPTIONS CONTAINED IN SCHEDULE B AND THE CONDITIONS AND STIPULATIONS HEREOF, SECURE TITLE INSURANCE CORPORATION, a California corporation, herein called the Company, insures the insured, as of Date of Policy shown in Schedule A, against loss or damage, not exceeding the amount of insurance stated in Schedule A, and costs, attorneys' fees and expenses which the Company may become obligated to pay hereunder, sustained or incurred by said insured by reason of:

1. Title to the estate or interest described in Schedule A being vested other than as stated therein;

2. Any defect in or lien or encumbrance on such title;

3. Unmarketability of such title; or

4. Any lack of the ordinary right of any abutting owner for access to at least one physically open street or highway if the land, in fact, abuts upon one or more such streets or highways;

and in addition, as to an insured lender only:

5. Invalidity of the lien of the insured mortgage upon said estate or interest except to the extent that such invalidity, or claim thereof, arises out of the transaction evidenced by the insured mortgage and is based upon

    a. usury, or

    b. any consumer credit protection or truth in lending law;

6. Priority of any lien or encumbrance over the lien of the insured mortgage, said mortgage being shown in Schedule B in the order of its priority; or

7. Invalidity of any assignment of the insured mortgage, provided such assignment is shown in Schedule B.

This Policy shall not be valid or binding until Schedule B is countersigned by an authorized officer or agent of the company.

IN WITNESS WHEREOF, THE SECURE TITLE INSURANCE CORPORATION has caused its corporate name and seal to be hereunto affixed by its duly authorized officers as of the date shown in Schedule A.

SECURE TITLE INSURANCE CORPORATION

BY: *Jack Harper*
PRESIDENT

ATTEST: *Russell Kennedy*
SECRETARY

SCHEDULE A

PREMIUM ____432.50_____

Case No:

Amount of Insurance: Date of Policy: Policy No:

$_100,000.00_   _August 10, 1990 at
8:00 A.M._   **CAS** -223346___

1.   Name of Insured:

     BRUCE B. BUYER AND BARBARA A. BUYER

2.   The estate or interest in the land described herein and which is covered by this policy is:
     A FEE

3.   The estate or interest referred to herein is at Date of Policy vested in:

     BRUCE B. BUYER AND BARBARA A. BUYER, his wife as
     Joint Tenants

4.   The land referred to in this policy is situated in the County of   Barrett   , State of
     California   , and is described as follows:

     Lot 142, as shown upon that certain map entitled, "Map of Barrett
     Bay Unit One, Boonville, California, " filed for record September
     22, 1960 in Volume 10 of Maps, at Page 78, Barrett County Records.

This policy valid only if Schedule B is attached.

WHAT SHOULD I LOOK FOR IN MY TITLE INSURANCE POLICY?

Be certain you check to see that the policy amount is correct, and that the date given on the policy is, in fact, the escrow's actual closing date, for this is the date when the policy becomes effective. Verify that the policy describes all of the property and all of the interests being acquired. If the buyer thought, for example, that he were buying two lots but the deed covered only one and the title policy described only that one, the title insurer would have no liability.

WHAT IS AN ALTA TITLE INSURANCE POLICY?

The American Land Title Association policy (ALTA) was primarily designed to meet the demands of the large national lending institutions for uniform title insurance protection across the country and for increased protection against risks which can only be ascertained by an inspection of the property. In effect, it extends the scope of the basic owner's policy to cover various matters not on record. In California, any lender, institutional or private, may obtain an American Land Title Association policy to insure against the same items which are in the standard CLTA owner's policy, as well as against any of the following: mechanics' liens not yet recorded, claims to water and mineral rights, unrecorded easements, unrecorded tax and assessment liens, and certain other matters. To determine whether a title company will insure against any other matters, the company will inspect public records and, for a fee, the property itself. These off-record investigations sometimes reveal a wide variety of encroachments: overhanging structures or architectural details, common walls, boundary fences, community driveways, etc., which will be shown by the title company as exceptions in the policy and not normally insured against.

An ALTA policy does provide a lender with some important protection few people ever think about, protection against the lender's deed of trust having been recorded other than when requested. This protection can become very important because the date, time, and order of recording determine a trust deed's priority, that is, whether it becomes a "first," "second," "third," or lesser trust deed. The security a lender seeks most is a valid lien with priority over other claims and interests, plus some assurance that the borrower and the owner of record are one and the same and that this borrower has valid title to the property which secures the loan.

Sometimes, however, a lender may require protection beyond that afforded by an ALTA policy. He may order that an endorsement or a special coverage be added to his policy, the most common of which are those covering violations of covenants, conditions, and restrictions (CC & R's) limiting the use of land and regulating the type and location of improvements; encroachment of property improvements which might extend onto a neighbor's property; damage from the exercise of mineral rights; and mistaken location and dimensions of the property as disclosed in county records. These endorsements expand the coverage of the title insurance policy and are usually added without charge. Any other endorsements requested by the lender in his escrow instructions will be added by the title company if they are insurable, and their costs will be charged to the borrower.

There are many other endorsements available, each suited to a particular situation or occurrence. As an example, say a zoning ordinance requires all houses to be set back ten feet from the property boundary at the street, and after escrow closes, the city discovers that your house is built only eight feet from the street. Should the city require this violation of its zoning ordinance corrected, resulting in actually moving the house two feet or else cutting two feet off the front of the house, the situation would be covered if the lender had requested an endorsement to cover it. Another example would be unrecorded mechanics' liens filed after the homeowner has moved in. While the previous owner is responsible for paying the lien, there would be legal expenses involved in finding the previous owner and serving him with the papers. Special policy endorsements may be written to cover numerous situations where an insured desires special insurance against a particular risk, whether based on recorded or unrecorded matters.

Owners may insure themselves with extended-coverage policies, too, the most common of which is the ALTA Owner's Policy. This policy insures against off-record matters, but it doesn't come cheap because it requires additional work, likely a physical inspection and maybe even a licensed surveyor's report.

WHAT IS THE TORRENS TITLE SYSTEM?

A few parts of the country, fewer than one percent, use a different system of guaranteeing title to real property. Under this system, called the Torrens Title System, the county recorder maintains a record of all encumbrances that exist on the title to each piece of property in the county. Before a piece of land can be sold or mortgaged, the buyer and seller must go to court for a hearing. The county recorder sends a notice of the hearing to anybody who, according to the county records, could possibly have a claim against the title. Anybody with a claim must sue to have his claim settled before title is passed to the buyer. The court dismisses or settles all the claims, orders the title to be registered in the buyer's name, and issues the new owner a Torrens Certificate, which lists any liens and encumbrances against the title. Once a Torrens Certificate is issued, the title is declared marketable and no undisclosed defects can be used later to cause a loss of title.

HOW DO DEEDS DIFFER?

In most states, deeds are either grant or quitclaim. In a grant deed, the seller or "grantor" states that he owns the property and that there are no liens, loans, or easements on the property other than those which he has told you about. In a quitclaim deed, the grantor conveys whatever interest he may have in a property without making any guarantees regarding liens, loans, or easements. If the seller has full title, the buyer will get full title. If he has nothing, the buyer will get nothing.

Whenever you buy real property, never accept a quitclaim deed as the sole transfer device. Someone could legally sell you his nonexistent interest in the Brooklyn Bridge, the Golden Gate Bridge, or the Pacific Ocean with such a deed. These deeds are commonly used only to eliminate a minor interest in a property.

Although most community-property states do have quitclaim deeds, not all states do. In community property states (once again, they are Arizona, California, Idaho, Louisiana, Nevada, New Mexico, Texas, and Washington), all assets acquired during marriage are jointly owned by the husband and wife regardless of whose name is on the grant deed. If you want to hold property as your "sole and separate property" in these eight states, you should always obtain a quitclaim deed from your spouse to prevent a later claim being made by your spouse.

Don't become as confused about quitclaim deeds as those many people have been who have asked me to execute a "quick-claim" deed for them, believing it to be a sort of hurry-up deed. It may be quick, but that has nothing to do with its name. "Quitclaim" simply means to be quit or rid of any claim on a property. That's all.

WHAT IS A WARRANTY DEED?

Warranty deeds, widely used in the Eastern and mid-Western states (see Appendix), define their warranties in explicit terms rather than implying them according to prevailing law. The grantors warrant that they have the lawful authority to sell and that the property is free of all encumbrances. They also agree that they will "defend the title against the just and lawful claims of all persons."

WHAT ARE CONDOMINIUMS, AND IS TITLE INSURANCE AVAILABLE FOR THEM?

A condominium, "condo" for short, is one individual unit within a larger complex of units which may be residential, industrial, or commercial. Each unit owner receives a deed to his own unit and may secure title insurance on it. Instead of owning land, though, he owns "air space," which is still considered real property, just as real as a house with the land it rests on. All the unit owners in the complex own an undivided interest in the common areas, parking areas, walkways, yards, pool, etc., and these common areas include such things as the bearing walls, utility lines, conduits, studs, sheetrock, wood paneling, all the pipes and wires in the walls, and the land beneath the units. Basically then, each owner has a "cube of airspace" together with the structural portions and the land, which are all owned in common.

A COMMON MISUNDERSTANDING: Believing that no one will object, Cliff decides to dig a basement under his condominium unit.

THE WAY THINGS REALLY ARE: Cliff forgot that he doesn't own the land under his unit and that he has no legal right to dig a basement there. He might go ahead and dig, pour the concrete, and turn the area into a great storage and rumpus room, but he might be required by his homeowners' association to remove the whole thing once they find out what he's done.

Each unit is assessed separately by the county tax collector, has its own assessor's parcel number, and receives a separate tax bill. Likewise, each unit has its own mortgage or loan, so if a neighbor defaults on his loan payments or property taxes, it doesn't affect you in the least.

To see that the common areas are maintained, that the fire insurance is kept current on the entire complex, and that other matters of common concern are looked after, a homeowner's association is created. This association may be either incorporated or unincorporated. If is is incorporated, the common areas will be owned by the association, and a board of directors will be responsible for maintaining them. The corporation draws up a set of by-laws to spell out the duties and obligations of the corporate body, and they become the guidelines used for running the association. If it is unincorporated, the unit owners own the common areas as tenants-in-common, and

the association is run by an elected majority of unit owners.

Each unit owner, of course, automatically becomes a member of the association, and the association charges each owner a monthly maintenance fee which is a pro-rata share of maintenance costs, insurance premiums, property taxes on common areas, special assessments, and any other common expenses.

Upon creating a condominium project, the developer will prepare and record a declaration of covenants, conditions, and restrictions which are normally incorporated in the deed and will set forth the rights, duties, and obligations of all the unit owners. Your preliminary title report will show the book and page where they are recorded in the official county records. You may obtain a copy from your escrow officer, the homeowners' association, or the recorder's office. Often the CC & R's are voluminous and complex to read, but do spend the time to read them, for they spell out the specific conditions binding each owner. If you know an attorney who is well versed in real estate, have him review them for you. If there is a restriction or condition that you cannot live with, such as a restriction against pets, don't expect the homeowner's association to change it just for you. If you are confused over any of the rules, ask your escrow officer or attorney to explain them to you.

The homeowner's association will also maintain fire and liability insurance for all of the common areas of the condominium development. Upon close of escrow, your escrow officer will obtain a fire insurance endorsement from the company holding the policy on the project, and you, as a buyer and new owner, will be named as an insured party. If you obtain a loan on the unit, your lender will require a copy of this "Loss Payee Endorsement" as proof that their investment is protected. This fire insurance policy won't, however, cover the personal contents of your unit or your unit itself, nor will it cover you if someone is hurt in your unit. You will have to provide that coverage yourself just as tenants who live in rental housing do.

HOW DO CONDOMINIUMS AND COOPERATIVES DIFFER?

Physically you couldn't tell the difference between a condominium and a stock cooperative or "co-op." They are exactly alike in appearance, but on paper they are really quite different. A co-op differs from a condominium development in that, unlike a condominium, each co-op shareholder does not own his individual unit, but rather he owns a share in the entire corporation, and the corporation holds title to the whole property. There is only one tax bill and one loan. Each shareholder must pay a monthly fee which covers his portion of the loan payment, property taxes, and building maintenance expenses. The corporation is run according to a set of bylaws which specify how the corporation is to govern itself. Read a copy of these bylaws before buying into a co-op, for they set down the shareholders' rights. In addition, ask to look at the corporation's budget, talk to other shareholders about the management of the units. Unlike a condo development, if your co-op neighbor defaults on his payments, it will have a deleterious effect on you. You and your fellow shareholders could have to contribute something to make up your deadbeat neighbor's payments. For this reason, co-ops are selective about admitting shareholders. Co-op membership committees interview prospective buyers and check into their backgrounds before deciding whether to accept or reject them.

Because co-op shareholders do not have deeds to their individual units, they do not buy title insurance, nor do they generally go through escrow, although they could certainly go through escrow if they wanted to.

WHAT IS TIME-SHARE OWNERSHIP, AND HOW DOES THE TIME-SHARE BUYER GET LEGAL CLAIM?

Time-sharing or interval ownership, as it is also called, is something becoming increasingly popular in vacation areas such as Florida, Hawaii, and California. It is a means for purchasing a portion of a house or condominium together with other people. Each "owner" buys a "share" based upon time.

Time-sharing began in the French Alps in the 1960's. In the United States the concept took hold around 1975 when eight resorts were organized as time-share developments. Today, more than 525,000 families have purchased shares in over a thousand time-share developments nationwide.

In the early years, less-than-honest, wheeler-dealer salespeople peddled time-share developments with the hard-sell approach and sometimes vanished with funds before the projects were completed. Today, all but four states regulate time-share developments and sales. Developers must make full disclosures, put down payments into escrow accounts until units have been completed, and allow buyers a certain amount of time to reconsider.

Commonly, each time-share unit is comprised of 52 shares in all, corresponding to the 52 weeks in a year, each share being for one specific week per year. The price of each share is determined by the type of dwelling involved and by the demand for a particular time; in Palm Beach, Florida, and Palm Springs, California, for example, shares during January and February are more desirable than those during July and August and hence command premium prices.

A resort management company maintains the entire property year-round, and each owner pays a yearly fee which goes toward management, maintenance, and taxes.

Just as with ordinary real estate, the time-share buyer gets a grant deed and may obtain title insurance. He may also finance his time-share unit with a down payment, typically 30%, and a loan for the balance, and if he should default on his payments, the lender would have the right to foreclose. Sounds familiar, doesn't it?

One of the advantages of time-sharing is that an owner may trade his vacation place one year for another place that year which is halfway around the world. An organization called Interval International Exchange (P.O. Box 2170, So. Miami, FL 33143), which charges a nominal subscription fee, facilitates these exchanges.

There's also a directory available which lists time-share resorts throughout the world. The subscription fee includes five bi-monthly issues and monthly issues in January and December. Write to Endless Vacations Publications, Inc., P.O. Box 80260, Indianapolis, IN 46209-8098.

Should you be inclined to become a time-share buyer, remember that time-shares are definitely not investments. The properties involved, if sold as a whole, would not be worth nearly as much as the sum of the 52 shares. Very few buyers ever sell their shares at a profit. Sometimes they cannot resell their shares at all. Essentially what you are doing when you buy a time-share is something quite different from what you would be doing if you were buying an ordinary piece of real estate. As a time-share buyer you are locking in a price for your future vacations. That's all, pure and simple.

If you still want to buy a time-share, consider the following tips:

• Do not buy time-shares from salespeople who use pressure tactics and promise free goodies like cameras and televisions. Buy a resale. Or, at the very least, find out what the resale market is for the time-share you're considering.

• Review all the documents with a hawk-eyed lawyer before signing, and make sure that the contract includes a "cooling-off period" during which you can change your mind and still get a full refund.

• Find out whether you would be buying under a fee-simple plan, which gives the buyer title to a fraction of the unit, or under a right-to-use plan, which entitles the buyer to use the unit for a specified period of time but includes no ownership rights.

• Keep in mind that there are hidden costs involved such as maintenance fees and taxes which generally range from $150-$350 per year.

• Remember that exchange programs aren't guaranteed. There may be time limits on exchange opportunities, and sometimes you have to request a trade long in advance.

• Check into the track record of the seller, the developer, and the time-share community's management company. Find out who takes care of the property and performs services such as fixing damage from leaky faucets and replacing furniture.

• Determine what your rights are if the builder or management company develops financial problems or defaults on the project altogether. Make sure the contract includes provisions which protect you from claims filed by a third party against the developer or manager.

8
DEBITS, CREDITS, AND PRORATIONS

WHAT SHOULD I KNOW ABOUT ESCROW SO FAR?

Hopefully you should now have a fair idea about what's involved in obtaining financing, searching the title, and securing title insurance, as well as about how to distinguish the four basic ways of taking title. If so, you have acquired the basics of escrow. If you should happen to forget what you've learned here or if you should ever have any questions or doubts about your own escrow, do see your escrow officer. She is there to help you, and, besides, you are paying for her services through part of your escrow fees whether you use her help or not.

HOW CAN I FIGURE OUT WHO OWES WHAT IN ESCROW?

You might think that you would have to be an accountant or at the very least a bookkeeper to understand all the calculations used in an escrow, but you don't have to be. You just need to have a basic comprehension of the various charges you will be obliged to pay. You should know why you have to pay each charge, how much you have to pay, and when you will have to pay it.

These most important figures are in your escrow instructions and will appear as columns of numbers, numbers related to debits, credits, and prorations, three words which are important to a full understanding of escrow. They are important because, whether you're a buyer or a seller, you will be asked to sign various documents, such as escrow instructions, loan documents, and deeds, and when you sign them, not only are you agreeing with your escrow officer's instructions of how to disburse the monies, but you are agreeing with the correctness of her escrow figures as well. Therefore, it's doubly important to understand the words, debit, credit, and proration.

- *Debit* means something you owe, an amount you will be charged in escrow; it's an item you must pay for; it's money that's coming out of your pocket.

- *Credit* is the opposite of debit; it's money owed to you, an amount paid to your account in escrow; it's a sum which the other party must pay you for something; it's money that's going into your pocket.

- *Proration* means to divide a debit or credit, that is, to divide a charge which has been paid in advance already or is due to be paid in arrears.

Whenever you look at an escrow instructions sheet, be sure to glance at the bottom and make sure that the debit and credit totals equal each other. If they don't, there's something wrong, for the two must balance to the penny. It's a good idea to do your own addition and subtraction of the columns, too, for escrow officers have been known to force a balance.

POSSIBLE CLOSING COSTS

BUYER'S SCALE		SELLER'S SCALE	
DEBITS	**CREDITS**	**DEBITS**	**CREDITS**
purchase price	deposits	old loan payoffs	sales price
title insurance	loans	escrow fees	prorations
escrow fee	prorations	prorations	miscellaneous
loan fees	miscellaneous	reconveyance fees	
fire insurance		transfer tax	
prorations		sales commission (if applicable)	
termite inspection fee			
recording fees			

Remember that the party who actually pays the various fees and taxes will vary from state to state and from geographical area to geographical area (see Appendix).

Before signing your escrow instructions, be sure to verify that what you have been charged is what you were told in the beginning that you would have to pay. If the termite report was originally quoted at $85, see that it is, in fact, $85. Take the checklist at the end of Chapter 10 and check off each item to be sure that the charges are what you expected and that everything else is as agreed upon before. You should know before escrow closes how much you will be expected to pay and you should check that you actually receive what you are paying for, too.

HOW DO PRORATIONS WORK?

While debits and credits are pretty straightforward and understandable, prorations tend to confuse people. Yet, prorations are not as complex as they may seem at first. They're really not difficult to understand or to compute either, so long as you think of them merely as dividing up an item of expense according to some definite date.

Prorations apply to any charges which one party or the other may have incurred in advance of the property's sale, charges which cover a period of time following the sale. Such things as property taxes, fire insurance premiums, rents, maintenance charges on condominiums, interest on loans, and impound accounts all might be prorated in escrow in the interest of fairness to both parties. They are either prepaid by the seller, necessitating a credit due him for the period the buyer will own the property from close of escrow to the date of the next payment due, or they might be paid after the sale by the buyer, thus necessitating a credit due the buyer for the period of time the seller owned the property. Those sums have to be adjusted, and prorations do the adjusting.

After you have mastered one proration, you will be able to use the same formula for any item you want to prorate. Let's try one involving taxes.

For any proration, you will have to know two dates, the date you will prorate from and the date you will prorate to. (Be sure you check the instructions to see whether the word used is "to" or "through." There's an important difference. If the instructions say to prorate "from January 1 to January 10," the prorations would cover nine days. If they say prorate "from January 1 through January 10," the prorations would cover ten days.) The most common date used for computing prorations is the date of close of escrow (C.O.E.) which is usually the date when documents are recorded and the actual change of ownership occurs.

All escrow prorations are normally based on a thirty-day month, except for interest, which is based instead on the actual number of days you are using to compute your calculations.

Let's say in our example that you are assuming ownership of a property on August 10th and that the first property tax installment is $130.56, and you want to figure out the prorations for both the buyer and the seller.

To begin with, we should take a look at property taxes as a whole, as they are commonly figured in one state, say California, and when we do, we find that taxes become an outstanding debt against property on the first day of March, even though they are not payable until considerably later. The full fiscal year for property taxes runs from July 1st to June 30th, and it is divided into two halves so that payments may be made in two installments. The first tax installment covers the six-month period from July 1st to December 31st; it is due on November 1st and is delinquent on December 10th, after which time a penalty is added. The second installment covers the six-month period from January 1st to June 30th; it is due on February 1st and becomes delinquent on April 10th.

Property taxes have priority over any mortgage or deed of trust or any lien or encumbrance except other taxes. Most mortgages and deeds of trust, therefore, have provisions to the effect that the failure to pay taxes when due can cause a default and give grounds for foreclosure. Assessment bonds and other taxes create a lien or encumbrance against a property also and, like property taxes, have priority over any deed of trust.

Should an owner fail to pay property taxes by the delinquent dates (December 10th or April 10th), the property will be given a tax sale number and placed on the delinquent tax roll published once a year on the 30th of June. After publication of this list, the owner has five years in which to pay the delinquent taxes, including penalties and interest. If he doesn't pay after five years, the state will auction off the property.

Now let's get back to our example. The first property tax installment is $130.56, and the close of escrow happens to be August 10. The first thing we must do to determine the buyer's and seller's tax prorations is figure how much the taxes are per day, and to do that, we figure out the taxes per month by dividing $130.56, six month's taxes by 6. That figure is $21.76. Then we divide $21.76 by 30 days, and get $0.72. Those math whizzes who liked to do word problems when they were in school and who want to skip steps can use another, more direct, way to calculate the taxes per day by dividing $130.56 by 180, which is the accepted number of days in a half year for calculating tax prorations. Either way you figure it, the answer is still the same, 72 cents, after you round off to the nearest lower cent.

Using that figure, you can calculate the property tax proration as follows: Since you, the buyer, take ownership on August 10th, you are liable for property taxes until the date they're due, and you will be making the payment for those taxes sometime between November 1st and December 10th, but the seller is liable from July 1st to August 10th, a period of forty days or one month and ten days. The seller must therefore credit you, the buyer, with that much in taxes, a total of $28.80. It will be credited to you on the escrow instructions and debited to him, the seller. On the escrow instructions, it looks like this:

	DEBIT	CREDIT
Buyer - Prorata Taxes 7/1 - 8/10		$28.80
Seller - Prorata Taxes 7/1 - 8/10	$28.80	

Note that often the prior year's tax bill has to be used as a basis for prorating the next fiscal year's taxes because there is no new tax bill available. When such is the case, it will be stated on your escrow instructions. Also, if the tax bill has already been mailed out, be sure to ask the seller or your escrow officer to get it for you because you as the new owner will be responsible for paying the property taxes whether you receive the actual bill or not.

HOW IS INTEREST PRORATED?

Interest generally is not paid in advance, but in arrears, that is, an August 1st mortgage payment pays for July's interest. This means that when you, the buyer or new owner, pay the payment due September 1st, you are actually paying interest for the month of August. Should a buyer take over the seller's existing loan either as an assumption or a subject to, the interest must be prorated. Since interest is usually paid monthly as it accrues, you, the buyer, will be credited and the seller debited for that portion of the month when the seller owned the property and paid the interest on it. Now, if escrow closes on the tenth of August, you didn't own the house for the first ten days of the month, so you should be credited for those ten days. The interest is prorated, meaning that the seller must pay you for those ten days. A seller can conserve his cash if escrow closes before a monthly mortgage payment falls due because escrow will pay it all for him. On the escrow instructions, a proration would look like this:

```
                                        DEBIT        CREDIT
Buyer - Interest on Existing Loan                    $XXX.XX
          8/1 - 8/10
Seller - Interest on Existing Loan      $XXX.XX
          8/1 - 8/10
```

HOW ARE RENTS PRORATED?

If you are buying an income property which already has tenants, the seller must credit you for the rents that he has collected or should have collected for the month. If the rents are all due August 1st, the seller must credit you, the buyer, whether he has collected those rents or not by the time escrow closes, for rents covering the period, August 10th through August 30th, assuming once again that escrow is closing August 10th. In addition, all the advance rent and security/cleaning deposits the seller has collected from his tenants must also be credited to you, the buyer, as well, and you become responsible for them. Make sure there is a "rent and deposit schedule" attached to your escrow instructions which shows the unit number, amount of rent and when last paid, rental due date, and deposits paid.

The seller of an income property should provide you, the buyer, with all the leases or rental agreements currently in force along with a written assignment assigning the rents to you, the new owner. Get these papers through your escrow officer, or directly from the seller, and you will save yourself considerable grief later.

You should know that in an income property transaction, the buyer has an advantage in closing escrow on a date *after* most of the rents are due because the buyer does not then have to bother collecting those rents, and the amount of cash the buyer needs to close escrow will be reduced by the amount of rent credited. In most cases, what this means is that the buyer has an advantage in closing escrow a few days after the first of the month, whereas the seller, on the other hand, has an advantage in closing escrow a few days before the first of the month.

Here is an example of one rent schedule:

RENT STATEMENT

IN ORDER THAT RENTS FOR THE PROPERTY I AM CONVEYING MAY BE CORRECTLY PRORATED, I HEREBY STATE THAT THE RENTALS AS TO AMOUNTS AND DATES TO WHICH THEY ARE PAID ARE AS FOLLOWS:

House/Apt. Number	Tenant's Name	Monthly Rent	Date Paid To	Credit Buyer Last Mo Rent	Deposits	Pro-Rata Amount
1	Smith	$300	Sept. 1		$150	$200.00
2	Jones	$200	Sept. 5		$200	$166.67
3	Appleby	$375	Aug. 15		$250	$ 62.50
			TOTALS:		$600	$429.17

HOW IS FIRE INSURANCE PRORATED?

Fire insurance policies are usually written for either a one-year or a three-year period. They may be paid in full in advance, on a percentage basis spread out over three years, or monthly. However they are paid, they are usually prepaid when a property is being sold and goes through escrow, and the seller is entitled to be compensated for the prepayment either directly from his insurance company or through escrow. Because most buyers prefer to secure their own fire insurance policies, it is not all that often that a buyer assumes the existing policy, but if one does, the premium must be prorated.

To prorate fire insurance premiums, as with property taxes, you must first figure the cost of the insurance per day before you can calculate each party's share. Let's figure an example where the policy's inception date is August 1st; the policy period is 36 months; the premium was paid last year for the entire 36 months; and the premium is $235 per year. We divide $235 by 12 months first and then divide $19.58 by 30 days, and we get the per-day rate of $0.65. If escrow closes August 10th, and the policy is paid for almost two more years, the buyer would credit the seller for two years (2 x $235) less ten days ($6.50), for a total of $463.50. That's all there is to it.

Naturally you should be sure to get an assignment from the fire insurance company, naming you as an insured party on the policy.

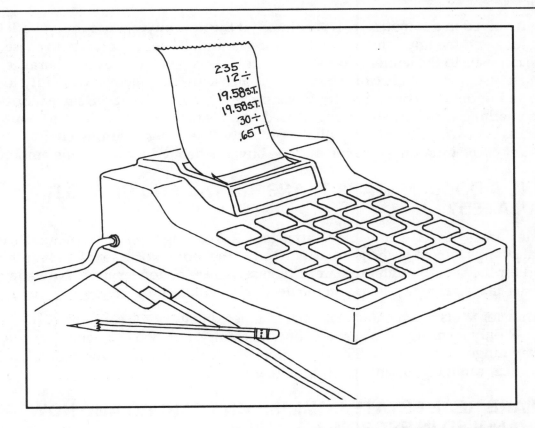

HOW ARE MAINTENANCE CHARGES AND HOMEOWNER'S DUES PRORATED?

This kind of proration applies generally if you are buying a unit in a planned development, condominium, or cooperative which has a homeowners' association that collects assessments from each unit to cover common expenses, such as maintaining parking lots, grounds, and swimming pools.

These association dues are usually paid monthly, so they, too, will have to be adjusted to debit or credit the buyer and seller according to the period for which they were last paid. For example, if the monthly maintenance dues are $65, and they are due on the first of each month and have already been paid by the seller, then when escrow closes on August 10th, the buyer will be debited for $43.20 (20 days @ $2.16 per day) and the seller will be credited for a like amount on his escrow instructions.

The seller is then credited because he has already paid the dues for the entire month of August, and the buyer reimburses him for those days because the buyer will own the property twenty days during that month.

HOW IS AN IMPOUND ACCOUNT ADJUSTED?

An impound account is a sum collected in advance by some lenders and held as a deposit for such things as property taxes and fire insurance premiums. Any existing balance is normally refundable when the loan is paid off. If there is an impound account involved in a transaction, it is adjusted if the new buyer is assuming both the existing loan and the impound account balance as well. If the seller has paid these advance deposits to the lender and they have not been used for taxes or insurance, the seller must be reimbursed because the buyer is also assuming the responsibility to provide an impound account. Strictly speaking, this is not a proration, since it doesn't divide something which has been partly used up. It is more like a savings account which transfers ownership along with the property. The seller is simply credited for the amount of the impound account, and the buyer is debited for that same amount.

WHAT IS A DOCUMENTARY TRANSFER TAX AND HOW IS IT CALCULATED?

In many areas the seller must pay a transfer tax. Years ago this tax was evidenced by actual stamps affixed to the grant deed. Today the term "documentary stamps" is still used for the tax although the stamps themselves are no longer used. Nowadays the transfer tax is generally stated on the deed by the dollar-amount only.

The transfer tax is a percentage tax, that is, a percentage of the sales price. It varies widely, not only from city to city and county to county, but also from state to state, and it may range from a low of $50 to a high of $300 or even sometimes more. Your escrow officer can tell you what the rate is in your area.

WHEN ARE REAL ESTATE COMMISSIONS EARNED AND HOW ARE THEY HANDLED IN ESCROW?

As a general rule, an agent has earned his commission when he has found a buyer who is ready, willing, and able to buy a property on the exact terms of the listing agreement or on terms acceptable to the seller, and the agent is usually entitled to his commission regardless of whether the sale is ever completed. Once the agent has found that willing and able buyer, he may sue the seller to get his commission if the seller changes his mind and decides not to sell the property.

A COMMON MISUNDERSTANDING: Tom and Evelyn decide that their real estate agent really didn't do that much work to sell their house. The day after they listed it, the agent brought someone over to look at it, and that person bought the place for the asking price. They decide that they just won't pay him his full commission because he didn't really do much to earn it.

THE WAY THINGS REALLY ARE: Tom and Evelyn's agent does have the legal right to collect his full commission so long as he has met the terms of the listing and purchasing agreements. They should be happy that he sold their house so quickly and got the full price they wanted for it.

Fortunately for them, agents don't often have to sue to get their commissions. They get paid through escrow, whether the commission is a stipulated dollar amount or a percentage of the sales price. Typically the seller pays the real estate commission, but since this fee is not set by law, it may be negotiated between the parties, and the percentage may be lowered or the burden shared by both buyer and seller.

Most real estate firms charge a standard percentage of the purchase price as their commissions, usually 6% for houses and 10% for raw land, and they use the same percentage for every similar property no matter what it sells for. Don't, however, be afraid to talk over this commission percentage with your agent because some agents are flexible. Often when there is only one agent representing both buyer and seller, the agent will reduce his commission one percent, but when there are two agents involved and they have to split the commission fifty-fifty, they may not be so willing to agree to lower the fee. Discuss it with the agent anyway. They are not compelled by law to stick to any specific percentage. An agent may even refund a portion of his commission back to a principal, either to the buyer or the seller, through escrow if the refund is approved in writing by both parties.

PLEASE NOTE WELL

Under no circumstances will your escrow officer pay the sales commission to the real estate agent before the close of escrow, and when it is paid, it will be paid to the agent's office, not to the agent directly.

When you sign a listing agreement with a real estate agent, be sure you understand all the terms and conditions with which you must comply. There are different ways to list a property, and you should ask the sales agent to explain them to you carefully.

To avoid any confusion, explain the exact terms of the commission to your escrow officer when escrow is first opened. The escrow officer needs to know precisely who is to be paid what, when, and how.

9
ESCROW INSTRUCTIONS

WHAT'S INVOLVED IN DRAWING UP ESCROW INSTRUCTIONS?

Escrow instructions differ greatly from transaction to transaction, but, whatever they are, they always result from the escrow officer's taking the purchase agreement and other pertinent information out of the opening file and then drawing up actual instructions detailing how the sale will take place. These instructions are, in essence, the written authorization to the escrow or title company, and they usually begin with the statement: "You are hereby authorized and directed to do the following..." Of course, the "you" here is the escrow or title company.

These instructions specify all the various conditions which must be met prior to the close of escrow. They state who will pay for what costs, and they authorize the escrow holder to disburse the monies to the proper parties and to record the necessary documents in order to close escrow when the parties involved have met all of the terms specified. Once opened, escrow remains open until the transaction is terminated according to the terms of the instructions.

Technically, you could, if you wanted to, draw up your own instructions, but they would have to meet the escrow holder's requirements. They would have to be written, signed by each party submitting them, legally binding, and revocable only by mutual consent.

Most escrow companies have standard pre-printed escrow-instruction forms which the escrow officer uses to accommodate an individual transaction. Often there is one

SECURE TITLE COMPANY
1220 Oak Park Blvd.
Boonville, CA 11002
Telephone 423-4567

ESCROW INSTRUCTIONS

Date: __August 10, 1990__
Order No. __12345__
Escrow Officer: __E. Edwards__

☒ BUYER'S   ☐ BORROWER'S

To: Secure Title Company
I/We hand you herewith
☒ Executed loan documents – First loan (approved by signature)
☒ Executed loan documents – Second loan (approved by signature)
☒ Balance of funds to close
☐ _____

☐ _____
☐ _____
☐ _____

which you are authorized to deliver and/or record when you have received for my account the following:

☒ Grant Deed
☒ **Bill of Sale covering personal property**
☐ _____

and when you can issue your standard coverage form policy of title insurance with a liability of $ __100,000.00__
on the property described in your Preliminary Title Report No. __12345__   dated __July 15__ . a copy of which
I/we have read and hereby approve. Commonly known as: __12 Allendale Ct.__
__Boonville,__ _____ ,California
showing title vested in __Bruce B. Buyer and Barbara A. Buyer,__
__his wife as Joint Tenants__

Subject to:
1. Printed exceptions and conditions in said policy.
2. ☒ all ☒ 2nd half   General and special taxes for fiscal year 19 __90__   19 __91__
3. Assessments and/or bonds not delinquent.
4. Exceptions numbered   __2 and 3__   as shown in your preliminary title report
   dated __July 15__ , 19 __90__ issued in connection with the above order number.
5. Deed of Trust in favor of: __First Federal Trust in the amount of $80,000.00__
6. Deed of Trust in favor of: __Samuel P. Seller, in the amount of $10,000.00__

	Debits		Credits	
Sales Price	100,000	00		
Paid outside of Escrow to				
Deposit by the undersigned			1,000	00
Encumbrance of Record				
Loan Trust Fund				
Assumption Fee				
New Loan			80,000	00
Deed of Trust ☐ 1st ☒ 2nd ☐ 3rd			10,000	00
Loan Charges: Loan Fee $ 1,200.00 Tax Res. $				
Appsl. Fee $ Ins. Res. $				
Cred. Rept. $ 35.00 FHA Prem. $				
Int. Est. @11.5% Fr 8/10 To 8/31 $ 536.55				
Total	1,771	55		
☒ Pay Fire Ins. Prem.	235	00		
☒ Pay Tax Service	17	50		
☐ Pay Taxes				
☐ Personal Property Tax				
☐ Pay Assessments or Bonds				
☒ Prorate Taxes Fr. 7/1 To 8/10 on $ 652.60 yr.			72	51
☐ Prorate Fire Ins. Fr. To on $				
☐ Prorate Int. @ % Fr. To on $				
☐ Prorate Rent Fr. To on $				
Pay Termite Inspection Fee	85	00		
ALTA Inspection Fee	20	00		
Draw Doc. $				
Notary Fee $ 4.00	4	00		
Title Prem. Std. $ 432.50 ALTA $ 96.50	529	00		
Escrow $ 160.00	160	00		
Recording $ 13.00	13	00		
Balance Due ☒ To Close ☐ The Undersigned			11,762	54
Totals	102,835	05	102,835	05

These instructions are effective until __September 10,__ 19 __90__ and thereafter unless revoked by written demand and authorization satisfactory to you. Incorporated herein and made a part hereof by reference are the "General Provisions" and any additional instructions appearing on the reverse side of this page.
Received: __August 10__   , 19 __90__

By *Edan Edward*

Bruce B. Buyer   Barbara A. Buyer
Bruce B. Buyer   Barbara A. Buyer
Address __12 Allendale Ct. , Boonville, CA__
Phone No. _____

SECURE TITLE COMPANY
1220 Oak Park Blvd.
Boonville, CA 11002
Telephone 423-4567

ESCROW INSTRUCTIONS

Date: __August 10, 1990__
Order No. __12345__
Escrow Officer: __E. Edwards__
Office: __Boonville__

☒ SELLER'S   ☐ LENDER'S

To: Secure Title Company

I/We hand you herewith

☒ Deed from __the undersigned__   To __Bruce B. Buyer and Barbara A. Buyer__
☒ Approved copy of Note   ☒ Request for Notices
☒ Approved copy of Deed of Trust   ☒ Bill of Sale
　 which you are authorized to deliver and/or record when you have   ☐ _____
　 received for my account the following:

☒ Pay balance of sale proceeds as per following statement.
☒ Original promissory note corresponding to attached copy. Interest to commence __August 10, 1990__
　 First payment due __Sept. 10, 1990__ . Maturity date __August 10, 1995__
☒ Evidence of Fire Insurance
☐ _____

and when you can issue your standard coverage form policy of title insurance with a liability of $ __10,000.00__
on the property described as in your Preliminary Title Report No. __12345__ dated __July 15__ , a copy of which
I/we have read and hereby approve. Commonly known as: __12 Allendale Ct.__
__Boonville,__ , California

showing title vested in __Bruce B. Buyer and Barbara A. Buyer,__
__his wife as Joint Tenants__

Subject to:
1. Printed exceptions and conditions in said policy.
2. ☒ all ☒ 2nd half   General and special taxes for fiscal year 19 __90__   19 __91__
3. Assessments and/or bonds not delinquent.
4. Exceptions numbered __2 and 3__   as shown in your preliminary title report
　 dated __July 15__ , 19 __90__ issued in connection with the above order number.
5. Deed of Trust in favor of: __First Federal Trust, in the amount of $80,000.00__
6. Deed of Trust in favor of: __Samuel P. Seller, in the amount of $10,000.00__

	Debits		Credits	
Sales Price			100,000	00
Deposit Retained (paid outside of escrow)				
Encumbrance of Record				
Loan Trust Fund				
Loan Discount Fee				
Deed of Trust ☐ 1st ☒ 2nd ☐ 3rd	10,000	00		
☐ Pay Taxes				
☐ Personal Property Tax				
☐ Pay Assessments or Bonds				
☒ Prorate Taxes Fr. 7/1 To 8/10 on $ 652.60 yr.	72	51		
☐ Prorate Fire Ins. Fr. To on $				
☐ Prorate Int. @ % Fr. To on $				
Pay Tender Termite Control for termite repair work	250	00		
Pay Commission Valley Real Estate License No.	6,000	00		
Pay Demand of Helpful Mortgage Company	5,013	80		
Principal $5,000.00				
Interest 8/1-8/10 13.80				
Pay Demand of Bankers Savings and Loan	47,175	70		
Principal $47,000.00				
Interest 8/1-8/10 120.70				
Reconveyance Fee 30.00				
Forwarding Fee 25.00				
Recon. $ 30.00	30	00		
Draw Doc. $				
Notary Fee $ 2.00	2	00		
Title Prem. Std. $ ALTA $				
Escrow $				
Documentary Transfer Tax $110.00	110	00		
Recording $ 12.00	12	00		
Balance to Seller ☐ Mail ☒ Will Call	31,333	99		
Totals	100,000	00	100,000	00

These instructions are effective until __September 10__ , 19 __90__ and thereafter unless revoked by written demand and authorization satisfactory to you. Incorporated herein and made a part hereof by reference are the "General Provisions" and any additional instructions appearing on the reverse side of this page.
Received: Aug. 10, 19 90

Samuel P. Seller
Samuel P. Seller
Address 4 Evelyn Ct., Sydney, Ill.

By *Edna Edward* _____   Phone No. _____

set of pre-printed forms used for a standard real estate transaction between buyer and seller and another somewhat more complicated set used for an exchange. Should an attorney represent one of the parties, he may want to draft his own escrow instructions, especially if the pre-printed forms do not include provisions for a complicated transaction. There is no legal requirement governing the format for escrow instructions, and so long as her company approves them, the escrow officer must receive and follow specially drafted instructions in the same way she does those which are on her company's own forms.

Whether they are entered on a form, drafted by an attorney, or drawn up by you, escrow instructions should give the escrow holder the following information:

- A listing of documents and/or monies which are to be deposited into escrow and by whom they are to be deposited;

- Conditions which must be met prior to close of escrow (loans, termite reports, etc.);

- A listing of items to be prorated, including such things as property taxes, insurance, interest, and rents; and

- An explanation of the fees to be paid by the buyer and/or seller.

The most important thing to remember about escrow instructions is that your escrow officer must know all the facts of the purchase so that she can carry out the expectations of all the parties concerned to their mutual satisfaction. Information given in the escrow instructions should never contradict those agreements reached between the parties in the purchase agreement. As a safety measure, however, both documents should indicate that an inconsistency is to be interpreted in favor of the escrow instructions because they are usually drawn up after the purchase agreement. When escrow instructions of buyer and seller are discovered to be materially different, the instructions may not be a contract between them at all, for their individual rights depend upon their mutual agreement.

A COMMON MISUNDERSTANDING: When Pete comes in to sign his seller's escrow instructions, he looks at what he's being charged for roof repairs, and he tells himself that he can't remember ever agreeing to pay that much. To be fair to himself, he decides to lower the figure, and he writes in a new amount. He then signs the instructions and thinks that the escrow officer has to abide by them.

THE WAY THINGS REALLY ARE: Pete's escrow officer must abide by both parties' escrow instructions, and those instructions must correspond with each other exactly. A debit of $685 for roof repair on Pete's instructions must show up as a $685 credit on his buyer's instructions. The buyer will have to approve Pete's change before escrow can close.

Although some escrow companies prefer not to keep a copy of the purchase agreement in the escrow file because of the legal complications it might cause, you should submit a copy of your own purchase agreement when you open escrow so your escrow officer will have the terms of the transaction at her disposal for clarification.

A COMMON MISUNDERSTANDING: Now that Erik's purchase is in escrow, he decides to delay the close of escrow for another three months because he doesn't want to be penalized for taking his money out of his timed money certificate before it matures. He's got the property all tied up anyway. It's in escrow, so he can't possibly lose it.

THE WAY THINGS REALLY ARE: Erik's purchase agreement and his bank loan commitment will determine how long he has to close escrow on the property. Both have specific expiration dates. He could easily lose the property.

Escrow instructions may be either unilateral (buyer signs one set of instructions and the seller signs another) or bilateral (buyer and seller sign the same set of instructions). Some areas follow the unilateral custom with the real estate agent playing a large part in getting information to the escrow company and seeing that the escrow instructions are complied with. The instructions are then normally drawn up after all the information is in and escrow is ready to close. Other areas follow the bilateral system, in which case the escrow instructions are generally drawn up and signed when escrow is first opened.

Amendments are drawn up and signed as necessary to reflect any changes in the original instructions as, for example, when the actual date of an escrow closing differs from the original date used for computing the prorations.

HOW DO EXCHANGES WORK AND HOW ARE THEIR ESCROW INSTRUCTIONS DRAFTED?

When a property owner trades a property for someone else's property, the transaction is called a real estate exchange or trade. Real estate exchanges are generally made when a seller wishes to postpone the taxation of capital gains resulting from the sale of his property, something commonly known as a "Section 1031 Tax-Deferred Exchange."

Whereas a sale is the transfer of property for money or the promise to pay money, an exchange is the transfer of property in return for other property with perhaps some money involved to balance the exchange. These balancing funds are sometimes called the "boot."

Your accountant or attorney will know whether it is to your advantage to participate in an exchange, and you would be wise to consult such an expert about the matter before you ever consider acquiring or disposing of an exchange property. Deferring the payment of taxes on capital gains realized from the disposal of real property is usually the best way for a property owner to preserve his capital, but it's not always the best way, for tax laws and the interpretations of those laws are constantly changing, and one's own financial situation changes as well. Together with an expert, analyze this option and look at your overall financial picture before the time when the sale or exchange will occur.

Your accountant or attorney can explain the conditions which must be met in order for either a principal residence or an income property to qualify for tax deferral. For escrow purposes, though, we are concerned about only two things:

- Making sure that the properties are of like kind, that is, that they are similar in use (is an apartment house being exchanged for an office building, or is a piece of machinery being exchanged for an office building? …the first would qualify; the second would not); and

- Closing and recording the escrows on the same day or within a reasonable period of each other (often the properties involved in an exchange are located in different counties, even in different states, and closing the two escrows concurrently, which is the general escrow practice, takes a fair amount of coordination, but concurrent closing is generally necessary for the exchange to qualify for tax-deferral unless, that is, the exchange is specifically set up to be delayed; more about delayed exchanges in a moment).

An exchange may be a simple transfer of properties between two parties as follows: Appleby is tired of all the hassles in running an apartment building and wants to trade it for some raw land; Bartleby is tired of holding onto his raw land, which yields no income, and wants to trade his equity for an apartment building which does yield income, so the two parties arrange to trade their properties. So-called two-way exchanges such as this do occur, but as a rule they occur far less frequently than do exchanges involving three or more parties, because locating a property owner who wants to trade his property for yours can be very difficult. The parties often agree to participate in a three-way exchange, with three or more parties involved, one of whom brings cash into the exchange and one of whom takes cash out.

Here's the way a three-way exchange works: Abbott wants to exchange his property for a property owned by Barnes, but Barnes does not want Abbott's property at all. Barnes wants instead to get all of his cash out of his property, although he says that he will participate in a three-way exchange in order to get the cash he wants. Cole, however, does want Abbott's property, and he can meet all of the terms specified by Abbott.

They put the exchange itself together in three steps like this: Abbott deeds his property to Barnes; Barnes deeds his property to Abbott; and Barnes deeds Abbott's property to Cole in exchange for cash and/or monied indebtedness. As a result of this three-way exchange, Abbott gets Barnes' property; Barnes gets cash and/or notes; and Cole gets Abbott's property. Everyone achieves his objective.

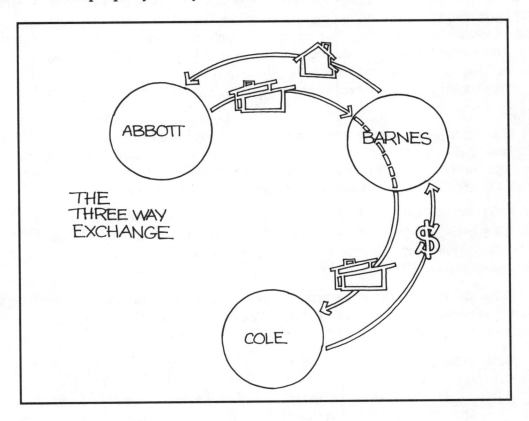

THE THREE WAY EXCHANGE

The escrow for a three-way exchange involves some extra paper work, but it solves the problem satisfactorily as follows: Abbott signs a set of exchange instructions in which he relinquishes title to his property and acquires title to Barnes' property; Barnes signs exchange instructions relinquishing title to his property, and he receives money or a note and the deed to Abbott's original property; Barnes also signs seller's instructions deeding Abbott's property to Cole; and lastly, Cole signs buyer's instructions and acquires title to Abbott's former property.

An exchange set up in this way should not only qualify for a tax deferral on the capital gains, but it also offers the convenience of buying and selling properties in a single transaction.

A COMMON MISUNDERSTANDING: Adele is exchanging a property in Los Angeles for one in Sacramento, and she figures that because an exchange is so complex, she'd better hire an attorney to draft the escrow instructions and help her sort out all the details.

THE WAY THINGS REALLY ARE: Escrow companies have pre-printed exchange instruction forms that will fit almost any tax-deferred property exchange. They also have an escrow officer who is proficient in handling exchanges. If the escrow officer believes that Adele needs an attorney, the officer will recommend that she secure one.

WHAT IS A DELAYED EXCHANGE?

A delayed exchange is a three-way exchange, but it involves concurrent recording of only two out of the three (or more) grant deeds; the third grant deed comes into play later. Delayed exchanges occur when one exchanger hasn't had enough time to find his property to exchange into, but he still wants to preserve the tax advantage of exchanging. He must leave the proceeds of the first part of his exchange in escrow as he continues looking for his "exchange" property. He can't touch those funds.

A COMMON MISUNDERSTANDING: Gary and Lyndy want to exchange their rental property in Lompoc for a rental property in Santa Barbara. They have found a buyer for the Lompoc house, but they haven't yet been able to find a suitable Santa Barbara property. They feel they can't put their buyer off any longer. Either they'll have to cancel the deal or they'll have to try getting their buyer to wait until they can find another property.

THE WAY THINGS REALLY ARE: As a result of the "Starker" decision, Gary and Lyndy now may leave their sales proceeds from the Lompoc house in escrow while they look for another property. They have 45 days after close of escrow on the house to identify a new property, and they have 180 days to close escrow on it.

The *Starker* decision gave some guidelines for IRS-acceptable delayed exchanges, and since that time such exchanges have become more formalized and more commonplace.

The *Starker* case involved a taxpayer who agreed in 1967 to convey certain of his real property to two lumber companies in exchange for certain other properties which hadn't yet been identified. The parties agreed on the value of Starker's property in April of 1967, and he conveyed that property to them at that time. Instead of getting any cash for his property, though, Starker accepted credits on the lumber companies' books with the proviso that he would have until April 1, 1972, to accept properties from them of equivalent value. If there were any balance left in his account then, he would receive it in cash. Over a three-month period, the lumber companies conveyed properties to Starker which were of equivalent value, and he received no proceeds in cash.

Although the parcels Starker selected were not owned by the lumber companies when they originally entered into their agreement, the court determined that Starker never received any cash in lieu of property, and therefore the transaction did indeed qualify for tax deferral under Section 1031.

Following the original *Starker* case, there were more court decisions involving IRS treatment of delayed exchanges, some favorable to taxpayers and some to the IRS. When all the dust of the combat had cleared, the taxpayers had won. Delayed, or what the courts called "non-simultaneous," exchanges were found to qualify for tax deferral. This decision has had a profound and substantial effect on the real estate market and on the tax planning involved in disposing of investment property. And, wonder of wonders, the dreaded Tax Reform Act of 1986, which dealt some brutal body blows to real estate investors, did nothing to diminish the significant tax advantages of the delayed three-way exchange.

There are now formal guidelines which exchanges must follow in order to qualify for tax-deferral benefits, and they're relatively simple, but they must be followed to the letter. The property to be acquired must be designated within 45 days following the disposition of the other property and must close escrow within 180 days *or* by the due date (including extensions) of the tax return covering the year of the disposition, *whichever comes first*.

Whether your tax-deferred exchange is delayed or simultaneous, the IRS wants you to spell out the details and the "intent" of the parties involved. To do so, include in the various purchase agreements the following statement: "This transaction is intended to be a 1031 TAX-DEFERRED EXCHANGE." That's enough.

HOW MIGHT I CHANGE A CONVENTIONAL SALE ALREADY IN PROGRESS TO A TAX-DEFERRED EXCHANGE?

If you should want to change a conventional sale to a tax-deferred exchange while everything is still in escrow, include the following addendum to your deposit receipt or escrow instructions:

"It is understood and agreed between the parties hereto that Seller's intent is to convert this transaction from a purchase and sale to a tax-deferred exchange (under Section 1031 of the Internal Revenue Code). The parties hereto therefore agree to cooperate fully, one with the other, in executing whatever additional documents or amendments may be required in order to effect a tax-deferred exchange properly, at such time as Seller has located other property acceptable to Buyer for the purpose of completing the exchange.

"The parties hereto further understand and agree that it is an express condition to Seller's obligation to convey the subject property to Buyer, that Seller has located acceptable exchange property and restructured this transaction as a multiple-party, concurrent-closing tax-deferred exchange. In the event Seller has not located his exchange property or is unable to close the acquisition of such property on or before the closing date of this escrow, this purchase and sale agreement shall be of no further force or effect, and the parties agree to cooperate in executing escrow cancellation instructions to reflect such termination."

CAN ANY ESCROW OFFICER HANDLE AN EXCHANGE?

By now many escrow officers have had experience handling exchanges and should be able to handle one competently. Exchanges are pretty commonplace nowadays, especially in the Western U.S.

Nonetheless, you should ask your escrow officer whether she has ever handled an exchange before and whether she has any doubts about her ability to handle yours. If she hesitates, ask to talk with someone who has the experience you feel you need. Most every escrow company has somebody who specializes in exchanges.

10
SIGNING YOUR ESCROW INSTRUCTIONS

WHAT HAPPENS AFTER ESCROW HAS TAKEN ITS NORMAL COURSE?

Once your escrow has taken its normal course, that is, after you have been notified that the loan has gone through and the termite clearance has been sent in and all the loan documents have been drawn up, you are finally ready for delivery. Generally an escrow's gestation and delivery takes a month or two, but it can take whatever time period the principal parties agree upon. Whichever time period yours has taken, thirty days, sixty-two days, or some other period, let's suppose now that the allotted time is nearly up. At this time your real estate agent or escrow officer should be telephoning you and saying, "Okay, everything's ready. You can come in and sign the escrow instructions." By that your escrow officer means that she has taken all of the facts and figures pertinent to your transaction and she has compiled them into instructions which apply to both the buyer and the seller. As mentioned before, those instructions may be bilateral or unilateral, that is, either as one separate set for the buyer and another for the seller or as a combined set for both together.

What's most important here is that you should be well aware that once you have signed your set of escrow documents, you may be subject to penalties, and perhaps even legal action, if you attempt to cancel for any reason whatsoever. Be certain, therefore, that you can abide by the agreements you are signing. Take time to read and review all the documents carefully. Take them home if necessary, and double-check for mathematical or clerical errors. Never let yourself be rushed through these procedures.

A COMMON MISUNDERSTANDING: Andrew and Judith don't have time to read all their documents at the escrow company. After all, their visit to the escrow company is eating into their lunch hour. They decide to sign all the papers just as they're presented and to review them later at home.

THE WAY THINGS REALLY ARE: If they don't have the time to look over their papers at lunch, Andrew and Judith should take the papers home overnight before signing. Once they have signed, it is too late for them to make any changes.

WHAT PAPERS WILL I HAVE TO SIGN AS A BUYER?

Although there are certain papers which must always be signed and there are certain others which will vary according to the lender's requirements, the answer to this question will depend primarily on the loan you have arranged. Some lenders require more documents than others, especially if there is any bureaucratic agency, like FHA or VA, involved.

No matter what kind of real estate transaction a buyer is involved in, though, he will always sign an original promissory note and an original deed of trust. In addition to those two, the papers will vary and may include a fire insurance requirement form, a Regulation "Z" Form (disclosure statement), a right of recision form (right to cancel the loan within three working days), a borrower's statement to the lender, and loan instructions.

Since your escrow officer has probably spelled out the details and conditions of your transaction on each of your escrow documents, you will want to be sure that you understand the intent of the documents you are signing, so we will examine each of them separately.

- *Original Note and Deed of Trust*—Your note is your "promise to pay." Read it over very carefully before signing it. Verify the loan amount, the interest rate, the monthly payment, and the due date. They all will affect your life for years to come.

- *Fire Insurance Requirement Form*—You might be asked to sign a statement agreeing to comply with the lender's requirements for fire insurance on the property. The lender will specify the kind of insurance, fire, flood, earthquake, etc., and how much coverage you must have. The lender will normally require you to obtain fire insurance in the amount of his loan and pay for one year's premium in advance, but for your own protection you will want to be sure that the buildings you purchase are adequately covered for their entire replacement value.

- *Regulation "Z" Form (Disclosure Statement)*—As a borrower, you will be given an "Estimated Statement of Loan Fees and Closing Costs." This statement is also called a "Regulation 'Z' Form" or a "Federal Truth in Lending Statement" (see Chapter 6). Its purpose is to give you a breakdown of all the loan items you will be charged for, including the total amount you will be paying over the life of the loan.

- *Right of Recision Notice*—This document allows you as borrower a last opportunity to cancel the loan within three working days. Oddly enough, you will probably be asked to sign this document twice, the first time when you sign your loan documents and the second time at the end of the three-day waiting period. The first time you are agreeing to the receipt of the notice, and the second time you are actually giving up your legal right to cancel the loan. The "Right of Recision" is normally limited to property which the borrower expects to use as his principal residence.

- *Lender's Escrow Instructions*—On this statement are the lender's instructions to the escrow company stating the conditions which must be met before their deed of trust can be recorded. You, the borrower, sign a copy of this statement signifying that you have read it and understood it and that you agree with its terms and conditions. Your escrow officer must follow these instructions exactly as they are written. They will direct her to do the following: See that all loan documents are properly executed by the borrower and returned to the lender, except for the deed of trust which is held until recorded and is returned to the lender after being recorded; obtain a policy of title insurance; confirm fire insurance coverage for the lender (generally the requirement is that a minimum of one year's coverage will be paid in escrow); and close escrow by a certain date or abort it and return all the documents.

- *Bill of Sale*—When you buy a property, sometimes the seller will include movable items such as a refrigerator, drapes, a stove, and a dog house as part of the deal. If so, you, the buyer, should obtain a bill of sale signed by the seller stating which items he agrees will be part of the property sale. This is a standard operating procedure and avoids the possible confusion later over what belongs to whom, what stays, and what goes along with the seller when he moves out.

- *Statement of Information*—Title insurance companies usually require a Statement of Information (sometimes referred to as a "Statement of Identity") on all individual grantors, grantees, and borrowers. These statements provide pertinent data on individuals. They serve as a safeguard against forgeries and help title companies eliminate such items as judgments and bankruptcies against parties with similar names. Information on these forms is kept strictly confidential, used only by the title company to insure that you aren't being confused with somebody else who goes by a similar or even an identical name. You needn't be concerned about your privacy when asked to provide this information.

At the end of this chapter there are buyer's and seller's checklists which should help you verify everything you need to know before you sign your escrow papers.

On the next page you'll find a summary of what both the buyer and the seller will probably be signing.

DOCUMENTS	BUYER	SELLER
Escrow Instructions	Original	Original
Note	Original	
Deed of Trust	Original	
Loan Documents	Original	
Grant Deed		Original
Bill of Sale		Original

WHEN DOES PERSONAL PROPERTY BECOME "REAL PROPERTY"?

Personal property becomes real property when it is nailed, bolted, screwed, plastered, cemented, or built into a structure. A chandelier, for example, is personal property when purchased at a lighting store, but when it is screwed to the ceiling, it becomes a fixture and is supposed to be included in the sale of a property unless specifically excluded. On the other hand, the chandelier's light bulbs remain personal property because they are not permanently attached to the structure, so a tightwad seller is within his rights in removing the light bulbs before relinquishing possession of the property.

When buyer and seller cannot agree whether something is real property or personal property, five legal tests are brought to bear on the situation.

The first and most important test is the method of attachment. If the item has been permanently attached with some sort of fastener, such as nails, screws, or bolts, or with some sort of bonding material, such as glue or cement, then it has become a fixture. Fixtures are real property and must be included in a sale.

The second test is the adaptability of a particular item for use with the property Built-in equipment which requires special wiring, such as an audio speaker or an intercom or a burglar alarm, is personal property which has been adapted to the property. It has become real property.

The third test is the intention of the buyer and seller, intention best made known in writing. If the microwave oven mounted over the stove has been mentioned in the listing agreement as "not included in sale," then there's no doubt about the seller's intention. Although it is obviously a fixture and ought to be included in the sale, that microwave oven, which has been screwed to the wall, needn't be left behind by the seller.

The fourth test is the actual agreement between buyer and seller. The purchase

BILL OF SALE

THIS BILL OF SALE is dated the 10th day of August, 1990

WITNESSETH:

That   SAMUEL P. SELLER

herein called the Seller, for good and valuable consideration, hereby sells, assigns, and transfers to

BRUCE B. BUYER AND BARBARA A. BUYER

herein called the Buyer, all that certain property which is hereinafter described.

IT IS HEREBY COVENANTED by the Seller, which covenant shall be binding upon the heirs, executors, and administrators of the Seller, that this sale is warranted. The sale of said property will be defended against any and every person who lawfully claims the same.

That property which is hereby sold, assigned and transferred is described as follows, to-wit [describe as precisely as possible and give location, if known]:

```
Hanging Tiffany lamp in breakfast nook
Oak towel bars in master bathroom
Crystal chandelier in dining room
Wooden decorator blinds in den
Frigidaire electric stove, model ES-142 in kitchen
Frigidaire refrigerator, model SF-32 in kitchen
Kenmore washer, model 89121, in garage
Kenmore electric dryer, model 12756, in garage


All items located at 12 Allendale Ct., Boonville, CA 11002
```

Signature of Seller: *Samuel P. Seller*
SAMUEL P. SELLER

agreement should list all the items which might cause controversy later on, and it should state exactly how each one will be handled. Sometime prior to close of escrow, the buyer should ask the seller to prepare a bill of sale for these items, too. There should be no doubt about whose they will be when escrow closes.

The fifth test is the relationship of the parties. In determining whose assumptions are correct in any litigation about whether something is personal property or real property, courts tend to favor buyers over sellers, tenants over landlords, and lenders over borrowers.

Don't let some unfortunate misunderstanding about personal and real property spoil what should be a happy occasion for you, the closing of a real property transaction. Get everything in writing.

A COMMON MISUNDERSTANDING: When Esther first looked at the house, she fell in love with the hanging Tiffany lamp, the wooden decorator blinds, and the oak towel bars. She was pleased that she would be getting all of these extras along with the house.

THE WAY THINGS REALLY ARE: Esther never thought about getting a bill of sale for these specific items. The seller took all of them with him when he moved out, the no-good skunk. He installed cheap replacements.

IS THERE ANYTHING MORE I CAN DO TO PROTECT MYSELF?

Yes, one last and very important step you should take before authorizing your escrow officer to close escrow is to inspect the property personally. Remember that you probably haven't seen the property for some time now. How do you know that all the personal property items, the refrigerator, stove, drapes, and light fixtures, are the same ones you saw originally and that they're now in the same condition as they were? When you inspected the property with the intention of buying it, the seller naturally had everything shined and polished to perfection. Everything was as neat as a pin—the lawn was mowed; the crystal chandelier was twinkling; and the dog was out visiting relatives. Who knows what the place looks like now and whether the items you agreed would be included in the bill of sale are still there? Find out for yourself.

Inspect everything again before you ever allow your money to be released to the seller, for once your escrow has closed and the seller has your money, you have little recourse to get any repairs or restitutions made. Whom would you call anyway? The escrow officer can't really pressure the seller, and the real estate agent probably doesn't want to get involved. You may try hassling with the seller yourself by taking him to small claims court or threatening to "make a federal case out of the matter," but who needs that kind of additional aggravation anyway? You will be busy enough just moving in without worrying about having to make repairs and recover missing items.

Avoid the post-escrow blues by making one final walk-through inspection just before escrow closes.

WHAT HAPPENS IF ONE OF THE PRINCIPALS ISN'T AVAILABLE TO SIGN THE PAPERS?

If the escrow instructions are ready to sign and suddenly your wife has to go to the hospital or the partner with whom you intend to buy the property must leave town, you will need to get a power of attorney, a document your hospitalized wife or departing partner signs to allow someone else—real estate agent, friend, or most often, the other person signing—to act in his stead and sign the papers for him. The person granted a power of attorney is known as an "attorney-in-fact."

The power of attorney may be either specific or general. A general power of attorney grants the right to sign all documents, no matter what kind, during a person's absence. A specific power of attorney specifies exactly what may be signed.

If you find that the person with whom you intend to buy a property must be absent, notify your escrow officer as soon as possible, and she will obtain the power of attorney for you in advance, inasmuch as it will have to be recorded with the county recorder either at the close of escrow or before.

There's no need to feel uneasy about using a power of attorney because it cannot possibly be used legally to allow drastic changes to occur. Your house cannot be given away, nor can any property be deeded to the holder of the power of attorney. The holder may not use the power for his personal benefit at all. The power of attorney is simply a document designed to solve a particular problem, namely, someone's

RECORDING REQUESTED BY:

Secure Title Co.

WHEN RECORDED, MAIL TO:

Bruce B. Buyer
12 Allendale Ct.
Boonville, CA 11002

302210

RECEIVED AUG 1 0 1990

RECORDED AT REQUEST OF
SECURE TITLE CO.

AT 8 O'CLOCK A M.
BARRETT COUNTY RECORDS

FEE $ 5   V. L. GRAVES
COUNTY RECORDER
Recorder's Use Only

302210

POWER OF ATTORNEY

Know All Men by These Presents: That ___ BARBARA A. BUYER ___
the undersigned (jointly and severally, if more than one) hereby make, constitute, and appoint ___
___ BRUCE B. BUYER ___
as my true and lawful Attorney for me and in my name, place, and stead and for my use and benefit:

(a) To ask, demand, sue for, recover, collect, and receive each and every sum of money, debt, account, legacy, bequest, interest, dividend, annuity, and demand (which now is or hereafter shall become due, owing, or payable) belonging to or claimed by me, and to use and take any lawful means for the recovery thereof by legal process or otherwise, and to execute and deliver a satisfaction or release therefor, together with the right and power to compromise or compound any claim or demand;

(b) To exercise any or all of the following powers as to real property, any interest therein, and/or any building thereon: To contract for, purchase, receive and take possession thereof and of evidence of title thereto; to lease the same for any term or purpose, including leases for business, residence, and oil and/or mineral development; to sell, exchange, grant, or convey the same with or without warranty; and to mortgage, transfer in trust, or otherwise encumber or hypothecate the same to secure payment of a negotiable or non-negotiable note or performance of any obligation or agreement;

(c) To exercise any or all of the following powers as to all kinds of personal property and goods, wares and merchandise, choses in action and other property in possession or in action: To contract for, buy, sell, exchange, endorse, transfer, and in any legal manner deal in and with the same; and to mortgage, transfer in trust, or otherwise encumber or hypothecate the same to secure payment of a negotiable or non-negotiable note or performance of any obligation or agreement;

(d) To borrow money and to execute and deliver negotiable or non-negotiable notes therefor with or without security; and to loan money and receive negotiable or non-negotiable notes therefor with such security as he shall deem proper;

(e) To create, amend, supplement, and terminate any trust and to instruct and advise the trustee of any trust wherein I am or may be trustor or beneficiary; to represent and vote stock, exercise stock rights, accept and deal with any dividend, distribution, or bonus, join in any corporate financing, reorganization, merger, liquidation, consolidation, or other action and the extension, compromise, conversion, adjustment, enforcement or foreclosure, singly or in conjunction with others of any corporate stock, bond, note, debenture, or other security; to compound, compromise, adjust, settle, and satisfy any obligation, secured or unsecured, owing by or to me and to give or accept any property and/or money whether or not equal to or less in value than the amount owing in payment, settlement, or satisfaction thereof;

(f) To transact business of any kind or class and, as my act and deed, to sign, execute, acknowledge, and deliver any deed, lease, assignment of lease, covenant, indenture, indemnity, agreement, mortgage, deed of trust, assignment of mortgage or of the beneficial interest under deed of trust, extension or renewal of any obligation, subordination or waiver of priority, hypothecation, bottomry, charter-party, bill of lading, bill of sale, bill, bond, note, whether negotiable or non-negotiable, receipt, evidence of debt, full or partial release or satisfaction of mortgage, judgment, and other debt, request for partial or full reconveyance of deed of trust and such other instruments in writing of any kind or class as may be necessary or proper in the premises.

Giving and granting unto my said Attorney full power and authority to do and perform all and every act and thing whatsoever requisite, necessary, or appropriate to be done in and about the premises as fully to all intents and purposes as I might or could do if personally present, hereby ratifying all that my said Attorney shall lawfully do or cause to be done by virtue of these presents. The powers and authority hereby conferred upon my said Attorney shall be applicable to all real and personal property or interests therein now owned or hereafter acquired by me and wherever situated.

My said Attorney is empowered hereby to determine in his sole discretion the time when, purpose for, and manner in which any power herein conferred upon him shall be exercised, and the conditions, provisions, and covenants of any instrument or document which may be executed by him pursuant hereto; and in the acquisition or disposition of real or personal property, my said Attorney shall have exclusive power to fix the terms thereof for cash, credit, and/or property, and if on credit with or without security.

The undersigned, if a married woman, hereby further authorizes and empowers my said Attorney, as my duly authorized agent, to join in my behalf, in the execution of any instrument by which any community real property or interest therein, now owned or hereafter acquired by my spouse and myself, or either of us, is sold leased, encumbered, or conveyed.

When the context so requires, the masculine gender includes the feminine and/or neuter, and the singular number includes the plural.

[ ] This is to be considered a general Power of Attorney.
[ ] Notwithstanding the aforesaid, this is to be considered a specific power of attorney limited to ___ that real property ___
___ located at 12 Allendale Ct., Boonville, CA 11002 ___ and expiring August 10, 1990
Witness my hand this ___5th___ day of ___August___, 19 90 .

_____

STATE OF   California   )
) s.s.
COUNTY OF Barrett   )
On_____ August 5th _____, 19 90 ,
before me, the undersigned, a Notary Public in and for said County
and State, personally appeared

Barbara A. Buyer

proved to me on the basis of satisfactory evidence to be the person__
whose name__ is (are) subscribed to the within instrument and
acknowledged that ___she___ executed the same.

Barbara A. Buyer
BARBARA A. BUYER

WITNESS my hand and official seal:

Edna Edwards

Notary Public in and for said County and State
NOTARY SEAL

OFFICIAL SEAL
EDNA EDWARDS
Notary Public

necessary absence. When the person returns, he merely records a cancellation of the power at the recorder's office.

WHICH ESCROW PAPERS SHOULD BE NOTARIZED?

As you probably know, a notary public is simply an official witness, one who acknowledges the signing of documents. This acknowledging is commonly called notarizing.

Not all documents relating to an escrow transaction have to be notarized. Only those which are to be recorded need be. For example, neither escrow instructions nor bills of sale have to be notarized. If you have any doubts about whether a certain document should be notarized, ask your officer. She's probably a notary herself.

If you have to sign any of your escrow documents on a weekend or holiday, do be sure you arrange to have your signatures acknowledged. It's a must. You'll find that notaries are listed in the Yellow Pages. You'll also find that real estate and insurance offices usually have notaries and are open on weekends.

A COMMON MISUNDERSTANDING: Mark's wife is busy getting ready to move into a new house some 300 miles away when she's needed to sign over the grant deed for the old house. Mark decides to forge her signature on the deed just as he sometimes endorses checks with her signature. He knows how she signs her name well enough so that nobody could tell the difference.

THE WAY THINGS REALLY ARE: Mark may secure a power of attorney from his wife so he can legally sign for her, but otherwise she will have to appear before a notary personally to have her signature on the grant deed acknowledged.

Many people think that notaries can certify just about anything—photographs, paintings, sweepstakes entries, hunting trophies—you name it. The truth is that notaries cannot certify just anything. Unless something includes certain wording, a signature, and a notarial certificate, it cannot be notarized.

Some people also think that a person's name may be changed on a whim. It can't be. A notary can accept only legal names as verified by an official identification card. Should a hairy hulk wearing a designer dress and heavy eye makeup want to sign as Harriet even though the ID produced says Harry, the notary must refuse to acknowledge the signature. This stranger of dubious gender must produce a valid driver's license or some other authoritative ID with the name Harriet in order to sign notarized documents as Harriet.

PLEASE NOTE WELL

At the closing you must be certain that everything is done exactly right and that the terms are just as you have negotiated them. Look for clerical errors and double-check all mathematical figuring. Never let yourself be rushed through these procedures. Never become casual about any part of your purchase, particularly these final and extremely important details.

BUYER'S AND SELLER'S CHECKLISTS

For your own protection, whether you are the buyer or the seller in a transaction, you might wish to use the checklists on the following pages before you sign your final escrow and loan documents. By using them, you can be reasonably certain that everything meets with your approval. They may save you much grief later, too.

BUYER'S CHECKLIST

☐ 1) Is the purchase price correct?

☐ 2) Have you been credited for all the loans and deposits put into escrow?

☐ 3) Is your name correct on the grant deed? Is it spelled correctly, and does it include the correct middle initial? Is the manner in which you will take title stated correctly? Is the legal description of the property correct? Does this description conform with the one given in the preliminary title report? Was the title cleared to your satisfaction?

☐ 4) Are the notes properly filled out? Are the loan amount, interest rate, due date, and prepayment terms all correct?

☐ 5) Is your name correct on the deed of trust? Is it dated correctly? Is the loan amount stated correctly?

☐ 6) If there is any personal property included, are you being given a bill of sale, and do you agree with the items included?

☐ 7) Are you paying for fire insurance yourself outside of escrow or through escrow? If through escrow, is the premium amount correct?

☐ 8) Are the prorations correct?

☐ 9) Is the termite inspection fee correct? Were you credited for any work that was agreed upon between you and the seller?

☐ 10) Is the correct date given for the close of escrow?

SELLER'S CHECKLIST

☐ 1) Is the sales price correct?

☐ 2) Are the old loans being paid off or assumed? Do you agree with the payoff loan amount?

☐ 3) Is the deed correct? Does it show the correct amount of transfer tax?

☐ 4) If there are any notes in your favor, are they correct?

☐ 5) If there will be a deed of trust recorded in your favor, ask to see a copy. Is it correct?

☐ 6) If you will be signing a bill of sale for any personal property, are all the agreed-upon items listed and correctly described?

☐ 7) If the buyer is assuming your old loan, were you given credit for the existing fire insurance premium and for the impound account?

☐ 8) Are the prorations correct?

☐ 9) Did you agree to credit the buyer for any termite work, structural damage, or other repairs to be done? Do these credits show up on your escrow instructions as debits?

☐ 10) Is the correct date given for the close of escrow?

11
CLOSING ESCROW

WHAT HAPPENS AFTER I HAVE SIGNED ALL THE NECESSARY ESCROW DOCUMENTS?

To begin with, your escrow officer must have the following in hand to close escrow:

- The final escrow instructions signed by buyer and seller;

- The signed loan documents;

- A certified check, money order, or pile of currency from the buyer for the full balance of the purchase price;

- A signed and acknowledged grant deed and, if applicable, a signed bill of sale; as well as

- Instructions from buyer and seller to record the deeds on a specific date.

When the escrow officer has all of these papers in her possession, then, and only then, may escrow close.

One of the first things the escrow officer does next is secure a check from the lender in order to pay off the seller for the balance owed on the property, including any old bills and loans. But institutional lenders are quite strict about disbursing funds. They will release their money only after they have received the entire escrow package, especially the loan documents. It's a kind of hand-to-hand business: "I'll give you this when you give me that." Consequently, the escrow officer usually hand-delivers the whole package. Moreover, lenders like to have this exchange completed 24 hours in advance of the actual recording date so they will have plenty of time to check over all their documents to be certain that everything is in order.

Your escrow officer drafts a "funding" or cover letter detailing all the documents in the package. This letter, together with the original loan documents, is called the funding or loan package.

The escrow officer must make sure that all the documents sent to the lender are properly filled out and properly executed. Should she find an error, regardless of how tiny, even, say a missing initial, she will call the party involved and have him sign or rectify the error. Lenders, in general, require a good deal of specific accuracy because they are audited often by governmental agencies. The lender, upon receiving and checking this package, will then call the escrow officer and give her the authorization to record the necessary papers with the county and release their check for the loan proceeds.

WHAT IS "RECORDING" AND WHY IS IT NECESSARY?

Throughout this book you have been reading about recording this or that document at the county recorder's office, and you've probably had a few questions about this subject which haven't been answered yet. Here are some answers to some of those questions you may have had.

Over centuries of land ownership, people began to recognize that somehow one had to make known his right to own a certain piece of real property. Because a simple bill of sale is easy to lose or forge and because it might be challenged by the heirs of a long-departed original seller, a bill of sale by itself wasn't enough. So someone decided that making ownership known publicly with a recorded document would solve the problem and ensure that a property belonged to its rightful owner. Over the years, this idea took root and became the accepted practice. Even in the Wild West, where the stakes were high and almost anything went, prospectors would make a beeline into town to record their gold claims to ensure that no one else would get the legal rights before they did.

The county recorder's office is now the place where documents are recorded and thus made secure. Once a document is recorded, the public is assumed to have knowledge of its existence. "Constructive notice" has been given.

The first written documents showing land transfers eventually evolved into what we now call deeds. Whereas title represents ownership of property, a deed is the instrument used to transfer title from one person to another. A person holding a deed to a parcel of land holds the title as represented by the writing in the deed.

A deed, remember, is not a contract between a buyer and a seller. Do not confuse a deed, which transfers title, with a deed of trust, which is used to secure a promissory note in some states.

Recording deeds has become an essential ingredient for the buyer and the lender.

Indeed, in most cases, the recorded instrument carries legal preference over the un-recorded instrument. For example, should a seller give a grant deed to two different buyers, the one holding a recorded deed would have valid claim to the property; the buyer with an unrecorded deed would lose out even if he received his deed from the seller before the recorded deed was given. Likewise, if more than one deed of trust were recorded, the first one on record would get the first opportunity at foreclosure.

To record the deeds and other necessary documents, the title company's "recorder" takes them to the county recorder's office. There she will have the necessary documents recorded to make your purchase official. This time of recording is considered the close of escrow—the day, hour, and minute when the property legally and rightfully changes hands.

Each county recorder sets definite times when documents may be recorded at that office. Escrow agents generally have special recording hours set aside for them, during which time the general public may record a document so long as they do not interrupt an escrow agent's series of document numbers. A county with a heavy workload generally requires escrow agents to record early in the morning in order to be sure the posting of all the documents is completed by closing time, whereas a county with a small workload may set the hours for escrow agents in the middle of the day. Likewise, these hours will vary from place to place. If you wish to find out exactly when escrow will close, check with your local county recorder or escrow officer for the recording times set aside for escrow agents in your area.

Escrow agents prefer to record at the earliest possible time of the day, preferably 8 a.m., and here's why: If a deed for a property is recorded at 10 a.m., and a lien affecting the same property were recorded by someone else an hour and a half earlier, the lien would prevent the title insurance company from being able to insure clear title, and it could delay the close of escrow.

The escrow agent's recording clerk must be sure that nothing was recorded on the same property or against the same persons named in her documents. She has to check all documents carefully, "run the title to date," up to exactly the minute she will record. Recording right after the recorder's office opens eliminates the possibility of an intervening document's being recorded. Remember that the first to record is the first in right.

A COMMON MISUNDERSTANDING: Steve's preliminary title report doesn't show the latest loan he took out only 12 days ago. If he doesn't say anything about it, he can go ahead and sell the property, and nobody will know about the loan.

THE WAY THINGS ARE: The title or escrow company will learn about this new loan when they run the title to date just before recording. The close of escrow will be delayed until either Steve has paid off the loan or the new buyer has agreed to assume it.

When there is an exchange of properties which are located in different counties or states, recording the transfer of ownership tends to become complicated because each party involved in the exchange wants the properties to record concurrently. The escrow agents involved make special reservations with the county recorders so that

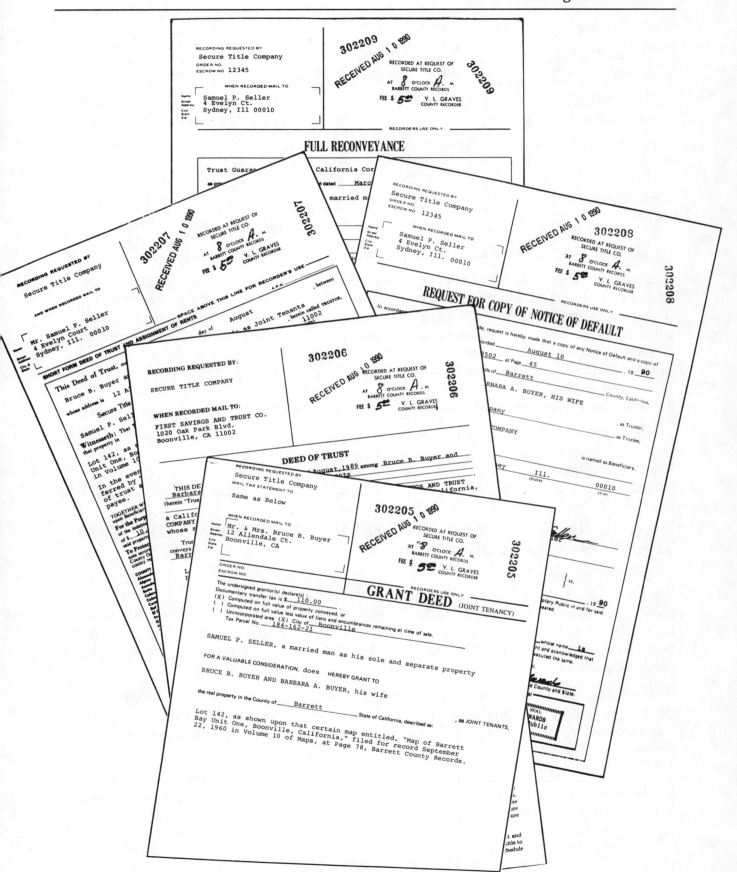

the recording times will coincide.

Before county recorders will record any document, they collect a recording fee. This fee is generally $5 for the first page and $2 for each additional page.

The escrow officer determines the exact recording sequence by following the order of each document's priority. A sample recording might follow this sequence:

- GRANT DEED—seller to buyer;

- DEED OF TRUST—buyer to 1st lender;

- DEED OF TRUST—buyer to 2d lender;

- REQUEST FOR NOTICE OF DEFAULT—2d lender's request on 1st loan; and

- DEED OF RECONVEYANCE—trustee to seller.

The recording itself consists of four steps: First, the county recorder enters in the upper right-hand corner of each document the filing number, the time of receipt (down to the minute), and the amount of fees collected; second, either she makes a photocopy of the original document and puts it in a large bound book or she micro-films it; third, she files and indexes her copy; and fourth, she returns the original document to the party whose name and address appears in the upper left-hand corner of the first page.

PLEASE NOTE WELL

Remember that all recorded documents become public records available to anyone who wishes to look at them at the county recorder's office or pay a fee to obtain a copy.

WHAT'S THE DIFFERENCE BETWEEN TRANSFERRING TITLE AND TRANSFERRING POSSESSION?

The title of real property changes legally at the time of recording, but actual possession may transfer at an earlier date or a later date. Sometimes a buyer wants to move in before close of escrow and pay rent, and sometimes a seller wants to remain for a while and rent the property back from the buyer. In either case, the terms should be spelled out on the original purchase agreement, with the monthly or weekly rental charge clearly stated.

Here's an example of a rent-back agreement clause: "If the seller has not vacated the premises upon recordation of the deed, seller agrees to pay purchaser $___ per day (week) from recordation to date of possession by the buyer. This sum is to be prorated in escrow."

HOW ARE THE FUNDS DISBURSED?

After all of the documents have been recorded, your escrow officer will release the monies which have been held in the escrow account. This involves paying everybody off—the seller, the holders of old loans, the termite companies, the real estate agents, and so on—according to the instructions. The escrow officer will issue checks using the figures (debits and credits) stated on the escrow instructions. She will release the escrow funds with great care, being absolutely sure that she has received all the

money due in escrow and that all personal checks have cleared the bank. She cannot take the risk of releasing checks without having funds sufficient to cover them.

I remember well one buyer who stopped payment on his check several days after escrow had closed because he was unhappy about the dirty kitchen which the seller had left and wanted to get back at the "dirty dog." The buyer thought that by stopping payment on his check the seller would suffer and not get his sales proceeds money. What the buyer failed to understand was that on the day escrow closes, the escrow officer disburses all of the monies held in escrow, and the seller had already been paid.

Precisely to avoid problems of this sort, most escrow companies require a cashier's check for money presented near or at the time of closing. Those companies which do accept personal checks will hold up the close of escrow until the personal checks have cleared, two or three days for local banks and longer for out-of-town banks. If you want to use a personal check, deposit it with your escrow officer well ahead of the

SECURE TITLE COMPANY
1220 Oak Park Blvd.
Boonville, CA 11002
Telephone 423-4567

DATE August 11, 1990   ORDER NO. 12345   ESCROW OFFICER E. Edwards

ESCROW CLOSING STATEMENT

· Bruce B. Buyer & Barbara A. Buyer
· 12 Allendale Ct.
· Boonville, CA
·

I T E M S	DEBITS	CREDITS
XXX/PURCHASE PRICE	100,000.00	
DEPOSITS		1,000.00
DEPOSIT XXXXXX		11,762.54
XXXXXX LOAN to Seller		10,000.00
NEW LOAN		80,000.00
PRO-RATA — TAXES 7/1-8/10		72.51
— INSURANCE		
— INTEREST		
— RENTS		
TITLE INSURANCE POLICY FOR $100,000.00	432.50	
ESCROW FEE	160.00	
XXXXXXXXXXXXX ALTA Title Insurance for $80,000.00	96.50	
XXXXXXXXXXXXX ALTA Inspection Fee	20.00	
NOTARY FEE	4.00	
TRANSFER TAX		
RECORDING: Deed + 2 Deeds of Trust	13.00	
TAX COLLECTOR		
COMMISSION		
INSURANCE Pay for One Year Premium	235.00	
Pay for Termite Inspection Report	85.00	
Loan Fees: Loan Fee $1,200.00		
Credit Report Fee 35.00		
Tax Service Fee 17.50		
Interest 8/10-8/31 536.55		
1,789.05	1,789.05	
CHECK HEREWITH		
BALANCE DUE		
T O T A L S	102,835.05	102,835.05

SAVE FOR INCOME TAX PURPOSES

close of escrow to prevent any delay in closing.

A COMMON MISUNDERSTANDING: Dan doesn't quite have enough funds in the bank on Friday to cover his personal check needed to close escrow, but he knows he'll have the money there first thing Monday morning. He goes ahead and gives his check to the escrow company on Friday.

THE WAY THINGS REALLY ARE: Before she deposits his personal check into the escrow account, the escrow officer calls the bank to verify that the check is good. Escrow cannot close until Dan's check has cleared.

Prodded by the California Land Title Association, California recently enacted a law governing the holding periods for escrow deposits. It makes the holding periods dependent upon the nature of the funds themselves when they're deposited into escrow. Funds deposited into escrow in the form of cash or an electronic transfer become available immediately for escrow disbursements. Funds deposited in the form of a cashier's check, a teller's check, or a certified check become available for escrow disbursements on the first *business* day following the deposit. Funds deposited in the form of personal or business checks become available for disbursements according to the holding periods set by the Federal Reserve Board.

The Federal Reserve Board allows local checks to be held for up to three *business* days and non-local checks to be held for up to seven *business* days. Generally, "local checks" are those drawn on a bank in the same metropolitan area as the escrow office. San Francisco and Los Angeles are certainly not in the same metropolitan area, while San Francisco, San Jose, and Oakland are. Should you wonder whether your check is local or non-local, ask the escrow officer for a determination, and ask her how long the check will be held before the funds which it brings into escrow are made available for disbursement. An escrow company does have some leeway under the law. Local checks may be held for *up to* three business days, and non-local checks may be held for *up to* seven business days. Your escrow company may hold them for less time but not for more.

Often the escrow officer uses a worksheet or disbursement form which shows exactly who gets paid what. By adding the total amount of the disbursements according to the closing statement, she can check that the money she took in equals the money she will pay out.

By now you probably think that the closing of escrow is a complex operation, and it is, to a degree. Fortunately for you, though, all of this behind-the-scenes work is done for you. It is explained here simply to keep you informed. Besides, it's useful information. The more you know about the inner workings of the curious rite of escrow, the better protected you are.

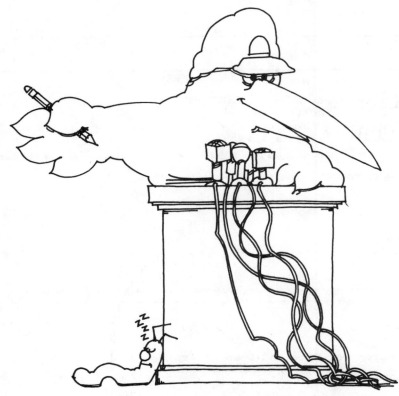

12
FINAL CLOSING STATEMENTS

WHAT HAPPENS AFTER THE RECORDING OF DOCUMENTS AND DISBURSEMENTS OF FUNDS?

At this point, your escrow officer considers the escrow closed, and she will proceed to draw up the final closing statements, tending to any last-minute adjustments and additional details. She will then mail out the title insurance policies, fire insurance policies, promissory notes, and any other pertinent documents, along with her closing letters, one to the buyer, one to the seller, and one to the lender.

WHAT DOCUMENTS DOES EVERYONE RECEIVE?

The little table below can best answer this question.

DOCUMENT	BUYER	SELLER	LENDER
CLTA Policy	Original		
ALTA Policy			Original
RESPA Statement	Copy	Copy	Original
Bill of Sale	Original		
Fire Insurance Policy	Copy	Old One	Original
Promissory Note	Copy		Original
Grant Deed	Original		
Deed of Trust			Original

SECURE TITLE COMPANY
1220 Oak Park Blvd.
Boonville, CA 11002
Telephone 423-4567

DATE August 11, 1990   ORDER NO. 12345   ESCROW OFFICER E. Edwards

ESCROW CLOSING STATEMENT

. Samuel P. Seller
. 4 Evelyn Ct.
. Sydney, Ill.
.

I T E M S	DEBITS	CREDITS
SALE/XXXXXXX PRICE		100,000.00
DEPOSITS		
DEPOSIT RETAINED		
EXISTING LOAN		
NEW LOAN Credit buyer for Note and Deed of Trust	10,000.00	
PRO-RATA — TAXES 7/1-8/10	72.51	
— INSURANCE		
— INTEREST		
— RENTS		
TITLE INSURANCE POLICY FOR $		
ESCROW FEE		
RECONVEYANCE FEE	30.00	
PREPARING DOCUMENTS		
NOTARY FEE	2.00	
TRANSFER TAX	110.00	
RECORDING: 2 Reconveyances + Request for Notice	12.00	
TAX COLLECTOR		
COMMISSION 6% of $100,000.00	6,000.00	
INSURANCE		
Pay for Termite Repair Work to be completed	250.00	
Pay off First Mortgage - Principal $47,000.00 Interest 120.70 Reconveyance 30.00 Forwarding 25.00	47,175.70	
Pay off Second Mortgage- Principal 5,000.00 Interest 13.80	5,013.80	
CHECK HEREWITH to Seller	31,333.99	
BALANCE DUE		
T O T A L S	100,000.00	100,000.00

SAVE FOR INCOME TAX PURPOSES

SECURE TITLE COMPANY
1220 Oak Park Blvd.
Boonville, CA 11002

Office: _____
Address: _____

Date _____ August 10, 1990 _____
Escrow No. __12345__

CREDITS	Amount	CREDITS
Deposit July 5, 1990		1 0 0 0 0 0
Deposit August 9, 1990		1 1 7 6 2 5 4
Deposit		
Deposit		
Funds to Hold in Escrow Termite Repair Fees	2 5 0 0 0	
Transfer of Funds		
Billing		
Loan Proceeds to Come From First Federal Trust		7 8 2 1 0 9 5

COMPANY

1. Policy Charge 432.50 + 96.50=   529.00
2. Escrow Fees   160.00
3. Recording Fees   25.00
4. Transfer Tax   110.00
5. Other Notary Fee + Inspection Fee 26.00

CHECKS TO BE DRAWN	CHECK NO.	Amount
Title Company - Escrow Fees		8 5 0 0 0
Insurance Company - One Year Premium		2 3 5 0 0
Termite Company - Termite Report Fee		8 5 0 0
Real Estate Company - Commission		6 0 0 0 0 0
Existing First Lender - Payoff in Full		4 7 1 7 5 7 0
Existing Second Lender - Payoff in Full		5 0 1 3 8 0
Trust Company - Trustee Fees		3 0 0 0
Seller - Sales Proceeds		3 1 3 3 3 9 9
TOTALS:		9 0 9 7 3 4 9 9 0 9 7 3 4 9

WHAT IS "RESPA"?

"RESPA" is an acronym for "Real Estate Settlement Procedures Act of 1974," which was passed to control real estate settlement costs on a national basis. "RESPA" and "HUD" are frequently used interchangeably for the same document used in escrow. "HUD" is another federal acronym, and it stands for "Department of Housing and Urban Development." The form itself is a consumer-protection-act form, and your escrow officer must fill one out if there is an institutional lender with federally insured deposits involved in the escrow. Unlike the Regulation "Z" Form, which is given to a borrower before his loan is completed, the RESPA form is given to a borrower after the loan is processed.

Everyone involved in a property transaction, buyer, seller, and lender, receives a RESPA statement. This form shows all the final debits and credits used to compute and close the escrow. These itemized statements are mandatory when there is a loan involved and when that loan is used, in whole or in part, to finance the purchase or transfer of title to dwellings housing one to four families, that is, for single-family dwellings through fourplexes. Most institutional lenders are obligated to comply with this 1974 act, so they issue a RESPA statement through the escrow company, which completes and mails out the form for them.

The only transactions exempt from this act, which applies to all federally insured lenders, are those involving loans used to finance or purchase property consisting of twenty-five acres or more, loans on vacant land, assumptions, all-cash transactions, and sales made subject to an existing loan.

PLEASE NOTE WELL

Because the RESPA statement contains your final closing figures, you should be sure to save it for income tax accounting. The figures given in the escrow instructions were mighty close approximations, but sometimes they have to be adjusted, as when the close of escrow did not occur on the very day when it was originally planned and the prorations all then had to be recomputed.

WHICH ITEMS GIVEN ON THE RESPA STATEMENT ARE TAX-DEDUCTIBLE?

The items given on your RESPA statement actually fall into three categories relative to your income taxes, and they are very important to you: tax-deductible in the current year, capitalized (added to the price paid for the property and thereby becoming part of your base for capital gains tax purposes when you sell), or neither (personal expense). The tax-deductible items are interest, points, loan-origination fees, and property taxes. Those items which are capitalized are the termite clearance costs, title insurance premiums, attorney's fees, appraisal fees, recording fees, notary fees, escrow fees, transfer taxes, and the ALTA inspection fee. The personal expense items are the fire insurance premium, private mortgage insurance, and any money put into an impound account.

WHAT HAPPENS WHEN ESCROW HAS TO BE CANCELED?

Occasionally a deal won't close and escrow must be canceled. The biggest concern, of course, is how the monies already held in escrow will be released. The funds could remain in escrow for a year or more unless you make proper provisions for their disposition.

A COMMON MISUNDERSTANDING: After his offer has been accepted, Nick does some double-checking and learns that the house he's buying, which is only 15 miles from work, is really a two-hour commute each way during the rush hours. He also realizes that he'll have to eat a lot more beans and spaghetti in order to meet the monthly payments. Even though he'd like to back out of the deal, he feels he has to go through with it now because it's already in escrow.

THE WAY THINGS REALLY ARE: Nick can always ask the seller to release him from the deal before escrow closes. By mutual consent, buyer and seller may cancel escrow.

When you signed your original purchase agreement with the seller, you probably agreed upon a time limit for closing, after which time penalties could be charged to the party responsible for the delay, or the escrow could be canceled altogether. In other words, if escrow does close within the time limit agreed upon, all is well, but if it has to be scheduled to close after the agreed-upon date, one of you will have to pay more, or you might agree to cancel the whole deal.

Escrow may be terminated by mutual consent of the buyer or seller for any number of reasons—inability to obtain financing, tight money, extensive structural damage to the property—or it may be terminated by a failure on the part of one party or another to satisfy certain of the escrow conditions within a specified time.

If a clause providing for a time limit within which to close escrow, say 30 or 60 days, is not included in your purchase agreement, the escrow could drag on for months, waiting for the buyer and/or seller to sign his papers and deliver his money.

Many times I have seen an escrow delayed by a buyer who gets "cold feet" and just can't get himself to sign all those loan documents or by a seller who has been offered more money by another buyer and tries to get the first buyer to back out of the agreement. Generally, however, once escrow has gone as far as to have all the legal documents drawn and signed, the parties eventually agree to close.

Most escrow instructions include a clause for cancellation which enables the buyer and seller by mutual agreement to cancel escrow by giving notice to the escrow holder.

Here's how it works if both parties are agreeable to canceling. The party deciding not to go through with the agreement writes or telephones the escrow officer and informs her of his reasons for requesting a cancellation. She then makes copies of this communication in the form of either the canceling party's letter or a cancellation agreement she has drawn up to reflect the telephone conversation, and she forwards these copies to the other parties involved so that everyone knows what's going on and so that any questions or disagreements may be resolved satisfactorily. In addition to reasons for the cancellation, this letter should state what is to happen to the monies already held in escrow, who gets the buyer's deposit, who pays any accumulated bills such as the termite report, and so on.

The escrow company may charge a cancellation fee covering the cost of preparing the preliminary title report and any leg work which the company may already have completed on the property, but that's all.

If you believe a cancellation of your escrow will be necessary, try to do the canceling before signing your escrow instructions, for once they are signed, cancellation is

much more complicated. Escrow instructions may be considered legally binding contracts and aren't revocable like purchase agreements because they generally do not have escape clauses.

Canceling escrow is relatively simple when both buyer and seller agree to end the transaction, but what if they should disagree? What happens when either the buyer or the seller does not live up to the original purchase agreement? Suppose the buyer continually stalls the close of escrow or decides at the last minute not to buy at all. What recourse does the seller have?

The purchase agreement and escrow instructions, like a rental agreement, are legally binding contracts, and their provisions are enforceable in a court of law. If the seller defaults on the contract, the buyer may sue the seller for "specific performance," which means that the court can order the seller to live up to his part of the contract and deliver the property to the buyer. If the buyer defaults, however, the seller sues for monetary damages only. In other words, a seller usually cannot force a buyer to buy. His only recourse is to retain the deposits, whereas the buyer might be able to force the seller actually to deliver the deed.

If this situation does arise in your own deal, consult your escrow officer, your attorney, and/or someone who specializes in real estate matters. And, by all means, make sure that your purchase agreement includes a clause providing for remedies which will forestall a default by either party.

IS THERE ANYTHING SPECIAL ABOUT BUYING PROPERTY FROM A FOREIGNER?

An amendment to the Foreign Investment in Real Property Tax Act (FIRPTA), which became effective January 1, 1985, requires anyone who buys non-residential property for more than $400,000 from a foreigner to set aside 10% of the purchase price for the I.R.S. According to I.R.S. Code 1445, the term "foreign persons" refers to foreign nationals who do not hold permanent resident visas.

Buyers and real estate agents are held liable if this 10% is not withheld, agents to the extent of their commission and buyers for the balance. Buyers are responsible for determining a seller's citizenship status and should require the seller to sign an affidavit of this status. If the seller is a foreigner, if the property's sales price exceeds $300,000, and if the property is not used as a residence, then the 10% must be withheld in escrow.

HOW DOES THE TAX REFORM ACT OF 1986 AFFECT ESCROWS?

The Tax Reform Act of 1986 now requires that all real estate transactions be reported to the Internal Revenue Service.

Whoever handles the closing, be it an escrow company, title company, financial institution, or attorney, that party must report the necessary information using IRS Form 1099. This form calls for the following on each seller or exchanger: name, taxpayer identification number (TIN), and forwarding address. In addition, it calls for the closing date, the sales price, the type of transaction, the real estate broker's name, address, and TIN, and the property's address, assessor's parcel number, and legal description.

WHERE CAN I GO TO COMPLAIN ABOUT MY ESCROW OR TITLE INSURANCE COMPANY?

Direct your escrow or title insurance complaints to the commissioner of corporations, to the state department of real estate, or to your local district attorney. If you used an independent escrow company, as is customary in Southern California, direct your complaint to the commissioner of corporations. The commissioner imposes strict regulations on independent escrow agents to ensure their impartiality and competence. Also make your complaint about an independent escrow agent known to the state escrow association if there is one (there is a California Escrow Association, which is devoted to better escrow practices and public relations). If you used a bank or savings and loan escrow department, direct your complaint to your state's bank or savings and loan commissioner or to whatever federal agency regulates the institution. If you have a complaint about a title insurance company, direct it to the insurance commissioner. Title insurance companies have to file their rates, policies, and endorsement forms with the state insurance commissioner, so that office should be knowledgeable enough to help you.

ARE THERE ANY OTHER QUESTIONS WHICH MIGHT BE OF CONCERN TO ME AS A BUYER OR SELLER AFTER CLOSE OF ESCROW?

There certainly are. After your escrow has closed, after the monies have been disbursed, and after the closing statements and documents have been distributed, you should take one last look at your new obligations to be certain you understand exactly what they are.

- Do you clearly understand when your loan payments are due? Be sure you get the loan payment book from the seller if you are assuming his loan, and verify both when the next payment is due and where it is to be made.

- Do you know when the property taxes come due? Be sure you get the old tax bill from the seller, and also be sure you contact the tax collector if you don't get a new tax bill by mail when it is due. Ignorance of the dates and amounts owed is no acceptable excuse for missing a property tax payment. The tax collector has heard them all. Be aware that in states which peg property taxes to sales prices the tax collector will be sending you at least one and sometimes two supplemental property tax bills. These bills cover the increase in property taxes from the old figure to the new one.

- Do you know when the next fire insurance premium will fall due?

- Do you know, if you bought a condo or co-op, when the homeowners' association fees must be paid?

If you have any uncertainties about these matters, even after escrow has closed, be sure you discuss them with your escrow officer. She will go over your new commitments with you and explain anything you don't understand.

One last and very important item to remember, one you should write in big red letters on your calendar, is that you should inquire about any monies which have been held in escrow after the close. More often than not, in the relief and joy of closing escrow, buyers and sellers forget that they still have money held back in their account, say $250 held for termite work. They think that since this amount has already been stated on the escrow instructions, that the matter is over and done with. It's not.

Some time ago I spent one entire week, eight hours a day, trying to release money which was held in various escrow accounts. I had a stack of more than a hundred old escrow files on my desk, each one with from $1.20 to $15,000 still in the escrow account. Many files were a year or more old, and most of the people involved had completely forgotten about the money! They, of course, were delighted to hear of their windfall checks that I would be sending them. Their money had been sitting there for months gathering dust, and they hadn't realized that they could have claimed it rightfully long before if they had only advised me that certain conditions had been met.

The reasons for holding their money were all different, ranging from money held for lawn repair and roof repair to money held for termite clearance and receipt of a new property assessment bill.

One of these files actually had $15,000 held in it. This was a deposit made on a large land purchase, which, believe it or not, was still pending after three years. I reminded the buyer about his $15,000 earnest money held in escrow, and I suggested that we put it into an interest-bearing savings account until the escrow closed. He replied that he had never thought of doing that. Had he requested three years before that we put his $15,000 into a bank account yielding a mere 6% interest, his escrow account would have been worth a whopping $17,700!

HOW DO I BEGIN LOOKING AFTER MY PROPERTY INVESTMENT?

You should begin looking after your property investment by keeping all of the property's papers organized. If you don't already keep a separate file folder for your monthly bills, now is a good time to begin. As each is paid, file it in that month's section, and put the bills ahead to the next month when they are to be paid. Keep a master list of all your bills in a special folder, and transfer this list each month with your other bills so you can't possibly overlook a payment.

Because you want to protect your credit and avoid having to pay late fees, you'll want to make your loan payments on time. To remind yourself of your obligations, you might want to write their due dates on your calendar over the next twelve months, or make up a master list for the periodic bills. It might be similar to the one shown here. It lists when the bills are due, when they are delinquent, how much they are, and to whom they are to be paid.

An institutional lender will usually give you a ten-to-fifteen-day grace period in which to make your loan payment, but after that you'll have to pay a very costly penalty, in some cases as much as $150. Be sure that your check is mailed to your lender well ahead of its delinquent date, though, because they expect to have received your payment by this date.

Property taxes, on the other hand, must be postmarked, not actually received, on or before the delinquent date given on the tax bill.

MASTER LIST FOR PROPERTY LOCATED AT:	12 Allendale Ct., Boonville		
TO WHOM PAYABLE	DUE DATE	DELINQUENT AFTER	AMOUNT PAID
Lender	First	Tenth	792.24
Seller	Tenth	Twentieth	212.48
Tax Collector	Nov 1	Dec 10	326.30
	Feb 1	Apr 10	326.30
Fire Insurance Company	Aug 12		243.88

WHAT IMPORTANT THINGS SHOULD I REMEMBER ABOUT ESCROW?

Remember that escrow means simply to involve a disinterested third-party holder in a specialized process to protect all the parties in a transaction.

Remember that the escrow officer is there to help you, whether you are the buyer or the seller or even the lender, so don't hesitate to ask her about anything related to your escrow.

A COMMON MISUNDERSTANDING: Two months after their escrow has closed, Max and Gertrude are talking with a new neighbor about one of their common fence lines. Later they begin to feel that the old owner may have misled them, and they begin looking more carefully into their title insurance policy. With certain questions in mind, they try to contact their real estate agent but learn that he is off visiting relatives. They decide to wait until he returns rather than bother their escrow officer. After all, she's been paid off and probably won't have any record of the matter anyway.

THE WAY THINGS REALLY ARE: Max and Gertrude should not hesitate to contact their escrow officer with their questions about title insurance, no matter whether it's days or years after escrow has closed.

Remember that your own escrow is never the only one in the office and that your escrow officer is usually dealing with fifteen to twenty escrows at once. She can't possibly remember your escrow number. So whenever you call your escrow officer, always identify yourself by name and escrow number, and you'll get the prompt service you want.

Remember that anyone with a qualifying document may record it at the county recorder's office, so if a situation should arise which does not necessitate the purchase of title insurance, a situation such as changing the manner of holding title or correcting a name on a deed, you can do the paperwork yourself, and if you should happen to encounter any difficulties doing it, you might even ask the escrow officer who last handled a real estate transaction for you to help you out.

MY FINAL CLOSING STATEMENT

I do hope that the information in this book has been of help to you. If at times the material may seem to have been too basic or overstressed, it was by design, for I have tried here to state things as simply as possible. I have always believed that escrow can be made simple and understandable and that people involved in escrow should know much more about what they're doing. In the same way that a well-insulated house conserves energy and saves on utility bills, so, too, does knowledge insulate. It conserves energy, saves grief and labor, and it insulates perhaps better than anything else. The knowledge you have gained here should insulate you well from many of the problems people encounter in escrow.

I realize that there may be some things about escrow which might have been clarified better and other things which may have been completely overlooked, so I would certainly welcome any replies that might help make this a better book. If you have any suggestions, please write me in care of ExPress.

FORMS

Some of the forms shown in the text appear here as blanks so that you may copy and use them as appropriate.

Before you copy them, fold over the corners of the pages where the tiny page numbers appear so the numbers will not show up on your copies.

On the next page is a list of these blank forms together with the page numbers indicating where they were introduced in the text.

NOTA BENE:

The author hereby grants permission to the purchaser of this book to copy any or all of these forms for personal use. Their reproduction for sale or distribution shall constitute an infringement of copyright.

The author assumes no responsibility for the legality or currency of these forms. Before using them, check with your escrow agent, real estate attorney, or closing agent to determine whether they are appropriate for your use.

	BLANK FORM ON PAGE NUMBER	INTRODUCED ON PAGE NUMBER
WORKSHEET FOR OPENING ESCROW	187	23
QUITCLAIM DEED	188	53
AGREEMENT TO CHANGE TITLE	189	56
LOAN SHOPPER	190	77
CASH-TO-CLOSE WORKSHEET	191	84
STRAIGHT NOTE	192	89
INSTALLMENT NOTE	193	90
ASSIGNMENT OF DEED OF TRUST	194	92
SUBSTITUTION OF TRUSTEE AND FULL RECONVEYANCE	195	109
BILL OF SALE	196	155
POWER OF ATTORNEY	197	158

WORKSHEET FOR OPENING ESCROW

DATE
PERSON OPENING ESCROW
ADDRESS
TELEPHONE
PROPERTY ADDRESS
OWNER
ADDRESS
TELEPHONE
BUYER
ADDRESS
TELEPHONE
SALES PRICE   DEPOSIT
TOTAL DOWN PAYMENT (INCLUDING DEPOSIT)
COMMISSION
% PAID TO
% PAID TO
1ST DEED OF TRUST – LENDER
AMOUNT   TERMS
2ND DEED OF TRUST – LENDER
AMOUNT   TERMS
TERMITE REPORT COMPANY
TERMITE REPORT COPIES SENT TO
BILL OF SALE (PERSONAL PROPERTY INCLUDED)
CLOSING DATE
CLOSING COSTS
TITLE INSURANCE PAID BY
ESCROW FEES PAID BY
TRANSFER TAXES PAID BY
TITLE
PURCHASER TO TAKE TITLE AS
MISCELLANEOUS

188

RECORDING REQUESTED BY:

MAIL TAX STATEMENT TO:

WHEN RECORDED, MAIL TO:

Recorder's Use Only

ORDER NO.

ESCROW NO.

QUITCLAIM DEED

DOCUMENTARY TRANSFER TAX $_____
_____COMPUTED ON FULL VALUE OF PROPERTY CONVEYED, OR
_____COMPUTED ON FULL VALUE LESS LIENS & ENCUMBRANCES
REMAINING THEREON AT TIME OF SALE.
_____Unincorporated Area_____City of _____
Tax Parcel No._____

FOR A VALUABLE CONSIDERATION,   HEREBY QUITCLAIM to:

the real property in the County of_____ , State of_____, described as:

Witness my hand this _____ day of _____, 19___.

_____   _____

STATE OF   )
) s.s.   WITNESS my hand and official seal:
COUNTY OF   )

On _____, 19___ ,   _____
before me, the undersigned, a Notary Public in and for said County   Notary Public in and for said County and State
and State, personally appeared

NOTARY SEAL

proved to me on the basis of satisfactory evidence to be the person__
whose name__ is (are) subscribed to the within instrument and
acknowledged that _____ executed the same.

MAIL TAX STATEMENT AS DIRECTED ABOVE

AGREEMENT TO CHANGE TITLE FROM JOINT TENANCY TO COMMUNITY PROPERTY

1) PARTIES:

Parties to this agreement are _____

and _____.

2) RECITALS:

   a) The parties hereto are husband and wife, residing in the County of _____

   _____, State of _____.

   b) They have heretofore held property in their common or separate names, and may hereafter do so.

   c) They hold portions of their property in joint tenancy only as a matter of convenience of transfer.

   d) This agreement is entered into with the full knowledge on the part of each party of the extent and probable value of all of the property and estate of the community, and of the separate and joint property of each other, ownership of which would be conferred by law on each of them in the event of the termination of their relationship by death or otherwise.

   e) It is the express intent of the parties hereto that all their common properties are and shall be their community property.

3. AGREEMENT THAT ALL PROPERTY SHALL BE COMMUNITY:

Each party hereby releases all of his or her separate rights in and to any and all property, real or personal and wherever situated, which either party now owns or has an interest in, and each party agrees that all property or interest therein owned heretofore or presently or hereafter acquired by either from common funds shall be deemed to be community property of the parties hereto, whether held in their separate names, as joint tenants, as tenants in common, or in any other legal form. The parties understand that this agreement will automatically, without other formality, transfer to the other a one-half interest in any separate property now owned and that such transfer could constitute a taxable gift under Federal and State law.

4. AGREEMENT MODIFIABLE IN WRITING ONLY:

This agreement shall not be modified except in writing signed by both parties, or by the mutual written surrender or abandonment of their said community interest in accordance with the laws of said State pertaining to the management of community property, or by the termination of their marriage by death or otherwise.

DATED: _____, 19___

_____

_____

LOAN SHOPPER

	Lender One	Lender Two	Lender Three
Initial interest rate on note			
Fixed, variable, graduated, other			
Amortization due date			
Points and other fees (total)			
Pre-payment penalty			
Assumability (specific requirements)			
Interest rate cap			
Index used			
Interest rate adjustments			
Co-borrowers allowed			
Maximum negative amortization			

CASH-TO-CLOSE WORKSHEET

ANALYSIS OF CASH TO CLOSE

Full purchase price of new house $\$$_____ A

Loan amount requested $\$$_____ B

Down payment needed (without closing costs) $\$$_____ C=A-B

Closing cost estimate (3-5% of loan amount) $\$$_____ D

_____

TOTAL CASH NEEDED TO CLOSE $\$$_____ E=C+D

SOURCES OF CASH NEEDED TO CLOSE

Amount from sale of present house $\$$_____ F

Amount of cash deposit $\$$_____ G

Amount from savings & checking accounts $\$$_____ H

Amount from gifts $\$$_____ I

Amount from stocks or other securities $\$$_____ J

Amount from other sources (secondary $\$$_____ K
financing, etc.)

_____

_____

_____

_____

TOTAL CASH AVAILABLE FOR CLOSING $\$$_____ L=F+G+
H+I+J+K

NOTE: "L" must be equal to or greater than "E."

STRAIGHT NOTE

$_____ _____ (city),

_____(state), _____ , 19___,

_____ after date, for value received,

I promise to pay to _____

_____ , or order, at

_____

the sum of _____DOLLARS,

with interest from_____, until paid at the

rate of _____ per cent per annum, payable _____

_____

Principal and interest payable in lawful money of the United States of America. Should default be made in payment of interest when due, the whole sum of principal and interest shall become immediately due at the option of the holder of this note. If action be instituted on this note, I promise to pay such sum as the Court may fix as Attorney's fees. This note is secured by a Mortgage Deed of a Deed of Trust of even date herewith.

_____   _____

_____   _____

_____   _____

When paid, this Note, if secured by a Deed of Trust, must be surrendered to Trustee for cancellation before reconveyance will be made.

DO NOT DESTROY

INSTALLMENT NOTE

(Combined Principal and Interest in Equal Installments)

_____ _____ (city),

_____(state), _____ , 19___,

OR VALUE RECEIVED, I promise to pay in lawful money of the United States of America to

_____

r order, at _____

he principal sum of_____DOLLARS,

vith interest in like lawful money from_____, 19_____

t _____ per cent per annum on the amounts of principal sum remaining unpaid from time to time. Principal and

iterest payable in installments of_____ DOLLARS, or more

ach, on the _____ day of each and every_____

eginning _____

_____

_____

_____

ach payment shall be credited first to the interest then due, and the remainder to the principal sum; and interest
hall thereupon cease upon the amount so paid on said principal sum. AND I agree that in case of default in the
ayment of any installments when due, then the whole of said principal sum then remaining unpaid, together with
he interest that shall have accrued thereon, shall forthwith become due and payable at the election of the holder of
iis note, without notice. AND I agree, if action be instituted on this note, to pay such sum as the Court may fix as
ttorney's fees. This note is secured by a Mortgage Deed or a Deed of Trust of even date herewith.

_____   _____

_____   _____

_____   _____

/hen paid, this Note, if secured by a Deed of Trust, must be surrendered to Trustee for cancellation before reconveyance will be made.

DO NOT DESTROY

RECORDING REQUESTED BY:

WHEN RECORDED, MAIL TO:

Recorder's Use Only

ASSIGNMENT OF DEED OF TRUST

FOR A VALUABLE CONSIDERATION, the undersigned hereby grants, assigns, and transfers to:

all beneficial interest under that certain Deed of Trust dated _____, 19__

executed by _____, as Trusto

to _____, as Trustee

and recorded as Instrument Number _____ on _____, 19__

in Book _____ at Page _____

of Official Records, in the office of the County Recorder of _____
together with the Promissory Note secured by said Deed of Trust and also all rights accrued or to accrue under said Deed of Trust.

Witness my hand this _____ day of _____, 19___.

_____

STATE OF   )
) s.s.
COUNTY OF   )

On _____, 19___,
before me, the undersigned, a Notary Public in and for said County and State, personally appeared

WITNESS my hand and official seal:

_____
Notary Public in and for said County and State

NOTARY SEAL

proved to me on the basis of satisfactory evidence to be the person__ whose name__ is (are) subscribed to the within instrument and acknowledged that _____ executed the same.

NOTE: This Assignment should be kept with the Note and Deed of Trust hereby assigned.

ECORDING REQUESTED BY:

WHEN RECORDED, MAIL TO:

Recorder's Use Only

SUBSTITUTION OF TRUSTEE AND FULL RECONVEYANCE

THE UNDERSIGNED, PRESENT BENEFICIARY under that certain Deed of Trust executed by:

_____, as Trustor,

_____, as Original Trustee,

and recorded as Instrument Number _____ on _____, 19_____

in Book _____ at Page _____ of Official Records, in the office of the County

Recorder of _____ County, State of _____,
hereby appoints and SUBSTITUTES the Undersigned as the new and substituted Trustee thereunder in accordance with the terms and provisions contained therein; AND

as such duly appointed and substituted Trustee thereunder, the Undersigned DOES HEREBY RECONVEY
to the person or persons legally entitled thereto, without warranty, all the estate, title, and interest acquired
by the Original Trustee and by the Undersigned as the said substituted Trustee under said Deed of Trust.

Wherever the text of this document so requires, the singular includes the plural.

Witness my hand this _____ day of _____, 19___.

Beneficiary and Substituted Trustee:

_____

_____

STATE OF _____)
) s.s.
COUNTY OF _____)

WITNESS my hand and official seal:

On _____, 19 _____,   _____
before me, the undersigned, a Notary Public in and for said County   Notary Public in and for said County and State
and State, personally appeared

NOTARY SEAL

proved to me on the basis of satisfactory evidence to be the person__
whose name__ is (are) subscribed to the within instrument and
acknowledged that _____ executed the same.

BILL OF SALE

THIS BILL OF SALE is dated the   day of

WITNESSETH:

That

herein called the Seller, for good and valuable consideration, hereby sells, assigns, and transfers to

herein called the Buyer, all that certain property which is hereinafter described.

IT IS HEREBY COVENANTED by the Seller, which covenant shall be binding upon the heirs, executors, and administrators of the Seller, that this sale is warranted. The sale of said property will be defended against any and every person who lawfully claims the same.

That property which is hereby sold, assigned and transferred is described as follows, to-wit [describe as precisely as possible and give location, if known]:

Signature of Seller: _____

197

RECORDING REQUESTED BY:

WHEN RECORDED, MAIL TO:

Recorder's Use Only

POWER OF ATTORNEY

Know All Men by These Presents: That _____
the undersigned (jointly and severally, if more than one) hereby make, constitute, and appoint _____
_____
as my true and lawful Attorney for me and in my name, place, and stead and for my use and benefit:

(a) To ask, demand, sue for, recover, collect, and receive each and every sum of money, debt, account, legacy, bequest, interest, dividend, annuity, and demand (which now is or hereafter shall become due, owing, or payable) belonging to or claimed by me, and to use and take any lawful means for the recovery thereof by legal process or otherwise, and to execute and deliver a satisfaction or release therefor, together with the right and power to compromise or compound any claim or demand;

(b) To exercise any or all of the following powers as to real property, any interest therein, and/or any building thereon: To contract for, purchase, receive and take possession thereof and of evidence of title thereto; to lease the same for any term or purpose, including leases for business, residence, and oil and/or mineral development; to sell, exchange, grant, or convey the same with or without warranty; and to mortgage, transfer in trust, or otherwise encumber or hypothecate the same to secure payment of a negotiable or non-negotiable note or performance of any obligation or agreement;

(c) To exercise any or all of the following powers as to all kinds of personal property and goods, wares and merchandise, choses in action and other property in possession or in action: To contract for, buy, sell, exchange, endorse, transfer, and in any legal manner deal in and with the same; and to mortgage, transfer in trust, or otherwise encumber or hypothecate the same to secure payment of a negotiable or non-negotiable note or performance of any obligation or agreement;

(d) To borrow money and to execute and deliver negotiable or non-negotiable notes therefor with or without security; and to loan money and receive negotiable or non-negotiable notes therefor with such security as he shall deem proper;

(e) To create, amend, supplement, and terminate any trust and to instruct and advise the trustee of any trust wherein I am or may be trustor or beneficiary; to represent and vote stock, exercise stock rights, accept and deal with any dividend, distribution, or bonus, join in any corporate financing, reorganization, merger, liquidation, consolidation, or other action and the extension, compromise, conversion, adjustment, enforcement or foreclosure, singly or in conjunction with others of any corporate stock, bond, note, debenture, or other security; to compound, compromise, adjust, settle, and satisfy any obligation, secured or unsecured, owing by or to me and to give or accept any property and/or money whether or not equal to or less in value than the amount owing in payment, settlement, or satisfaction thereof;

(f) To transact business of any kind or class and, as my act and deed, to sign, execute, acknowledge, and deliver any deed, lease, assignment of lease, covenant, indenture, indemnity, agreement, mortgage, deed of trust, assignment of mortgage or of the beneficial interest under deed of trust, extension or renewal of any obligation, subordination or waiver of priority, hypothecation, bottomry, charter-party, bill of lading, bill of sale, bill, bond, note, whether negotiable or non-negotiable, receipt, evidence of debt, full or partial release or satisfaction of mortgage, judgment, and other debt, request for partial or full reconveyance of deed of trust and such other instruments in writing of any kind or class as may be necessary or proper in the premises.

Giving and granting unto my said Attorney full power and authority to do and perform all and every act and thing whatsoever requisite, necessary, or appropriate to be done in and about the premises as fully to all intents and purposes as I might or could do if personally present, hereby ratifying all that my said Attorney shall lawfully do or cause to be done by virtue of these presents. The powers and authority hereby conferred upon my said Attorney shall be applicable to all real and personal property or interests therein now owned or hereafter acquired by me and wherever situated.

My said Attorney is empowered hereby to determine in his sole discretion the time when, purpose for, and manner in which any power herein conferred upon him shall be exercised, and the conditions, provisions, and covenants of any instrument or document which may be executed by him pursuant hereto; and in the acquisition or disposition of real or personal property, my said Attorney shall have exclusive power to fix the terms thereof for cash, credit, and/or property, and if on credit with or without security.

The undersigned, if a married woman, hereby further authorizes and empowers my said Attorney, as my duly authorized agent, to join in my behalf, in the execution of any instrument by which any community real property or interest therein, now owned or hereafter acquired by my spouse and myself, or either of us, is sold leased, encumbered, or conveyed.

When the context so requires, the masculine gender includes the feminine and/or neuter, and the singular number includes the plural.

[ ] This is to be considered a general Power of Attorney.

[ ] Notwithstanding the aforesaid, this is to be considered a specific power of attorney limited to _____
_____ and expiring _____

Witness my hand this _____ day of _____, 19_____.

_____   _____

STATE OF   )
) s.s.
COUNTY OF   )
On_____, 19_____,

before me, the undersigned, a Notary Public in and for said County
and State, personally appeared

proved to me on the basis of satisfactory evidence to be the person__
whose name__ is (are) subscribed to the within instrument and
acknowledged that _____ executed the same.

WITNESS my hand and official seal:

_____
Notary Public in and for said County and State
NOTARY SEAL

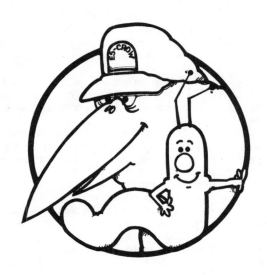

APPENDIX
ESCROW PROCEDURES AROUND THE UNITED STATES

This summary is merely a general reference guide. Contact a local title company or real estate attorney for specific information.

ALABAMA–Attorneys handle closings. Conveyance is by warranty deed. Mortgages are the customary security instruments. Foreclosures are non-judicial. Foreclosure notices are published once a week for three weeks on a county-by-county basis. The foreclosure process takes a minimum of 21 days from the date of first publication. After the sale, there is a one-year redemption period. Alabamans use ALTA policies to insure titles. Buyers and sellers negotiate who's going to pay the closing costs and usually split them equally. Property taxes are due and payable annually on October 1st.

ALASKA–Title companies, lenders, and private escrow companies all handle real estate escrows. Conveyance is by warranty deed. Deeds of trust with private power of sale are the customary security instruments. Foreclosures take 90-120 days. Alaskans use ALTA owner's and lender's policies with standard endorsements. There are no documentary or transfer taxes. Buyer and seller usually split the closing costs. Property tax payment dates vary throughout the state.

ARIZONA–Title companies and title agents both handle closings. Conveyance is by warranty deed. Whereas deeds of trust are the security instruments most often used, mortgages and "agreements for sale" are used approximately 20% of the time. Foreclosure depends upon the security instrument. For deeds of trust, the foreclosure process takes about 91 days. Arizonans use ALTA owner's and lender's policies, standard or extended, with standard endorsements. The seller customarily pays for the owner's policy, and the buyer pays for the lender's policy. They split escrow costs otherwise. There are no documentary, transfer, or mortgage taxes. The first property tax installment is due October 1st and delinquent November 1st; the second half is due March 1st and delinquent May 1st. Arizona is a community-property state.

ARKANSAS–Title agents handle escrows, and attorneys conduct closings. Conveyance is by warranty deed. Mortgages are the customary security instruments. Foreclosure requires judicial proceedings, but there are no minimum time limits for completion. Arkansans use ALTA policies and endorsements and receive a 40% discount for reissuance of prior policies. Buyers and sellers pay their own escrow costs. The buyer pays for the lender's policy; the seller pays for the owner's. In addition, the seller pays the state documentary tax. Property taxes come due three times a year as follows: the third Monday in April, the third Monday in July, and the 10th day of October.

CALIFORNIA–Not only do escrow procedures differ between Northern and Southern California, they also vary somewhat from county to county. Title companies handle closings through escrow in Northern California, whereas escrow companies and lenders handle them in Southern California. Conveyance is by grant deed. Deeds of trust with private power of sale are the security instruments used throughout the state. Foreclosure requires a three-month waiting period after the recording of the notice of default. After the waiting period, the notice of sale is published each week for three consecutive weeks. The borrower may reinstate the loan at any time prior to five business days before the foreclosure sale. All in all, the procedure takes about four months. Californians have both ALTA and CLTA policies available. In Southern California, sellers pay the title insurance premium and the transfer tax. Buyer and seller split the escrow costs. In the Northern California counties of Amador, Merced, Plumas, San Joaquin, and Siskiyou, buyers and sellers share title insurance and escrow costs equally. In Butte County, sellers pay 75%; buyers pay 25%. In Alameda, Calaveras, Colusa, Contra Costa, Lake, Marin, Mendocino, San Francisco, San Mateo, Solano, and Sonoma counties, buyers pay for the title insurance policy, whereas sellers pay in the other Northern California counties. Each California county has its own transfer tax; some cities have additional charges. Property taxes may be paid annually on or before December 10th, or semiannually by December 10th and April 10th. California is a community-property state.

COLORADO–Title companies, brokers, and attorneys all may handle closings. Conveyance is by warranty deed. Deeds of trust are the customary security instruments. Public trustees must sell foreclosure properties within 45-60 days after the filing of a "notice of election and demand for sale," but they will grant extensions up to six months following the date of the originally scheduled sale. Subdivided properties may be redeemed within 75 days after sale; properties described by metes and bounds may be redeemed within 6 months after sale. Foreclosures may be handled judicially. Coloradans have these title insurance policy options: ALTA owner's, lender's, leasehold, and construction loan; endorsements are used, too. Although they are negotiable, closing costs are generally paid by the real estate agent. Sellers pay the title insurance premium and the documentary transfer tax. Property taxes may be paid annually at the end of April or semiannually at the ends of February and July.

CONNECTICUT–Attorneys normally conduct closings. Most often conveyance is by warranty deed, but quitclaim deeds do appear. Mortgages are the security instruments. Judicial foreclosures are the rule, either by a suit in equity for strict foreclosure or by a court decree of sale. Court decreed sales preclude redemption, but strict foreclosures allow redemption for 3-6 months, depending upon the discretion of the court. There are lender's and owner's title insurance policies available with various endorsements. Buyers customarily pay for examination and title insurance, while sellers pay the documentary and conveyance taxes. Property tax payment dates vary by town.

DELAWARE–Attorneys handle closings. Although quitclaim and general warranty deeds are sometimes used, most conveyances are by special warranty deeds. Mortgages are the security instruments. Foreclosures are judicial and require 90-120 days to complete. ALTA policies and endorsements are prevalent. Buyers pay closing costs and the owner's title insurance premiums. Buyers and sellers share the state transfer tax. Property taxes are on an annual basis and vary by county.

DISTRICT OF COLUMBIA–Attorneys, title insurance companies, or their agents may conduct closings. Conveyances are by bargain-and-sale deeds. Though mortgages are available, the deed of trust, containing private power of sale, is the security instrument of choice. Foreclosures require at least six weeks and start with a 30-day notice of sale sent by certified mail. ALTA policies and endorsements insure title. Buyers generally pay closing costs, title insurance premiums, and recording taxes. Sellers pay the transfer tax. Property taxes fall due annually or if they're less than $100,000, semiannually, on September 15th and March 31st.

FLORIDA–Title companies and attorneys handle closings. Conveyance is by warranty deed. Mortgages are the customary security instruments. Foreclosures are judicial and take about 3 months. They involve service by the sheriff, a judgment of foreclosure and sale, advertising, public sale, and finally issuance of a certificate of sale and certificate of title.

ALTA policies are commonplace. Buyers pay the escrow and closing costs, while county custom determines who pays for the title insurance. Sellers pay the documentary tax. Property taxes are payable annually, but the due and delinquent dates are months apart, November 1st and April 1st.

GEORGIA—Attorneys generally take care of closings. Conveyance is by warranty deed. Security deeds are the security instruments. Foreclosures are non-judicial and take little more than a month because there's a power of attorney right in the security deed. Foreclosure advertising must appear for 4 consecutive weeks prior to the first Tuesday of the month; that's when foreclosure sales take place. Georgians use ALTA title insurance policies, including owner's and lender's, and they use binders and endorsements. Buyers pay title insurance premiums and also closing costs usually. Sellers pay transfer taxes. Property tax payment dates vary across the state.

HAWAII—By law, only attorneys may prepare property transfer documents, but there are title and escrow companies available to handle escrows and escrow instructions. Conveyance of fee-simple property is by warranty deed; conveyance of leasehold property, which is common throughout the state, is by assignment of lease. Sales of some properties, whether fee simple or leasehold, are by agreement of sale. Mortgages are the security instruments. Hawaiians use judicial foreclosures rather than powers of sale for both mortgages and agreements of sale. These foreclosures take 6-12 months and sometimes more, depending upon court schedules. Title companies issue ALTA owner's and lender's policies and make numerous endorsements available. Buyers and sellers split escrow fees. Sellers pay the title search costs and the conveyance tax. Buyers pay title insurance premiums for the owner's and lender's policies. Property taxes come due twice a year, on February 20th and again on August 20th.

IDAHO—Closings are handled through escrow. Conveyance is by warranty deed or corporate deed, though often there are contracts of sale involved. Either mortgages or deeds of trust may be the security instruments. Deeds of trust which include power of sale provisions are restricted to properties in incorporated areas and properties elsewhere which don't exceed 20 acres. After the notice of default has been recorded, deed-of-trust foreclosures take at least 120 days, and there's no redemption period. Judicial foreclosures for mortgages take about a year, depending upon court availability, and there's a 6-12 month redemption period after that, depending on the type of property involved. Idahoans use ALTA policies and various endorsements. Buyers and sellers split escrow costs in general and negotiate who's going to pay the title insurance premiums. There are no documentary taxes, mortgage taxes, or transfer taxes, but there are property taxes, and they're due annually on December 20th or semiannually on December 20th and June 20th. Idaho is a community-property state.

ILLINOIS—Title companies, lenders, and attorneys may conduct closings, but only attorneys may prepare documents. Lenders generally hire attorneys and have them prepare all the paperwork. Conveyance is by warranty deed. Recorded deeds must include a declaration of the sales price. Mortgages are the customary security instruments. Judicial foreclosure is mandatory and takes at least a year from the filing of the default notice to the expiration of the redemption period. Illinoisans use ALTA policies. Buyers usually pay the closing costs and the lender's title insurance premiums; sellers pay the owner's title insurance premiums and the state and county transfer taxes. Property tax payment dates vary. Larger counties typically schedule them for March 1st and September 1st, and smaller counties schedule them for June 1st and September 1st.

INDIANA–Title companies, lenders, real estate agents, and attorneys handle closings. Conveyance is by warranty deed. Mortgages are the customary security instruments. Judicial foreclosures are required; execution of judgments varies from 3 months after filing of the complaint in cases involving mortgages drawn up since July 1, 1975, to 6 months for those drawn up between January 1, 1958, and July 1, 1975, to 12 months for those drawn up before that. Immediately following the execution sale, the highest bidder receives a sheriff's deed. Hoosiers use ALTA policies and certain endorsements. Buyers usually pay closing costs and the lender's title insurance costs, while sellers pay for the owner's policy. There are no documentary, mortgage, or transfer taxes. Property taxes fall due on May 10th and November 10th.

IOWA–Attorneys may conduct closings, and so may real estate agents. Conveyance is usually by warranty deed. Mortgages and deeds of trust are both authorized security instruments, but lenders prefer mortgages because deeds of trust do not circumvent judicial foreclosure proceedings anyway. Those proceedings take at least 4 -6 months. Since Iowa is the only state which does not authorize title insurance, Iowans who want it must go through a title company in another state. Buyers and sellers share the closing costs; sellers pay the documentary taxes. Property taxes are due July 1st based upon the previous January's assessment.

KANSAS–Title companies, lenders, real estate agents, attorneys, and independent escrow firms all conduct closings. Anyone who conducts a title search must be a licensed abstracter, a designation one receives after passing strict tests and meeting various requirements. Because many land titles stem from Indian origins, deeds involving Indians as parties to a transaction go before the Indian Commission for approval. Conveyance is by warranty deed. Mortgages are the customary security instruments. Judicial foreclosures, the only ones allowed, take about 6 months from filing to sale. Redemption periods vary, the longest being 12 months. Kansans use ALTA policies and endorsements. Buyers and sellers divide closing costs. Buyers pay the lender's policy costs and the state mortgage taxes; sellers pay for the owner's policy. Property taxes come due November 1st, but they needn't be paid in a lump sum until December 31st. They may also be paid in two installments, the first on December 20th and the second on June 20th.

KENTUCKY–Attorneys conduct closings. Conveyance is by grant deed or by bargain-and-sale deed. Deeds must show the name of the preparer, the amount of the total transaction, and the recording reference by which the grantor obtained title. Mortgages are the principal security instruments because deeds of trust offer no power-of-sale advantages. Enforcement of any security instrument requires a decree in equity, a judicial foreclosure proceeding. Kentuckians use ALTA policies and endorsements. Sellers pay closing costs; buyers pay recording fees. Responsibility for payment of title insurance premiums varies according to locale. Property taxes are payable on an annual basis; due dates vary from county to county.

LOUISIANA–Either attorneys or corporate title agents may conduct closings, but a notary must authenticate the documentation. Conveyance is by warranty deed or by act of sale. Mortgages are the security instruments generally used in commercial transactions, while "vendor's liens" and "seller's privileges" are used in other purchase money situations. Foreclosures are swift (60 days) and sure (no right of redemption). Successful foreclosure sale bidders receive an "adjudication" from the sheriff. Louisianians use ALTA owner's and lender's policies and endorsements. Buyers generally pay the title insurance and closing costs. There are no mortgage or transfer taxes. Property tax payment dates vary from parish to parish (parishes are like counties). Louisiana is a community-property state.

MAINE–Attorneys conduct closings. Conveyance is by warranty or quitclaim deed. Mortgages are the security instruments. Foreclosures may be initiated by any of the following: an act of law for possession; entering into possession and holding the premises by written consent of the mortgagor; entering peaceably, openly, and unopposed in the presence of two witnesses and taking possession; giving public notice in a newspaper for three successive weeks and recording copies of the notice in the Registry of Deeds, and then recording the mortgage within 30 days of the last publication; or by a bill in equity (special cases). In every case, the creditor must record a notice of foreclosure within 30 days. Judicial foreclosure proceedings are also available. Redemption periods vary from 90-365 days depending on the method of foreclosure. Mainers use ALTA owner's and lender's policies and endorsements. Buyers pay closing costs and title insurance fees; sellers pay the documentary transfer taxes. Property taxes are due annually on April 1st.

MARYLAND–Attorneys conduct closings, and there has to be a local attorney involved. Conveyance is by grant deed or bargain-and-sale deed, and the deed must state the consideration involved. Although mortgages are common in some areas, deeds of trust are more prevalent as security instruments. Security instruments may include a private power of sale, so it naturally is the foreclosure method of choice. Marylanders use ALTA policies and endorsements. Buyers pay closing costs, title insurance premiums, and transfer taxes. Property taxes are due annually on July 1st.

MASSACHUSETTS–Attorneys handle closings. Conveyance is by warranty deed in the western part of the state and by quitclaim deed in the eastern part. Mortgages with private power of sale are the customary security instruments. Creditors forced to foreclose generally take advantage of the private power of sale, but they may foreclose through peaceable entry (entering unopposed in the presence of two witnesses and taking possession for 3 years) or through the rarely used judicial writ of entry. People in Massachusetts use ALTA owner's and lender's title insurance policies and endorsements. Buyers pay closing costs and title insurance fees, except in Worcester, where sellers pay. Sellers pay the documentary taxes. Property taxes are payable in two installments, November 1st and May 1st.

MICHIGAN–Title companies, lenders, real estate agents, and attorneys may conduct closings. Conveyance is by warranty deed which must give the full consideration involved or be accompanied by an affidavit which does. Many transactions involve land contracts. Mortgages are the security instruments. Private foreclosure is permitted; it requires advertising for 4 consecutive weeks and a sale at least 28 days following the date of first publication. The redemption period ranges from 1 to 12 months. Michiganders use ALTA policies and endorsements. Buyers generally pay closing costs and the lender's title insurance premium, and sellers pay the state transfer tax and the owner's title insurance premium. Those property taxes which pay for city and school expenses fall due July 1st; others (county taxes, township taxes, and some school taxes) fall due on the first of December.

MINNESOTA–Title companies, lenders, real estate agents, and attorneys may conduct closings. Conveyance is by warranty deed. Although deeds of trust are authorized, mortgages are the customary security instruments. The redemption period following a foreclosure is 6 months in most cases; it is 12 months if the property is larger than 10 acres or the amount claimed to be due is less than 2/3 of the original debt. This is a strong abstract state. Typically a buyer will accept an abstract and an attorney's opinion as evidence of title, even though the lender may require title insurance. People in the Minneapolis-St. Paul area use the Torrens system. Minnesotans use ALTA policies. Buyers pay the lender's and owner's title insurance premiums and the mortgage tax. Sellers usually pay the closing fees and the transfer taxes. Property taxes are due on May 15th and October 15th.

MISSISSIPPI–Attorneys conduct real estate closings. Conveyance is by warranty deed. Deeds of trust are the customary security instruments. Foreclosure involves a non-judicial process which takes 21-45 days. Mississippians use ALTA policies and endorsements. Buyers and sellers negotiate the payment of title insurance premiums and closing costs. There are no documentary, mortgage, or transfer taxes. Property taxes are payable on an annual basis and become delinquent February 1st.

MISSOURI–Title companies, lenders, real estate agents, and attorneys may conduct closings. Conveyance is by warranty deed. Deeds of trust are the customary security instruments and allow private power of sale. Foreclosure involves publication of a sale notice for 21 days, during which time the debtor may redeem the property or file a notice of redemption. The foreclosure sale buyer receives a trustee's deed. Missourians use ALTA policies and endorsements. Buyers and sellers generally split the closing costs. Sellers in western Missouri usually pay for the title insurance polices, while elsewhere the buyers pay. There are no documentary, mortgage, or transfer taxes. Property taxes are payable annually and become delinquent January 1st for the previous year.

MONTANA–Real estate closings are handled through escrow. Conveyance is by warranty deed, corporate deed, or grant deed. Mortgages, deeds of trust, and unrecorded contracts of sale are the security instruments. Mortgages require judicial foreclosure, and there's a one-year redemption period following sale. Foreclosure on deeds of trust involves filing a notice of default and then holding a trustee sale 120 days later. Montanans use ALTA policies and endorsements. Buyers and sellers split the escrow and closing costs; sellers usually pay for the title insurance policies. There are no documentary, mortgage, or transfer taxes. Montanans may pay their property taxes annually by November 30th or semi-annually by November 30th and May 31st.

NEBRASKA–Title companies, lenders, real estate agents, and attorneys all conduct closings. Conveyance is by warranty deed. Mortgages and deeds of trust are the security instruments. Mortgage foreclosures require judicial proceedings and take about 6 months from the date of the first notice when they're uncontested. Deeds of trust do not require judicial proceedings and take about 90 days. Nebraskans use ALTA policies and endorsements. Buyers and sellers split escrow and closing costs; sellers pay the state's documentary taxes. Property taxes fall due April 1st and August 1st.

NEVADA–Escrow similar to California's is used for closings. Conveyance is by grant deed, bargain-and-sale deed, or quitclaim deed. Deeds of trust are the customary security instruments. Foreclosure involves recording a notice of default and mailing a copy within 10 days. Following the mailing there is a 35-day reinstatement period. After that, the beneficiary may accept partial payment or payment in full for a 3-month period. Then come advertising the property for sale for 3 consecutive weeks and finally the sale itself. All of this takes about 4 1/2 months. Nevadans use both ALTA and CLTA policies and endorsements. Buyers and sellers share escrow costs. Buyers pay the lender's title insurance premiums; sellers pay the owner's and the state's transfer tax. Property taxes are payable in one, two, or four payments, the first one being due July 1st. Nevada is a community-property state.

NEW HAMPSHIRE–Attorneys conduct real estate closings. Conveyance is by warranty or quitclaim deed. Mortgages are the customary security instruments. Lenders may foreclosure through judicial action or through whatever power of sale was written into the mortgage originally. Entry, either by legal action or by taking possession peaceably in the presence of two witnesses, is possible under certain legally stated conditions. There is a one-year right-of-redemption period. The people of New Hampshire use ALTA owner's and lender's policies. Buyers pay all closing costs and title fees except for the documentary tax; that's shared with the sellers. Property tax payment dates vary across the state.

NEW JERSEY–Attorneys handle closings in northern New Jersey, and title agents customarily handle them elsewhere. Conveyance is by bargain-and-sale deed with covenants against grantors' acts (equivalent to a special warranty deed). Mortgages are the most common security instruments though deeds of trust are authorized. Foreclosures require judicial action which take 6-9 months if they're uncontested. New Jerseyites use ALTA owner's and lender's policies. Property taxes are payable quarterly on the first of April, July, October, and January.

NEW MEXICO–Real estate closings are conducted through escrows. Conveyance is by warranty or quitclaim deed. Deeds of trust and mortgages are the security instruments. Foreclosures require judicial proceedings, and there's a 9-month redemption period after judgment. New Mexicans use ALTA owner's policies, lender's policies, and construction and leasehold policies; they also use endorsements. Buyers and sellers share escrow costs equally; sellers pay the title insurance premiums. There are no documentary, mortgage, or transfer taxes. Property taxes are payable November 5th and April 5th. New Mexico is a community-property state.

NEW YORK–All parties to a transaction appear with their attorneys for closing. Conveyance is by bargain-and-sale deed. Mortgages are the security instruments in this lien-theory state. Foreclosures require judicial action and take several months if uncontested or longer if contested. New Yorkers use policies of the New York Board of Title Underwriters almost exclusively, though some use the New York State 1946 ATA Loan Policy. Buyers generally pay most closing costs, including all title insurance fees and mortgage taxes. Sellers pay the state and city transfer taxes. Property tax payment dates vary across the state.

NORTH CAROLINA–Attorneys or lenders may handle closings, and corporate agents issue title insurance. Conveyance is by warranty deed. Deeds of trust with private power of sale are the customary security instruments. Foreclosures are non-judicial and take 45-60 days. North Carolinians use ALTA policies, but these require an attorney's opinion before they're issued. Buyers and sellers negotiate the closing costs, except that buyers pay the recording costs, and sellers pay the document preparation costs. Property taxes fall due annually on the last day of the year.

NORTH DAKOTA–Lenders, together with attorneys, conduct closings. Conveyance is by warranty deed. Mortgages are the security instruments. Foreclosures require about 6 months, including the redemption period. North Dakotans base their title insurance on abstracts and attorneys' opinions. Buyers usually pay for the closing, the attorney's opinion, and the title insurance; sellers pay for the abstract. There are no documentary or transfer taxes. Property taxes are due March 15th and October 15th.

OHIO–Title companies and lenders handle closings. Conveyance is by warranty deed. Mortgages are the security instruments. Judicial foreclosures, the only kind allowed, require about 6 months. People in Ohio use ALTA policies; they get a commitment at closing and a policy following the recording of documents. Buyers and sellers negotiate who's going to pay closing costs and title insurance premiums, but sellers pay the transfer taxes. Property tax payment dates vary throughout the state.

OKLAHOMA–Title companies, lenders, real estate agents, and attorneys may conduct closings. Conveyance is by warranty deed. Mortgages are the usual security instruments. Foreclosures are by judicial action only. Oklahomans use ALTA policies and endorsements. Buyers and sellers share the closing costs, except that the buyer pays the lender's policy premium, the seller pays the documentary transfer tax, and the lender pays the mortgage tax. Property taxes may be paid annually on or before the last day of the year or semi-annually by December 31st and March 31st.

OREGON–Closings are handled through escrow. Conveyance is by warranty or bargain-and-sale deed, but land sales contracts are common. Mortgage deeds and deeds of trust are the security instruments. Oregon attorneys usually act as trustees in non-judicial trust-deed foreclosures. Such foreclosures take 5 months from the date of the sale notice; defaults may be cured as late as 5 days prior to sale. Judicial foreclosures on either mortgages or trust deeds allow for a one-year redemption period following sale. Oregonians use ALTA and Oregon Land Title Association policies. Buyers and sellers split escrow costs and transfer taxes; the buyer pays for the lender's title insurance policy, and the seller pays for the owner's policy. Property taxes are payable the 15th of November, February, and May; if paid in full by November 15th, owners receive a 3% reduction.

PENNSYLVANIA–Title companies, real estate agents, and approved attorneys may handle closings. Conveyance is by special or general warranty deed. Mortgages are the security instruments. Foreclosures take 1-6 months from filing through judgment plus another 2 months or more from judgment through sale. Pennsylvanians use ALTA owner's, lender's, and leasehold policies. Buyers pay closing costs and title insurance fees; buyers and sellers split the transfer taxes. Property tax payment dates differ across the state.

RHODE ISLAND–Attorneys usually conduct closings, but banks and title companies may also conduct them. Conveyance is by warranty or quitclaim deed. Mortgages are the usual security instruments. Foreclosures follow the power-of-sale provisions contained in mortgage agreements and take about 45 days. Rhode Islanders use ALTA policies and endorsements. Buyers pay title insurance premiums and closing costs; sellers pay documentary taxes. Property taxes are payable annually, semi-annually, or quarterly with the first payment due in July.

SOUTH CAROLINA–Attorneys customarily handle closings. Conveyance is by warranty deed. Mortgages are most often the security instruments. Foreclosures are judicial and take 3-5 months depending on court schedules. Foreclosure sales take place on the first Monday of every month following publication of notice once a week for 3 consecutive weeks. South Carolinians use owner's and lender's ALTA policies and endorsements. Buyers pay closing costs, title insurance premiums, and state mortgage taxes; sellers pay the transfer taxes. Property tax payment dates vary across the state from September 15 to December 31.

SOUTH DAKOTA–Title companies, lenders, real estate agents, and attorneys may handle closings. Conveyance is by warranty deed. Mortgages are the usual security instruments. Foreclosures may occur through judicial proceedings or through the power-of-sale provisions contained in certain mortgage agreements. Sheriff's sales follow publication of notice by 30 days. The redemption period allowed after sale of parcels smaller than 40 acres *and* encumbered by mortgages containing power of sale is 180 days; in all other cases, it's a year. There's a unique statute which stipulates that all land must be platted in lots or described by sectional references rather than by metes and bounds unless it involves property described in documents recorded prior to 1945. South Dakotans use ALTA policies and endorsements. Sellers pay the transfer taxes and split the other closing costs, fees, and premiums with the buyers. Property taxes come due May 1st and November 1st.

TENNESSEE–A title company attorney, a party to the contract, a lender's representative, or an outside attorney may conduct a closing. Conveyance is by warranty or quitclaim deed. Deeds of trust are the customary security instruments. Foreclosures, which are handled according to trustee sale provisions, are swift, that is, 22 days from the first publication of the notice until the public sale, and there is normally no right of redemption after that. Tennesseans use ALTA policies and endorsements. The payment of title insurance premiums, closing costs, mortgage taxes, and transfer taxes varies according to local practice. Property taxes are payable annually on the first Monday in October.

TEXAS–Title companies normally handle closings. Conveyance is by warranty deed. Deeds of trust are the most common security instruments. Following the posting of foreclosure sales at the local courthouse for at least 21 days, the sales themselves take place at the courthouse on the first Tuesday of the month. Texans use only Texas standard policy forms of title insurance. Buyers and sellers negotiate closing costs. There aren't any documentary, transfer, or mortgage taxes. Property taxes are due October 1st. Texas is a community-property state.

UTAH–Lenders handle about 60% of the escrows and title companies handle the rest. Conveyance is by warranty deed. Mortgages and deeds of trust with private power of sale are the security instruments. Mortgage foreclosures require judicial proceedings which take about a year; deed-of-trust foreclosures take advantage of private power-of-sale provisions and take about 4 months. Utahans use ALTA owner's and lender's policies and endorsements. Buyers and sellers split escrow fees, and sellers pay the title insurance premiums. There are no documentary, transfer, or mortgage taxes. Property taxes are payable November 30th.

VERMONT–Attorneys take care of closings. Conveyance is by warranty or quitclaim deed. Mortgages are the customary security instruments, but large commercial transactions often employ deeds of trust . Mortgage foreclosures require judicial proceedings for "strict foreclosure"; after sale, there is a redemption period of one year for mortgages dated prior to April 1, 1968, and 6 months for all others. Vermonters use ALTA owner's and lender's policies and endorsements. Buyers pay recording fees, title insurance premiums, and transfer taxes. Property tax payment dates vary across the state.

VIRGINIA–Attorneys and title companies conduct real estate closings. Conveyance is by bargain-and-sale deed. Deeds of trust are the customary security instruments. Foreclosure takes about 2 months. Virginians use ALTA policies and endorsements. Buyers pay the title insurance premiums and the various taxes. Property tax payment dates vary.

WASHINGTON–Title companies, independent escrow companies, lenders, and attorneys may handle escrows. Conveyance is by warranty deed. Both deeds of trust with private power of sale and mortgages are used as security instruments. Mortgages require judicial foreclosure. Deeds of trust require that a notice of default be sent first and 30 days later, a notice of sale. The notice of sale must be recorded, posted, and mailed at least 90 days before the sale, and the sale cannot take place any earlier than 190 days after the actual default. Sellers generally pay the title insurance premiums and the "revenue" tax; buyers and sellers split everything else. Property taxes are payable April 30th and October 31st. Washington is a community-property state.

WEST VIRGINIA–Attorneys conduct escrow closings. Conveyance is by warranty deed and bargain-and-sale deed. Deeds of trust are the customary security instruments. Foreclosures are great for lenders; they take only a month. West Virginians use ALTA policies and endorsements. Buyers pay the title insurance premiums and sellers pay the documentary taxes; they divide the other closing costs. Property taxes may be paid in a lump sum after July 6th or in two installments on September 1st and March 1st.

WISCONSIN–Lenders and title companies conduct what are called "table closings." Conveyance is by warranty deed, but installment land contracts are used extensively, too. Mortgages are the customary security instruments. Within limits, the actual mortgage wording determines foreclosure requirements; redemption varies from 3 months for abandoned property to a full year in some cases. Lenders generally waive their right to a deficiency judgment in order to reduce the redemption period to 6 months. Wisconsinites use ALTA policies and endorsements. Buyers generally pay closing costs and the lender's policy fees; sellers pay the owner's policy fees and the transfer taxes. In transactions involving homesteads, conveyances may be void if not joined into by the spouse. Property taxes may be paid in full on February 28th, or they may be paid half on January 31st and half on July 31st. Wisconsin is a quasi-community-property state.

WYOMING–Real estate agents generally conduct closings. Conveyance is by warranty deed. Mortgages are the usual security instruments. Foreclosures may follow judicial or power-of-sale proceedings. Residential foreclosures take around 120 days; agricultural foreclosures, around 10 months. Wyomingites use ALTA owner's and lender's policies and endorsements. Buyer and seller negotiate who's going to pay the various closing costs and title insurance fees. There are no documentary, mortgage, or transfer taxes. Property taxes may be paid annually December 31st or semi-annually September 1st and March 1st.

GLOSSARY

These are basic explanations of escrow terms. They are not intended to be strict, legal definitions.

Abstract of Title—a listing of all documents affecting title to any particular real property; used in some areas instead of a preliminary title report.

Acceleration Clause—provision added to a note or deed of trust causing it to become due and payable under certain conditions, such as in the event of the sale of the property; also called a due-on-sale clause.

Accrue—to increase or accumulate; interest on loans is said to accrue daily.

Acknowledgment—a formal declaration before a notary public or qualified officer that the signing of a document is your voluntary act using your legal name and signature; popularly called notarizing.

Adverse Possession—acquisition of title to real property through continued occupation over a period of time (usually 5 years); title acquired in this way is not considered marketable until established by court proceedings against the owner of record.

Agreement of Sale—see "Land Contract."

Alienation Clause—a clause which calls for the entire loan balance to be paid upon the sale, loan, or transfer of title; an acceleration clause.

All-Inclusive Deed of Trust—a deed of trust which includes within its terms the obligations owing under a prior deed of trust; used in wraparound loans.

ALTA Title Insurance Policy—"ALTA" stands for the American Land Title Association; ALTA title insurance is a combination of various policies and endorsements which lenders usually require when making a loan; expands normal coverage to include unrecorded mechanics' liens, unrecorded physical easements, facts not revealed by a physical survey, water and mineral rights, and the rights of parties in possession such as buyers who have unrecorded claims and tenants.

Amendment—a change made to correct an error or to alter or augment part of an agreement without changing its principal idea or essence.

Amortize—pay off a debt in installments.

Amortized Loan, Fully—a loan which is paid off in a series of installments covering both principal and interest.

Annual Percentage Rate (A.P.R.)—the annual yearly rate of interest on a loan.

Appraisal—value of a property determined usually by someone knowledgeable about the sales of similar properties.

Appurtenant—belonging to.

Appurtenance—anything incidental or belonging to land which might be considered part of the property, such as an improvement or an easement for ingress and egress.

Arrears—that which is behind; used when describing payment of past-due interest and loan payments.

Assessed Value—value placed on property by the county assessor; used as a basis for computing property taxes; California law states that the assessor must value property for tax purposes at 25% of the fair market value; assessments are made a matter of record on March 1st.

Assessment Bond—an obligation to pay for costs of local improvements such as sidewalks, sewers, or street lighting.

Assignment—a transfer in writing of one's interest in something, as to assign an interest in a promissory note and deed of trust.

Assumption—taking over another person's financial obligation; taking title to a property with the buyer assuming liability for paying an existing note secured by a deed of trust against the property.

Attorney-in-Fact—a person given the power to act in place of another; that person is said to have the power of attorney; written authorization of this power should always be recorded in the county where the power is to be used.

Balloon Payment—the final payment which pays a note in full; much larger than the preceding payments.

Bargain-and-Sale Deed—a deed which includes the consideration together with the necessary language for conveying real property; depending on the state involved, it may or may not imply warranties.

Beneficiary—the recipient of benefits, often from a deed of trust; usually the lender of a sum of money.

Bilateral Escrow Instructions—a single set of escrow instructions signed by both the buyer and seller (as practiced in Southern California); often signed at the opening of escrow, not at the end.

Bill of Sale—signed document which transfers ownership of personal property from the seller to the buyer.

Binder—written confirmation of insurance coverage provided by an insurer prior to issuance of the actual policy.

Boot—profit realized in a tax-deferred exchange upon which income tax is not deferred; may be in either cash or paper.

Borrower's Statement to the Lender—document prepared by the lender authorizing him to perform certain acts (complete your loan, etc.) signed by the borrower; usually included in the loan package.

Breach—failure to fulfill a specific promise or obligation or to perform a specified duty.

Canceling Escrow—to terminate escrow by mutual written instructions.

Cap—a ceiling on interest rate increases.

CC & R's—covenants, conditions, and restrictions which control the owner's rights to the use of owned and common areas in a condominium subdivision or planned unit development.

Certificate of Title—written opinion by an attorney that ownership of a particular property is as stated in his certificate.

Chain of Title—the history of ownership of a parcel of real estate; each deed or other instrument transferring the title is called a link, and all of these links make up the chain of title.

Chattel—personal property.

Chattel Mortgage—a lien or security instrument against personal property.

Close of Escrow (C.O.E.)—the date when documents are recorded and title passes from seller to buyer; on this date buyer becomes the legal owner and title insurance becomes effective.

Closing Costs—costs, apart from the purchase price, which are payable at the close of escrow and include loan fees, title insurance fees, escrow fees, recording fees, notary fees, prorated items, etc.

Closing Statement—a final accounting of the closed escrow showing the actual figures used to compute the completed escrow; may be filled out on a "RESPA" or "HUD" form.

Cloud on Title—a claim appearing in some legal form on the title, but which is likely invalid; adversely affects a title's marketability until cleared.

Collateral—marketable real or personal property pledged by a borrower as security for a loan.

Commission—a real estate agent's earnings for handling a property transaction; usually computed as a percentage of the selling price and negotiable between the seller and the agent.

Commitment of Title—similar to a preliminary title report; guarantees that a title company will issue title insurance.

Common Areas—all the areas in a condominium or planned unit development which are not specifically reserved to the individual owners; include walkways, parking lots, and yards.

Community Property—a way to hold title which exists in community-property states and is presumed unless property is acquired by husband or wife as separate property specifically; neither spouse may sell community property without the consent of the other.

Competent—legally qualified.

Concurrently—occurring simultaneously, at the same time; real estate exchanges often must be recorded concurrently.

Conditions—specifications detailed in a deed; they may cover such things as setbacks, types of dwellings, etc.

Condominiums—apartments or other types of property in which the owner has fee title to the part actually occupied, with a proportionate interest in areas used by all occupants, such as walkways and parking areas.

Consideration—amount of money a buyer is willing to give a seller to purchase property.

Constructive Notice—notice given to the general public by the county records.

Contract—agreement to perform certain acts; may be legally binding.

Contract of Sale—agreement to purchase property wherein legal title is retained by the seller until the buyer has paid the purchase price in accordance with the terms of the contract.

Convey—to transfer title in property from one person to another.

Cooperative—multiple-family housing with each occupant being entitled to perpetual use of his own unit and receiving a share certificate giving him a proportionate interest in the entire property.

Co-tenancy—ownership shared by more than one person; tenancy-in-common and joint tenancy are both co-tenancy arrangements.

County Records—a system for recording documents in permanent books at the county court house; maintained by each county and provided by law; open to public examination.

Covenant—a written agreement to control the use of property by future owners.

Credit—an item in your favor; what is owed to you; also, your financial ability to borrow money.

Credit Application—a statement provided by a borrower for a prospective lender in order to establish or exhibit financial stability.

Debit—a charge; an item you must pay for; what you owe.

Deed—a written document which transfers title to property; there are several different types: a grant deed, the most common, is simply used to convey property; a gift deed is used to make a gift of property; a quitclaim deed is used to transfer an interest owned in a property and, incidentally, contains no warranties; a tax deed is used to convey title held by the state; and a deed of reconveyance is used to convey legal title back to the borrower from the trustee.

Deed of Trust—security for a property loan; deeds the property to a third party (trustee) to hold until the loan is paid.

Default—failure to make good on a promise, such as failure to make payments on a note or to live up to the terms of a contract.

Deficiency Judgment—a personal judgment in a foreclosure action for whatever amount remains owing after the foreclosure sale of an encumbered property.

Demand—specification by a lender as to what will cause them to call a loan balance due.

Demise—a transfer of an estate to another person for a specified period of years, for life, or at will.

Deposit—a sum of money usually given to bind an agreement or an offer on a property.

Description—a reference to certain maps, plats, and other instruments which are recorded with the county and serve to make a positive property identification.

Devise—to give property by will; a devisee is the person to whom a property is willed.

Disbursement—the release of monies held in an escrow account; usually on the day when escrow closes.

Documentary Stamps—tax applicable to property transfers and affixed to the grant deed; varies from county to county, city to city; sometimes called a transfer tax.

Double Escrow—a real estate transaction procedure in which the closing of one escrow is dependent upon the closing of another one; also called a concurrent escrow; commonly used in exchanges and in instances where the buyer depends on funds he expects to get from the sale of another property.

Due-on-Sale Clause—a clause which calls for an obligation to become due upon the sale of a property previously put up as collateral for a promissory note; frequently broadened to become a "due-on-transfer" clause; also called an acceleration clause.

Earnest Money—a deposit made to bind an agreement between buyer and seller.

Easement—a right of one person to make limited use of another's property; for example, the right to cross a property and maintain a road or right-of-way or the right to install and maintain public utility services.

Easement Appurtenant—created for the benefit of a parcel of land; belongs with the land.

Easement in Gross—an easement created for the benefit of an individual apart from the ownership of the land; a public utility easement is one example.

Egress—a means for departing from one's own property without trespassing on another person's property, as applied to an easement.

Encroachment—extension of an improvement onto the land of another person.

Encumbrance—a general term for something which restricts the title of real property; encumbrances may be liens, leases, mortgages, judgments, deeds of trust, or easements.

Endorsement—an addition to a CLTA or ALTA Policy of Title Insurance which either expands or lessens the standard coverage; special coverages for specified concerns, such as mechanics' liens, which may be obtained for an additional fee.

Equity—the difference between fair market value of a property and the debts owing on it; the owner's interest in a property.

Escrow—the depositing of papers and funds with a third party along with instructions to carry out an agreement; the entire transaction of depositing items with an impartial party.

Escrow Instructions—instructions from a buyer, seller, or lender to the escrow company as to what conditions must be met before escrow can close.

Escrow Number—the file number assigned to an escrow by the escrow officer for identification purposes.

Escrow Officer—also known as an escrow agent; someone qualified to perform all the steps necessary to prepare and carry out escrow instructions, which might involve such tasks as obtaining title insurance; securing payoff demands; prorating taxes, interest, rents, etc.; and disbursing the funds held in escrow.

Estate—the degree, quantity, nature, and extent of a person's interest in property.

Exceptions—conditional items listed on a preliminary title report and affecting the title; would be excluded from coverage by a title insurance policy.

Execute—to give validity by signing documents so that an intention may be completed.

Fee Simple Estate—the greatest interest one may hold in real property; usually means ordinary ownership of real estate and is sometimes called fee title.

FHA—Federal Housing Administration, a federal agency that insures institutional lenders against losses resulting from defaults on loans which are made according to the agency's requirements.

FHLMC—Federal Home Loan Mortgage Corporation, also called Freddie Mac; an affiliate of the Federal Home Loan Bank which creates a secondary market in conventional residential loans and in FHA and VA loans by purchasing mortgages from members of the Federal Reserve System and the Federal Home Loan Bank System.

Fiduciary—someone entrusted with financial responsibility in someone else's behalf.

File and Use—title insurers in most states file rate schedules, policy forms, and endorsement forms with the state insurance department; they may then use those rates and forms after a specified waiting interval; rates so filed are mandatory.

Finance Charges—all costs the borrower must pay directly or indirectly to obtain credit for a specific loan.

Financing Real Estate—securing a loan by giving real property as collateral for payment of the debt.

Fire Insurance Requirement Form—a form included in loan papers that a borrower must sign, in which the borrower agrees to obtain fire insurance coverage to protect the property and insure the lender.

FNMA—Federal National Mortgage Association, also called Fannie Mae; a federally sponsored private corporation which provides a secondary market for housing mortgages.

Foreclosure—a legal process which deprives a mortgagor of his interest in a property because he has failed to comply with the terms of the mortgage.

Funding—the release of loan funds from a lending institution to the escrow company, generally on the closing day of escrow or recordation.

Funding Letter—written request to a lender for release of loan funds; also called the "Request for Loan Proceeds."

Grant—to convey title of property by means of a deed; a grantor conveys a property to a grantee.

Grantee—one who acquires title to property by means of a grant deed; usually the buyer.

Grantor—one who transfers title of a property by means of a grant deed, usually the seller.

Hazard Insurance—fire insurance policy which often includes liability insurance and extended coverage insurance.

Homeowner's Association—a nonprofit association created to own or lease common areas and make improvements in a condominium or planned unit development; serves as the administrative and legislative arm of the unit owners.

Homeowner's Endorsement—an addition to a policy of title insurance that extends the normal policy to cover items other than those stated in the standard policy; may include such items as mineral rights and mechanics' liens.

HUD Form—HUD itself means "Department of Housing and Urban Development"; a final accounting of closing costs, itemizing buyer's and seller's closing costs separately; a consumer protection form.

Impound Account—a trust account established by a lender for the accumulation of borrower's funds to meet periodic payment of taxes, FHA mortgage insurance premiums, and future insurance premiums required to protect the property acting as security for a loan; the borrower pays impounds with the loan payment.

Indemnity—a guarantee against loss; a building contractor may, for example, give a title company an indemnity agreement that renders the title company harmless against any liens which may arise due to the contractor's failure to pay his bills.

Individual Lender—seller, third parties, or real estate agent; any person or group of persons other than institutional lenders.

Inflation Endorsement—an additional coverage which may be added to the standard owner's policy of title insurance; it adjusts the amount of coverage according to the cost-of-living index.

Ingress—a right to enter someone else's property without being a trespasser.

Installment Note—a promissory note with payments of principal and interest made at designated intervals.

Institutional Lenders—savings and loan associations, banks, life insurance companies, and mutual savings banks.

Instrument—a written legal document such as a contract, promissory note, deed, or grant.

Insurable Title—a property title which a title insurance company is willing to insure.

Interest Rate—cost of borrowing money expressed as a percentage of the amount borrowed and usually paid over the life of a loan.

Interval Ownership—see "Time Sharing."

Joint Protection Policy—a title insurance policy insuring the interest of both owner and lender.

Joint Tenancy—one way for several persons to hold title; joint tenants own an undivided equal interest and have equal rights to use the entire property; they are said to have the "right of survivorship," that is, they inherit the property automatically upon the death of the other joint tenant; this right is the principal distinction between a joint tenancy and a tenancy in common.

Joint Tenancy Deed—a deed which gives title to grantees as joint tenants.

Judgment—a court's final decree, generally resulting in a lien; may encumber the sale of a property and must be satisfied before it can be sold.

Judicial Foreclosure—type of foreclosure which requires court proceedings; mortgage foreclosures require court proceedings while deed-of-trust foreclosures generally do not; state laws dictate.

Junior Mortgage—a mortgage which is subordinate to another mortgage.

Jurat—certificate of an officer, such as a notary public or magistrate, who has witnessed someone's signature to a sworn document; also, that part of an affidavit stating by whom, where, when, and before whom it was sworn to.

Land Sale Contract—an agreement providing that the seller retains legal title until the purchaser has made required payments.

Leasehold Estate—an estate created by a lease for a certain period of time; in contrast to a fee simple estate, it is a lesser interest.

Legal Description—a description of land recognized by law and based on government surveys, spelling out the exact boundaries of the entire piece of land; should so thoroughly identify a parcel that it cannot be confused with any other.

Lender's Escrow Instructions—a lender's instructions to the escrow company giving specific conditions which must be met before escrow can close or the deed of trust can be recorded.

Lien—a legal claim upon property for the payment of a debt; a money encumbrance; there are numerous types, some of them overlapping: general liens, which affect all property of an owner; involuntary liens, which can be placed on a property without the necessity of the owner's consent, such as property taxes; specific liens, which affect specific property of an owner, such as a deed of trust; voluntary liens, which are placed on a property by the owner, such as a deed of trust; tax liens, which put a claim on property when its taxes are not paid; judgment liens, which are general liens resulting when a person suing another person wins a judgment from a court for the sum owing him; mechanics' liens, which are claims made by subcontractors, laborers, or materials suppliers who file with the county to obtain payment for their services.

Life Estate—use of property only during a person's lifetime; this interest may be sold, encumbered, or leased, but only for the term of the life estate.

Lis Pendens—legal notice that litigation is pending on a certain property and that anyone obtaining an interest in the property after the notice date may be bound by the judgment.

Loan Application—a lender's initial source of information on a borrower/applicant and the collateral involved; stipulates the amount of money requested and the repayment terms.

Loan Commitment—a lender's agreement to lend a specified amount of money; must be exercised within a certain time limit.

Loan Fees—costs charged by a lender for giving out a loan; may include points, tax service fees, appraisal fee, etc.

Lot Book Report—a short title company report providing the property owner's name, the vesting, the property's legal description, and a plat map.

Maturity Date—the end of a loan repayment period; a specific date in the future when full payment for a loan becomes due.

Mechanic's Lien—a lien which a subcontractor, laborer, or supplier of materials may put on a property after having furnished labor or materials to improve the property without being paid.

Metes and Bounds—boundary lines of land given in terminal points and angles.

Mineral Rights—ownership of minerals found on a property.

Mortgage—a two-party contract which pledges specific property as security for payment of a debt; commonly used to refer to a property loan.

Mutual Consent—approval of both parties to terms of a contract.

Negotiable—capable of being assigned or transferred by endorsement; checks, drafts, and notes are all negotiable.

Notary Public—person who acknowledges oaths, such as the signing of a grant deed or deed of trust; must be duly appointed by the proper authorities.

Note—a written promise to pay; straight notes have payments which cover interest only, and installment notes have payments which cover the interest plus some of the principal.

Notice of Completion—document recorded to give constructive notice that a building job has been completed.

Notice of Default—a formal recorded declaration that a default has occurred; starts foreclosure proceedings.

Official Records—a master set of books kept by the county recorder in which copies of all recorded documents in that county are stored; may be microfilmed.

Opinion of Title—an attorney's written evaluation of the condition of title to real property, based upon a careful examination of the abstract of title.

Paper—notes in lieu of cash; sellers frequently "take back paper" when they can't or don't wish to get all their equity out of a property in cash.

Parcel—land fitting a single description.

Partial Reconveyance—the release of part of someone's interest in real property secured by a mortgage or deed of trust.

Payee—one who receives money.

Payoff Check—final disbursement check to a lender to pay off a loan in full.

Payor—person who pays the sum due on a note to the payee.

Personal Property—that which is not real property; curtains, furniture, appliances, and other items not attached permanently to the property.

PITI Payment—the monthly payments necessary to cover principal, interest, taxes, and insurance.

Plant Department—department in a title company where research materials and copies of official documents are kept.

Plat Map—map of a land subdivision or housing development.

Points—as referred to on a loan, a point is equal to 1% of the loan amount and would be included in loan costs.

Possession—day the buyer actually moves onto the property; may be different from the close-of-escrow or recording date.

Power of Attorney—the authority given one person by another to act on his behalf.

Preliminary Title Report—a report showing current status of a property and condition under which a title company is willing to insure title as of a specified date.

Prepayment Penalty—fine charged by a lender when a borrower pays off a loan before the due date; sometimes called a prepayment bonus by those involved in creative financing.

Prescription—doctrine by which easements are acquired through long, continuous, and exclusive use or possession of property.

Price—the amount of money or other consideration given for a property; agreed upon between buyer and seller; also called purchase price or sales price.

Principal—the amount borrowed or financed; the unpaid balance of a loan; also, a main party to a transaction or a party handling a property transaction on his own behalf.

Priority—taking place in rank or order; taking precedence over; in real estate transactions, priority is established by the order in which documents affecting a property are recorded and also by the language contained in those documents.

Promissory Note—document with a promise to pay a sum of money; may be an installment note or a straight note.

Proration—a method of dividing up taxes, interest, and other sums proportionately between buyer and seller according to a certain date (usually close of escrow).

Public Records—records which by law give constructive notice of matters relating to property.

Quiet Title—court action brought to establish undisputed title; removal of a cloud on the title.

Quitclaim Deed—a deed in which the grantor releases any claim he may have on a property; most commonly used between spouses and in partnerships.

Real Property—term used to describe land and that which is permanently attached to the land.

Recision—see "Right of Recision."

Reconveyance—transfer of title from the trustee back to the real owner of property; occurs when a loan has been paid in full; releases the trustor (borrower) from any further liability for that debt.

Recordation—process of placing a document on file with the county recorder for everyone to see; said to give constructive notice of the document's existence; claims against property usually are given a priority on the basis of the time and date when they are recorded.

Redemption—reclaiming real property from someone who has taken legal title to it.

Redemption Period—period of time in which borrower may redeem his property.

Refinance—to renew, revise, or reorganize an existing loan by obtaining a new loan; usually pays off the existing loan.

Regulation "Z"—an estimated breakdown of costs that will be incurred in obtaining a loan; given to borrower by an institutional lender before the loan is taken out; a consumer protection form.

Remainder—future interest in a property.

Remainderman—person who holds a future interest which exists in favor of a party other than the grantor or his successors, as in a life estate relationship.

Reservation—a particular right withheld by a grantor when conveying property.

RESPA—settlement statement showing the final closing figures used to complete an escrow; also called a "HUD" statement.

Restriction—a limit on the use of property, usually imposed by a previous owner.

Rider—an addition to a document.

Right of Recision—a borrower's right to cancel a credit contract within three business days from the day he entered into the loan contract.

Right of Survivorship—a right created by joint tenancy which states that upon the death of one owner, the other immediately becomes the owner of the property.

Right of Way—the right to cross or pass over a parcel of land; may be a right to use a road or driveway, a right to construct power lines through the property, or a right to put pipes underground.

Right, Title, and Interest—term used in deeds to denote that the grantor is conveying all claims to a property.

Secondary Financing—a loan taken out in addition to a first loan; usually obtained from an individual lender.

Security—property pledged to insure payment of a debt; collateral.

Separate Property—that property which is held singly by either a husband or wife, described on a deed as "sole and separate property."

Setback—a portion of property which must be set aside and not built on to keep building improvements a certain distance from lot boundaries.

Short-Term Rate—a reduced rate for title insurance applicable in cases where the owner of a property has been insured previously or where any lender has been insured somewhat recently on the property.

Specific Performance—a legal doctrine which enables a court to compel someone to perform according to his agreement.

Statute of Limitations—law specifying time limits for initiating enforceable legal action.

Straight Note—a promissory note whose interest is payable in specified payments at various intervals and whose principal (original sum) is payable in one lump sum.

Subdivision—a tract of land surveyed and divided into lots.

Subject To—to take title without paying off the existing loan or deed of trust; original borrower remains ultimately responsible for repaying the loan; the buyer (new borrower) does not make a formal agreement with the lender.

Subordinate—that which takes second place; to be of lessor priority, such as a newly created deed of trust being subordinate to an existing one.

Subordination Agreement—a written agreement which changes the priority of documents, making, for example, one deed of trust subordinate to another.

Swing Loan—a short-term loan to bridge the gap between the purchase of a new home and the subsequent sale of an old one.

Tax-Deferred Exchange—a method for postponing capital gains when disposing of real property by trading one property for another of like kind.

Taxes (Real Property)—an assessment on real property which can become a lien against that property if not paid at the appropriate time.

Tax Sale Number—a number assigned to a property when property taxes are not paid on time; identifies that property on the delinquent tax roll.

Tenancy-in-Common—a form for taking title when two or more people buy property and own it together with either equal or unequal shares; if any one of the tenants-in-common dies, his interest passes to his heirs, not to the remaining tenants.

Termite Report—a statement made by a licensed pest control company indicating corrective work to remedy a structure's current infestation and preventive work to inhibit future or threatened infestation.

Time-Sharing—partial interest in a property allowing exclusive use for a specific time period.

Title—evidence of a person's right to property.

Title Company—company authorized to issue title insurance, as well as to serve escrow needs.

Torrens System—a governmental title registration system which uses certificates of title issued by a public official (called the registrar of title) as evidence of title.

Transfer Tax—see "Documentary Stamps."

Trustee—person or corporation appointed to hold title for another until repayment of an obligation has been made; a trustee for a deed of trust holds title to the property until the amount owing has been paid.

Trustor—person who executes a deed of trust; the borrower on a note.

Truth-in-Lending—name given to the federal statutes and regulations form (Regulation "Z") provided to borrowers prior to entering into a loan contract.

Undivided Interest—unsegregated interest of a co-owner in a whole property owned in common.

Unilateral Escrow Instructions—separate sets of escrow instructions, one for the buyer and one for the seller; normally drawn up after all the information is in and escrow is ready to close.

Unsecured Note—a loan granted solely on the strength of a borrower's signature; no security is pledged, and no deed of trust is recorded.

Usury—charging an interest rate above that which is allowed by state law.

VA—VA stands for Veterans Administration; the VA guarantees loans to qualified veterans; like the FHA loan, a VA loan guarantees payment to the lender if the borrower should default.

Variable Interest Rate—an interest rate which may fluctuate up or down over the life of a loan; changes occur generally at six-month intervals.

Vendee—the buyer.

Vendor—the seller, one who disposes of something.

Vest—to confer or bestow upon, as in the expression, "Title shall vest in..."

Vestee—current recorded owner.

Warranty Deed—deed with written guarantees of title.

Wraparound Loan—a loan that is really a combination of loans, the existing loan(s) and a new second loan.

Zoning—city or county regulations governing the use of property.

INDEX

ORDER FORMS

ExPRESS, P.O. BOX 1639, EL CERRITO, CA 94530-4639

Dear ExPress:
   I'm not a property owner yet, but I think I'd like to be one some day, and I'd certainly like to know what I'm doing. Show me.

Please send me _____ copies of *Landlording* @ $19.95 $_____
_____ copies of *The Eviction Book for California* @ $17.95 $_____
_____ copies of *All About Escrow* @ $14.95 $_____
_____ copies of *Landlording*™ *(The Forms Diskette)* @ $39.95 $_____
   >>> CALIFORNIA RESIDENTS, add applicable sales tax >>> $_____
Shipping and handling $ 2.00
   Make check or money order payable to ExPRESS.   TOTAL DUE $_____
Please specify diskette format: IBM 5 1/4__, IBM 3 1/2 __, or Apple Macintosh __
SEND TO

_____

_____

_____ZIP_____

ExPRESS, P.O. BOX 1639, EL CERRITO, CA 94530-4639

Dear ExPress:
   I'm an unscrupulous property owner who's merciless, lowdown, and greedy, and I'll pay double the usual price for your stuff just to lay my hands on all that great information. It may even reform me. Who knows?

Please send me _____ copies of *Landlording* @ $39.90 $_____
_____ copies of *The Eviction Book for California* @ $35.90 $_____
_____ copies of *All About Escrow* @ $29.90 $_____
_____ copies of *Landlording*™ *(The Forms Diskette)* @ $79.90 $_____
   >>> CALIFORNIA RESIDENTS, add applicable sales tax >>> $_____
Shipping and handling $ 4.00
   Make check or money order payable to ExPRESS.   TOTAL DUE $_____
Please specify diskette format: IBM 5 1/4__, IBM 3 1/2 __, or Apple Macintosh __
SEND TO

_____

_____

_____ZIP_____

ExPRESS, P.O. BOX 1639, EL CERRITO, CA 94530-4639

Dear ExPress:
   I'm a scrupulous property owner, and I'd like copies of your materials for my very own. Hurry up with my order. I need all the help I can get right now.

Please send me _____ copies of *Landlording* @ $19.95 $_____
_____ copies of *The Eviction Book for California* @ $17.95 $_____
_____ copies of *All About Escrow* @ $14.95 $_____
_____ copies of *Landlording*™ *(The Forms Diskette)* @ $39.95 $_____
   >>> CALIFORNIA RESIDENTS, add applicable sales tax >>> $_____
Shipping and handling $ 2.00
   Make check or money order payable to ExPRESS.   TOTAL DUE $_____
Please specify diskette format: IBM 5 1/4__, IBM 3 1/2 __, or Apple Macintosh __
SEND TO

_____

_____

_____ZIP_____

WHAT THEY'VE SAID ABOUT *ALL ABOUT ESCROW*

"*All about Escrow* by Sandy Gadow is that rarity, an easy-to-read book about the complicated subject of escrow...In addition to escrow information, Gadow provides advice about inspections, financing, condominiums, and cooperatives."

—*Los Angeles Times*

"...a sprightly and attractive handbook...truly a comprehensive guide to this necessary rite of purchase, written for the layperson but detailed enough to be of aid to the real estate professional."

—*San Diego Union*

"This book delivers on the promise of its title...The lavish use of illustrations and charts enhances readability. A real bonus for me was the summary of escrow and closing procedures in each of the states...This is a 'user friendly' guide that will help you understand better how escrow really works."

—Kenneth W. Edwards, author of *Your Successful Real Estate Career*

"Your new book is fantastic! I'm a real estate instructor, developer, and investment advisor. I constantly search for great reference materials. In all my years of real estate involvement, I have found no book that is as concise, clear, and easy-to-read, with filled-in blanks and forms. In short, it's wonderful. It practically teaches my entire course."

—James A. Hadley, Jr.

"...written by an escrow officer, this book is the best we've ever seen for explaining the mechanics of real estate transactions. A must!"

—R.G. Stewart